"On arriving in camp we heard of the daring and successful exploit of the notorious Earl. . . . This was characteristic of the man. He courts danger for the sport of the thing, and he is eminently successful, that is the beauty of the thing."

> — L. C. Bartlett, a member of the 4th Wisconsin,
> in a letter to the Sheboygan Falls, Wisconsin,
> *Evergreen City Times,* November 12, 1864

1864 Statement recommending Lieutenant Isaac N. Earl for brevet promotion to major:

"With small parties of 25 to 30 men he has penetrated the enemy's country in almost every direction, has gained information of incalculable importance, made captures of rebel officers of high rank, of mails, dispatches, flags, horses, mules, boats, supplies of all kinds, and large quantities of cotton. The money values of his captures will far exceed half a million dollars, but the real value of some of the captures, and of the information gained by him, cannot be estimated in money.

"He is a young man of strict moral habits, modest, brave, as kind to a prisoner as he is fierce when engaged in battle, and as true to the Union and the laws of honor as man can be. I know of no one whom I can [more] heartily recommend to the favorable consideration of the President."

> — Major General E. R. S. Canby
> Commander, Federal Military Division
> of West Mississippi

The Notorious Isaac Earl and His Scouts

UNION SOLDIERS, PRISONERS, SPIES

Gordon L. Olson

To Wendy & Omar,
Thanks for the
interest and the conversation!
Gordon Olson
2014

WILLIAM B. EERDMANS PUBLISHING COMPANY
GRAND RAPIDS, MICHIGAN / CAMBRIDGE, U.K.

© 2014 Gordon L. Olson

Published 2014 by
Wm. B. Eerdmans Publishing Co.
2140 Oak Industrial Drive N.E., Grand Rapids, Michigan 49505 /
P.O. Box 163, Cambridge CB3 9PU U.K.

Printed in the United States of America

20 19 18 17 16 15 14   7 6 5 4 3 2 1

ISBN 978-0-8028-6801-5

www.eerdmans.com

To Viola and Clifford Olson,

who taught their children to love reading and value books

Contents

Acknowledgments

I FIRST ENCOUNTERED LIEUTENANT ISAAC NEWTON EARL AND HIS
Special Scouts over forty years ago in the Area Research Center at the
University of Wisconsin, River Falls, while I was working on my master's
degree. Dr. James T. King, my advisor and head of the center, called my
attention to a new acquisition, the memoir of Civil War soldier Lucien
Bennett, and at his suggestion I made it the focus of my thesis research.
Bennett had been a member of Earl's Special Scouts, and his memoir introduced me to the remarkable tale of the Scouts' campaign to disrupt illegal
trade and guerrilla activities along the lower Mississippi River in 1864.

After completing my master's degree, I continued on to the PhD program at the University of Wyoming and then embarked on a public history
career as museum administrator, city historian, and teacher. Occasionally,
when time permitted, I revisited Earl and his scouts, taking advantage of
new scholarship and distant archival collections that were being made
computer-accessible to add new information and interpretations to my
original research. Likewise, I mentioned Earl's Scouts to friends and colleagues from time to time, and was encouraged to pursue a book-length
treatment of their story. Particularly, Dr. Frank (Mickey) Schubert, my
good friend and fellow historian, and I spent hours talking about why and
how to tell the story of Isaac Earl and the Scouts, he urging me to get at it.
He has more recently read and offered comments on preliminary drafts
of the manuscript. Others who read the manuscript and offered their reactions and ideas include Dr. Perry Jamieson, Dr. William Dobak, Michael
Lloyd, Gary O'Neal of Natchez, Mississippi, Michael Martin, author of
a detailed and very useful history of the Fourth Wisconsin Infantry and

Cavalry, genealogist Susan Dolan, whose research led me to the O'Neal family of Baton Rouge, and my neighbor and friend Joseph Martin, who is not only an avid reader of history but makes some of the best maple syrup in Michigan.

I am also indebted to my brother, Gary, with whom I spend time each year at my cabin in northern Minnesota, and who has listened to hours of my retelling of the story of Earl's Scouts. Gary also helped with research and did the lion's share of the driving when we traveled to Natchez, Mississippi, in the spring of 2013 to visit sites frequented by Earl and the Scouts in 1864. While in Natchez, we enjoyed the hospitality and regional knowledge of Gary O'Neal and his wife, Karen. Gary O'Neal spent two days guiding us along back roads that connect Natchez, Fayette, Union Church, and Woodville, out along the old Palestine road, and down to Natchez-Under-The-Hill, where the road and several buildings near the Mississippi River date from the Civil War era. O'Neal, who has written a detailed genealogy/history of the O'Neal family and is the great-great-grandnephew of Jane O'Neal, also read and commented on the manuscript.

I have also benefited from the assistance, advice, and knowledge of their collections provided by staff members of archival institutions large and small, including the National Archives, State Historical Society of Wisconsin, Wisconsin Veterans Museum, University of Wisconsin River Falls Library, Milwaukee Public Library, Port Hudson, Louisiana State Historic Site, Coe Library at the University of Wyoming, and the public library of Grand Rapids, Michigan. While in graduate school at the University of Wyoming, it was my good fortune to take a Civil War seminar class from E. B. Long. He and his wife, Barbara, were researchers for Bruce Catton and the authors of *The Civil War Day by Day*. Long examined my estimates of the value of goods captured by the Scouts, and he offered me many useful suggestions; thanks to his input, it is a more accurate reflection of their work. When the manuscript was complete, it needed maps to help readers envision the region where Earl's Scouts operated. For that essential aid to geographical understanding, Chris Gray produced clear and useful renderings of Baton Rouge, Louisiana, Natchez, Mississippi, and landings along the Mississippi River in Louisiana, Mississippi, and Arkansas.

Even with all that help, I might still be researching and rewriting, had it not been for William B. Eerdmans, head of Grand Rapids' Eerdmans Publishing Company. Bill offered both a contract and a deadline for the book — the two items I most needed to get it finished. And once the manuscript was in the hands of the Eerdmans staff, matters proceeded quickly and smoothly. Editor and friend Reinder Van Til took what I said and fashioned it into what I wanted to say — no mean feat. With manuscript and illustrations ready, Eerdmans designer Klaas Wolterstorff produced the book I have imagined for years, and with which I am very pleased.

Having called attention to the many people who have assisted my efforts, I wish also to extend a special acknowledgment to Christine, who has patiently tolerated my moody moments and erratic hours during the forty-five years we have been married, and has always been ready with encouragement when I needed it most.

Finally, I remind readers that any errors of fact or interpretation that remain, despite the best efforts of friends and professional colleagues, are my responsibility alone.

GORDON L. OLSON
Grand Rapids, Michigan

An Occupation Army

Through a moonless September 1864 night, the steamboat *Ida May*, its lights doused and windows covered, slid quietly down the Mississippi River, past sandbars and floating debris, as its captain carefully navigated the broad river's ever-changing channels. Aboard were 1st Lieutenant Isaac Newton Earl and his Special Scouts — thirty Union soldiers whose mission was to patrol the Mississippi River, gathering information about Confederate troop activity, and to "break up smuggling or any other mischief that may be going on," making arrests and forcing guerrillas and outlaws to seek refuge away from the river.[1]

A Busy Morning at St. Joseph

On this night Earl's Scouts' destination was St. Joseph, Louisiana, a small village on the west bank of the great river, about fifty miles south of Vicksburg, Mississippi. Laying out their town around a village green, St. Joseph's founders had sought to replicate a quiet New-England-style town. Instead, by 1864 it had become a hotbed for guerrillas and smugglers, among them a plantation owner named John Powell, who regularly ferried Confederate personnel, correspondence, and contraband goods back and forth across the Mississippi.

At about 2:00 a.m., the *Ida May*'s captain eased his vessel against the

---

1. Byron Kenyon to his parents, June 16, 1864, Byron Kenyon Letters, Port Hudson State Historic Site, Jackson, LA.

bank a few miles above St. Joseph and lowered the gangplank. As soon as their bridge to shore touched earth, Earl and his waiting scouts led their horses off the boat and set off at a brisk trot for St. Joseph, reaching the town less than an hour later. Without slowing, they wheeled right and rode five more miles west to Powell's home, where they surprised the still-sleeping homeowner and two other men, and seized a "half bushel" of Confederate mail. After securing their prisoners and the captured mail, Earl and his Scouts continued another mile down the plank road to another house, where they captured a Confederate soldier and three horses. Earl placed both the soldier and the homeowner under arrest, and before going further, he sent his five prisoners and the captured mail back to the *Ida May*, which in the meantime had proceeded downstream and docked at St. Joseph.

When the detail of Scouts and their prisoners arrived at St. Joseph, they found that the boat's crew and guards were waiting with more prisoners. Lt. James Butler, of General James Slaughter's staff, and two others had been captured when they carelessly rode up to the *Ida May*, unaware that it was a Union vessel and that the men in civilian garb around the boat were Union soldiers and civilian employees of the army.

Meanwhile, with their prisoners and captured mail on their way to the *Ida May*, Earl and the remaining Scouts rode on through the night. They were now more than ten miles inland and rather than proceed further on the plank road, Earl decided to skirt quietly behind several plantations on a less-used trail. He had been told that about twenty-five Confederates were in the area, and he hoped to catch them unaware. Thus far, Earl and the Scouts had been operating under cover of darkness; now, just as the rising sun was beginning to dispel the darkness, they saw a flickering campfire in front of a distant house. Spurring their mounts forward, advance scouts Newton Culver and Charles Fenlason managed to get between the startled men, who were preparing breakfast in the plantation house's front yard, and their nearby horses and weapons. With Culver and Fenlason preventing them from reaching their rifles and sabers, which were stacked on the porch, and Earl and the remaining Scouts charging up behind them, the Confederates, who claimed to be "mechanics" (skilled craftsmen) on their way from Georgia to Texas, had little option but to surrender. The Scouts destroyed their prisoners' rifles, strapped their sabers to their saddles, bound the men and put them aboard their horses, and began leading them back to the *Ida May*.

As they turned onto the plank road, Earl observed fresh, deep ruts and realized that several heavily loaded wagons had recently passed through, and the Scouts set off after the slow-moving wagons. Little more than a mile down the road, they started hearing the creak and squeak of the wagons ahead of them. Newton Culver and Charles Fenlason were in their usual place as advance riders, and Culver described in his diary what happened next. As he and Fenlason cautiously rounded a bend in the road, they came upon a sleepy horseman riding casually behind the rear of several wagons. Before the rider realized what was happening, he found himself facing Culver's revolver with no option but to surrender. Quietly, Culver and Fenlason rode up behind the other guards, capturing them along with the black muleskinners. The six wagons, each pulled by six mules and loaded with wool from Texas, which was to be turned into cloth for the Confederacy, were a serious loss at a time when the Confederacy was undergoing debilitating shortages.

The capture of the wagon train marked the completion of a remarkably productive morning. Before their adversaries knew they were in their neighborhood, the night-traveling Scouts had seized a valuable batch of mail, arrested a contingent of soldiers, and then captured a wool wagon train poised to cross the Mississippi River. In raw numbers, the St. Joseph raid netted thirty-five prisoners, nine horses, thirty-six mules and their harnesses, and six wagons loaded with about nine tons of wool. In addition, a collection of official and unofficial Confederate mail was now in Union hands. With jail awaiting them, three of the civilian captives immediately swore an oath of allegiance and were freed; the remaining thirty-two were slated to be turned over to the provost marshal in Natchez, Mississippi, where the Scouts were headquartered.

The Scouts added to their already impressive haul when they discovered a small ferryboat and a skiff partially hidden at the river bank. The two boats were waiting to take the loaded wagons, the mules and their drivers, and the guards across the Mississippi. With the *Ida May* already packed to the gunwales with captured wool wagons, prisoners, horses and mules, plus the scouts and their horses, there was no room to haul the ferryboat and skiff. Unwilling to leave them on the river bank, Earl ordered them set ablaze, and as the *Ida May* pulled away from the landing and headed downriver to Natchez, the smaller boats burned in the background.[2]

2. Accounts of the raid on St. Joseph are found in Lucien B. Bennett, "Sketch of the Military Service of L. B. Bennett, Private, Co. I, 4th Wisconsin Infantry," Area Research

3

First Lieutenant Isaac Newton Earl
(State Historical Society of Wisconsin)

Twenty-four-year-old Isaac Earl was a confident soldier at the peak of his abilities as he led his Scouts in the fall of 1864. Although their St.

Center, Wisconsin State University, River Falls, p. 13 (hereafter cited as Bennett, "Sketch of Military Service"); Newton Culver, Diary, entries for Sept. 18-19, 1864, State Historical Society of Wisconsin (hereafter cited as Culver, Diary, with date); Newton Culver, "Brevet Major Isaac N. Earl: A Noted Scout of the Department of the Gulf," *Proceedings of the Historical Society of Wisconsin* (1917), pp. 327, 329; *Daily True Delta* (New Orleans), Sept. 25, 1864: www.Genealogybank.com (accessed Sept. 19, 2013); Lt. I. N. Earl to Col. C. T. Christensen, Sept. 20, 1864, with accompanying Trimonthly Report for Sept. 10-20, 1864; *The War of the Rebellion: A Compilation of the Official Records of the Union and Confederate Armies* (Washington, DC: Government Printing Office, 1880-1901), ser. 1, vol. 41, part III, pp. 263-64 (hereafter cited as O.R., with series, volume, part, and page numbers). Original reports found in Trimonthly Reports submitted by Lt. Earl and Lt. Warren P. Knowles, Records of the Provost Marshall General's Bureau (Civil War), Record Group 110, National Archives and Records Service, Washington, DC (hereafter cited as Trimonthly Report, with submitting officer's name and days covered).

Joseph, Louisiana, raid was their most successful up until then, there had been others, and they had all been well received by Major General E. R. S. Canby, to whom Earl reported. Canby detested the smuggling and guerrilla activity that was rampant along the river, and Earl's successful raids had confirmed the general's conviction that a small but well-equipped squad of veteran soldiers could be an important component of the Union Army's response to such illegal activity. Unlike the war's eastern theater, where large armies engaged in epic battles and extensive campaigns, much of the work of the western army was occupation duty, a role that had begun with President Lincoln's determination to keep border states from seceding and had expanded as the entire Mississippi River valley came under Union control. New Orleans fell to troops led by General Benjamin F. Butler in May 1862, and slightly more than a year later, on July 4 and July 8, forces led by Generals U. S. Grant and Nathaniel P. Banks captured Vicksburg and Port Hudson, respectively, establishing federal control over the entire Mississippi. From mid-July 1863 until the end of the war, the primary mission of the western troops was to patrol the river's more than one thousand meandering miles from St. Louis to the Gulf of Mexico, keeping Confederate troops away from strategic points and preventing insurgents and outlaws from disrupting commercial and passenger traffic. Army leaders stationed infantry and cavalry regiments at key points along the Mississippi, while naval commanders assigned "brown-water" sailors aboard naval gunboats to patrol its waters. This arrangement often created tense command issues between army officers on land and naval leaders on the water, leaving army generals convinced that land and water forces should be under their overall command.

Occupying the Lower Mississippi

Neither the lower Mississippi's geography nor its people bent easily to outside control. America's largest river flowed wide and unpredictable, and together with its Missouri and Ohio tributaries, it created a delta of vast lowland swamps and bogs that regularly flooded for miles beyond its banks. Each spring, silt-laden floodwaters deposited rich organic soil and a thick tangle of grasses, brush, and trees along the river and its bayous. Nineteenth-century plantation owners used their slaves to clear these verdant lowlands, break the soil, and raise abundant crops that they then transported to river landings for shipment further down the river. When

Confederate forces lost Vicksburg and Port Hudson, their last two bastions on the Mississippi, in 1863, they ceded the heart of this commercial network to Union dominance.

Seceding states across the South had sent volunteers to the Confederate Army following Abraham Lincoln's election in 1860. At the same time, some states also established home guard units made up of men with farm or business obligations and dependent families to police and defend their home territories. Officially recognized as part of their state's commitment to the South's total military force, these units were led by local commanders, and the latter had great latitude in defining their priorities and strategies. However, other than occasional bounties for capturing draft dodgers and deserters, states provided little in the way of equipment, training, or pay.

When the presence of federal troops pushed Confederate forces back from the river, Southern authorities added another level to their military by giving official sanction to partisan units, whose aim was to harass and resist the occupiers. In April 1862, the Confederate Congress passed the Partisan Ranger Act, which provided army structure, pay, rations, and quarters to units recruited for service in or near Union-occupied areas. Governors in Mississippi and Louisiana moved quickly to authorize these state units, which often incorporated home-guard units.

While Southerners most often referred to these Confederate irregular fighters as partisans and gave them state designations such as Powers' Regiment of Louisiana Cavalry, Union officials naturally identified them quite differently. Although the irregulars began with military structure and discipline, partisan ranger recruitment and deportment changed as they took in deserters and draft dodgers and engaged in guerrilla and outlaw behavior later in the war. Union leaders and soldiers generally thought of and referred to these "partisans" as "guerrillas" who had little regard for the rules of warfare.

Acting individually and in coordination with other partisans, these irregular units became a determined insurgency that poked and prodded their occupiers, attacking small inland patrols, sniping at passing riverboats, planting explosive devices (called "torpedoes") that they could detonate under vessels, and even firing light artillery pieces from the river's edge. Other irregulars became outlaws and smugglers in pursuit of loot and profit rather than concerned with military objectives. These latter often earned the enmity of local residents of the South as well as of Union soldiers.

Worried that the lack of discipline among partisan groups produced more civilian damage than military good, Confederate leaders began questioning their decision to authorize the use of irregulars. On February 17, 1864, the Confederate Congress — with the endorsement of General Robert E. Lee and others — changed course and repealed the Partisan Ranger Act, exempting only Colonel John Singleton Mosby's and Captain John Hanson McNeill's ranger units that were operating in western Virginia, West Virginia, and Maryland.

For their part, federal officials began the war with a "soft," conciliatory policy toward the Confederacy, hoping to hold any wavering border states in the Union, while leaving the latchstring out for those that had left. Over time, Union policy tightened and became more punitive. By the last year and a half of the war, in response to increased guerrilla activity, conciliation gave way to what has been termed "hard war" and "punitive" use of military force for retribution.[3]

Many Union officers along the lower Mississippi shared policymaker's views that those engaged in irregular warfare and illegal activity deserved to be arrested and punished. Men in the enlisted ranks held similar, if not stronger, opinions. An Illinois infantryman spoke for many when he characterized guerrillas as "thieves and murderers by occupation, rebels by pretense, soldiers only in name, and cowards by nature." Published correspondence and reports variously describe as "guerrillas" everyone from state infantry and cavalry units, to partisan groups operating with only local authorization, to organized bands of outlaws.[4]

---

3. Sources for the discussion of the sanctioning and use of Confederate partisans and guerrillas were: "Proceedings of the First Confederate Congress: First and Second Sessions," *Southern Historical Society Papers* 45 (May 1925), pp. 122, 128-29, 153, 160-61, 191, 253; "Proceedings of the First Confederate Congress: Second Session," pp. 4-8, 48, 184, and "Proceedings of the First Confederate Congress: Fourth Session," pp. 401, 427-28, 440, 450; Mark Grimsley, *The Hard Hand of War: Union Military Policy toward Southern Civilians, 1861-1865* (New York: Cambridge University Press, 1995), pp. 2-5; Robert R. Mackey, *The Uncivil War: Irregulars in the Upper South, 1861-1865* (Norman: University of Oklahoma Press, 1994), pp. 197, 203, 205-8; Clay Mountcastle, *Punitive War: Confederate Guerrillas and Union Reprisals* (Lawrence: University Press of Kansas, 2009), p. 2; Daniel E. Sutherland, *A Savage Conflict: The Decisive Role of Guerrillas in the American Civil War* (Chapel Hill: University of North Carolina Press, 2009), pp. x, xi, 43-44, 93-94, 110-12, 116, 237-38.

4. Albert O. Marshall, *Army Life: From a Soldier's Journal, Incidents, Sketches, and Record of a Union Soldier's Army Life in Camp and Field, 1861-1864* (Joliet, IL: 1884), p. 157, cited in Mountcastle, *Punitive War*, p. 2; Sutherland, *Savage Conflict*, pp. xi-xii; Mackey, *Uncivil War*, pp. 6-9.

General Canby and Lieutenant Earl

As guerrillas became more active, Union military leaders along the lower Mississippi developed tactical responses to match their mobile, deceptive foes. In mid-1864, responsibility for establishing occupation strategies in the lower Mississippi fell to Maj. Gen. E. R. S. Canby, commander of the Federal Military Division of West Mississippi. An 1839 West Point graduate, Canby had broad experience with insurgents and irregular fighters. As a young second lieutenant, he had fought in Florida's Second Seminole War, and had later engaged insurgents during the war with Mexico. He also served in the Utah War (1857-1858), which pitted the U.S. Army against Mormon militiamen who stampeded army animals, burned supply trains, and blocked roads. Posted to New Mexico on the eve of the Civil War, he had engaged Navajo warriors whose raiding parties constantly harassed the skirts of his columns.[5]

Soon after arriving in New Orleans and assuming command, Canby formed Earl's Special Scouts to actively confront guerrillas and smugglers on the Mississippi River. The idea of such a unit was not totally new to the Union Army. Captain Richard Blazer had led a similar (but larger) unit in West Virginia as part of General George C. Crook's army of West Virginia. Blazer's scouts initiated several confrontations with John S. Mosby's Rangers. Another group, General Alfred W. Ellet's Mississippi Marine Brigade, organized in early 1863, consisted of about 350 men aboard lightly armored riverboats. The brigade attacked Rebel guerrillas along the Mississippi and discharged marines from the boats in pursuit of guerrillas, outlaws, and smugglers.

Yet, though it successfully disrupted illegal activity, the marine brigade was part of the ongoing dispute between Union Army and Navy leaders about whose authority would prevail on inland waterways. The internecine squabbling — together with charges that captured goods had "disappeared" while in their possession — led to the disbanding of the marine brigade shortly after Gen. Canby assumed command of the Military Division of West Mississippi. Canby likely viewed Earl's Scouts as a replacement group, having the same mobility and battle experience as the marines but one over which he exercised sole control.[6]

5. Max L. Heyman Jr., *Prudent Soldier: A Biography of Major General E. R. S. Canby, 1817-1873* (Glendale, CA: Arthur H. Clark, 1959), pp. 27-136.

6. Gen. Crook developed tactics in the mountains of West Virginia that he later used

Nothing in his early life suggested that Lt. Isaac Newton Earl, the man Canby selected to command the scouts, would be an exceptional soldier. The oldest of three orphaned brothers, whose parents had died when they were not yet adolescents, Earl was twenty-one years old and had no formal schooling when he responded to President Lincoln's call for Union Army volunteers following the Confederate firing on Fort Sumter. He had worked in lumber camps and as a farm laborer, but had never lived outside the rugged hills of central Wisconsin. Two years later, he was a war hero who had been captured at the siege of Port Hudson and had escaped a few days later with valuable information about conditions inside the battlements. He had received a promotion to first lieutenant for his efforts. During the last half of 1863 and into 1864, Earl established a reputation for eagerly and aggressively leading 4th Wisconsin Cavalry patrols into the Mississippi River countryside east of Baton Rouge. Captured once again in early 1864, he cemented his reputation as a daring and determined soldier by escaping from the Confederate prisoner-of-war camp in Cahaba, Alabama, making his way to the Gulf of Mexico and eventually back to Baton Rouge. This reputation for bravery and spirit under fire proved to be a valuable asset when Gen. Canby issued his call for volunteers to serve under Earl in the special scouting unit Canby was forming. More than one hundred veterans of the 4th Wisconsin Cavalry volunteered for the thirty available slots.[7]

Earl's Scouts functioned in a region with distinct political, social, and economic divisions. When the South made its secession decision and war came, most who had been opposed to secession gave up their resistance in the name of sectional solidarity. A few refused to abandon their adherence to the Union, and for them the years 1861 and 1862 were a difficult time; but as the Union army closed in from north and south, they began to feel more secure about proclaiming their allegiance to the Union. A small number of determined pro-Unionists met the Union army as it moved into the lower Mississippi River valley, and many stepped forward to assist occupation efforts. When Earl's Scouts were organized in 1864, a total of fifteen Southerners became part of the group. Several mustered into the

---

in the Indian Wars. For full accounts of these two units, see Darl L. Stephenson, *Headquarters in the Brush: Blazer's Independent Union Scouts* (Athens: Ohio University Press, 2001); Chester G. Hearn, *Ellet's Brigade: The Strangest Outfit of All* (Baton Rouge: Louisiana State University Press, 2000).

7. Bennett, "Sketch of Military Service," p. 13; Culver, "Brevet Major Isaac N. Earl," p. 319.

Anna Jane O'Neal
(photo courtesy Amy O'Neal)

army, while others worked undercover, gathering intelligence throughout the region.

Among those who gathered intelligence for the occupation troops was Jane O'Neal, the oldest daughter of Baton Rouge farmer Peter O'Neal, who had been killed by outlaws east of that city in 1862. O'Neal met Earl in 1863, and they formed a working partnership in which Jane initially provided information about guerrilla and partisan forces that were active east of Baton Rouge; in return, she received payments that very likely went toward helping her mother maintain the family's farm. Jane may have also been motivated by a desire to even accounts with outlaws she believed were responsible for her father's death. Even so, at that same time her brother was a soldier in the Confederate army. At some point during the time that O'Neal was a spy and informant for Earl, their working relationship blossomed into something more.

Union occupation squad leaders like Isaac Earl also turned to former slaves for information. As soon as the blue-uniformed soldiers arrived along the lower Mississippi, slaves began leaving plantations and making their way to Union camps. Overlooked and ignored by Southern whites, slaves passed on information to the Union forces and served as guides. Their knowledge of back roads, river crossings, and shortcuts was especially helpful to Earl and his Scouts. Several times they led the Scouts to guerrilla hiding places, and in one instance, former slaves hid one of Earl's wounded Scouts from pursuing Rebels, caring for him until he could be rescued. Although no black men served as members of the Scouts, ten black teamsters and laborers cared for their horses and equipment and traveled with them as hands aboard their steamboat.

When they were formed, Earl's Scouts received the best weapons and equipment the Union Army could offer. Along with the carbines, pistols, and swords, each man received two horses; these horses did not have the army brand, making it easier for their riders to pass themselves off as civilians. For the same purpose, they wore civilian clothes within Union lines, saving the uniforms for those times when they passed beyond their lines so that they would not be treated as spies if they were captured. A series of steamboats, most of them armed with small cannon, and all with quarters for the men and horses, enabled the scouts to operate along nearly 600 miles of the Mississippi River — from Laconia Landing, north of the White River in Arkansas, to Union headquarters in New Orleans.

During their ten months of action, Earl's Scouts traveled up and down the lower Mississippi, disembarking wherever they had been informed guerrillas were present. Over time, they developed a variety of tactics to deceive Rebel spotters along the river and on inland roads. They traveled in unmarked steamboats and landed at remote points above or below their destination, and then proceeded overland to their target. When on land, they would usually leave a town on one road and, once away from town, change direction and cross over to another road. Within Union lines, they behaved as civilians; on at least one occasion, when they were beyond their lines, they passed themselves off as Rebel guerrillas in order to surprise their foes and seize contraband goods. In some instances they arrested men who were operating beyond the scope of their licenses to trade, angering Union officers who favored increased trade along the river. At all times, Earl knew that if their authority was challenged, Gen. Canby would defend them as Union soldiers acting under his direct orders.

Earl's Scouts have an important place in the story of the Union occupation of the lower Mississippi and the army's response to guerrilla warfare. There was no other group like them. They represented the determination of Northern generals like Canby and veteran troops like those led by Isaac

Earl to apply their personal training and experience to the twin problems of guerrilla warfare and illegal trade. Earl's Scouts were three-year veterans when they signed on for an additional year of special duty. Like most young soldiers, they had initially volunteered to preserve the Union; upon encountering slavery, many had made its termination their mission as well. When offered the opportunity to join the Scouts, they found two more incentives to extend their service: first, their monthly pay increased from $16 to $50; equally important, they had an opportunity to serve under Isaac Earl, whose exploits and courage under fire veterans of the 4th Wisconsin Cavalry had often heard about.

Earl's Scouts experienced high points and low moments. They made important seizures and arrests, seizing more than $1 million in contraband goods and arresting more than 200 prisoners. But they were once arrested themselves by a Union general who was angry at them for disrupting river trade that he had encouraged. And on one occasion, several of their number were captured by Confederates and confined as prisoners of war. But considering that these men were ordinary farmers and workers when they enlisted, they had made a remarkable transformation into a specialized unit established to carry out Union anti-insurrection and antismuggling policies along the lower Mississippi by the waning months of the Civil War. They were an important element in Gen. Canby's occupation plan for the lower Mississippi, and their performance as members of Earl's Scouts was a unique adventure that was recalled by many for decades after the war.

CHAPTER ONE

President Lincoln's Call

ISAAC EARL'S SHORT BUT EXTRAORDINARY LIFE AS A SOLDIER — "A military career of which movies are made," one writer called it — began modestly enough when he joined neighbors and friends in central Wisconsin to answer President Lincoln's call for volunteers after the Confederate bombardment and seizure of Fort Sumter. Twenty-one years old at the time, he left his yearly routine of farm work in summer and logging in winter to join the 4th Wisconsin Infantry. Sent initially to Maryland, the regiment accompanied General Benjamin Butler to the Gulf of Mexico, where it participated in the capture of New Orleans on May 1, 1862. Subsequently, the unit participated in the battles of Baton Rouge and Port Hudson that opened the Mississippi from its source to its mouth for Union traffic.[1]

Although central Wisconsin was a remote region, without a local newspaper, intimations of the growing sectional conflict penetrated the area in the decade before the election of 1860. People around Isaac Earl talked about what could happen if the growing national crisis was not resolved, and they considered what they would do if the nation went to war with itself. Those discussions took on a new urgency when Southern states

---

1. Thomas J. McCrory, *Grand Army of the Republic, Department of Wisconsin* (Black Earth, WI: Trails Books, 2005), p. 193; Michael J. Martin, *A History of the 4th Wisconsin Infantry and Cavalry in the Civil War* (El Dorado Hills, CA: Savas Beatie, 2006). See also Wisconsin Adjutant General, *Roster of Wisconsin Volunteers, War of the Rebellion, 1861-1865*, 2 vols. (Madison, WI: Democrat Printing Company, 1886); William DeLoss Love, *Wisconsin in the War of the Rebellion: A History of Regiments and Batteries the State Has Sent to the Field* (Chicago: Church and Goodman, 1866).

began seceding shortly after Abraham Lincoln was elected President, and state leaders began preparing for armed conflict. Prior to the bombardment of Fort Sumter, Wisconsinites had been split over the issue of secession; but after the first Confederate cannons roared, patriotism ruled the day. At Governor Alexander Randall's urging, the Wisconsin legislature had appropriated $100,000 to equip seventy-five militia companies. As soon as telegraphs brought the news that Sumter had been attacked, legislators authorized the state to borrow an additional $200,000. The shelling at Sumter had scarcely stopped, and telegraph wires were still humming with President Lincoln's call for volunteers, when Gov. Randall confidently responded to the President that his request for troops would be "promptly met, and further calls when made." He then issued a call to the young men of the state for a single regiment of 780 men to serve for three months, as the President had requested.

Gov. Randall's confidence was not misplaced. His call for volunteers prompted an enthusiastic response. Young men, anxious that the war might end before they could prove their mettle, hurried to sign up. Their energy and excitement quieted any opposition to Lincoln's call. When an editor in Manitowoc stood up to defend Jefferson Davis, a shouting crowd drowned out his words. While a few militia groups hesitated momentarily as their members considered the reality of leaving families and communities for the uncertainty of war, ten militia companies from the populous southeast corner of the state quickly stepped forward to meet Wisconsin's initial obligation. Several others moved a bit too slowly and were turned away.

Initially, central Wisconsin had not contributed many soldiers, but as Gov. Randall and other Northern governors urged the President to expand his call for troops, militia companies organizing in more remote regions of the state sent a steady flow of volunteer offers to the governor's desk. President Lincoln responded by asking Northern governors for forty additional regiments to be filled with three-year enlistees "subject to the laws and regulations governing the army of the United States." In this second wave of volunteers were Isaac Newton Earl, his brothers, Joseph and William, and thousands of their fellow Wisconsin farmhands, store clerks, lumberjacks, and similar ordinary citizens.[2]

2. Richard N. Current, *The History of Wisconsin*, vol. 2: *The Civil War Era, 1848-1873* (Madison: State Historical Society of Wisconsin, 1976), pp. 296-99, 300-301.

The Earl Family in Wisconsin

The Earl brothers had lived in Wisconsin for slightly more than a decade when they volunteered for military duty. Their parents appear to have been part of a small group of families that had left New York's Finger Lakes region and migrated to Wisconsin by way of Illinois in the late 1830s and early 1840s. Settling first in Jefferson County, a farming area midway between Milwaukee and Madison, the families moved further northwest a few years later to the remote Dell Prairie area. The boys' parents died in about 1850, leaving three sons — Isaac, about ten, and Joseph and William, slightly younger. Thereafter the three brothers lived and worked on the Adams County farms of their mother's brothers, Nathaniel, Edwin, Elisha, and William Crosby. For a time, William and Isaac lived with Uncle Elisha and his wife, Sophia, and their four children on their farm in rural Adams County, while Joseph moved in with Uncle Edwin's family in nearby Pine Bluff.

Healthy and sturdy young men, the brothers followed the routine of many farmhands: working the fields in spring, summer, and fall, and spending their winters in nearby lumber camps. Early spring brought the greatest adventure: great log drives rafted tens of thousands of logs down the Wisconsin River to waiting sawmills, where they became boards, beams, and shingles for new homes for the expanding populace. As was true for many rural youngsters of the time, formal education had little part in the Earl brothers' formative years. Any education they received came at home. In fact, up until 1850, when Isaac was ten, Adams County had no schools. Its first school was located in Dell Prairie, several miles from Elisha Crosby's farm, but the boys probably learned rudimentary reading, handwriting, and arithmetic skills at home. Their cousin Ann Crosby, Elisha and Sophia's daughter, is listed in the 1860 census as a nineteen-year-old teacher. Most likely, she developed the skills needed to teach others at her home, where her younger male cousins would have had the same opportunity — when they were not working outdoors. Whatever the degree of informal instruction the Earl brothers received at home, Newton Culver's description of them as "unendowed with the knowledge derived from books but . . . grounded in that of woodcraft" is probably accurate.[3]

3. Information about the Earl family is limited. Former Scout Newton Culver describes the death of the parents and the time the brothers spent with their uncle Elisha Crosby and his family. Crosby came to Wisconsin from Courtland, New York, where he and his wife lived near several families with the Earl surname. Although no record has been found thus far identifying the Earl brothers' parents, it is not unreasonable to think

Lumber rafts on the Wisconsin River after the Civil War. The process was unchanged from the prewar days when Isaac Earl and other members of his Scouts rode similar rafts downriver.
(T.A. Taylor, *100 Years of Pictorial and Descriptive History of Wisconsin Rapids, Wisconsin* [1934]; photo by H. H. Bennett [1886])

Deciding to volunteer for military service in 1861, Isaac and Joseph joined an informal group at Kilbourn City who had designated themselves

that they came from the same region as did the Crosbys. Interestingly, Lewis Hatch, an eighteen-year-old farm laborer who also lived with the Crosbys, joined the 4th Wisconsin volunteers with Isaac and Joseph Earl and later joined the Scouts. U.S. 1830 Census: *Cortlandville, Cortland County, New York*, NARA Microfilm Publication No. 19, Roll 88, p. 82; U.S. 1840 Census: *Cortland, New York*, NARA Microfilm Publication No. 704, Roll 275, p. 83; 1850 U.S. Census: *Waterloo, Jefferson County, Wisconsin*; NARA Microfilm Publication No. 432, Roll 1000, p. 68A; U.S. 1860 Census: *Dell Prairie, Adams County, Wisconsin*; NARA Microfilm Publication No. 653, Roll 1399, p. 30; *Illustrated Historical Atlas of Wisconsin* (Milwaukee: Snyder, Van Vechten, and Co., 1878); Culver, "Brevet Major Isaac N. Earl," pp. 311-12.

the Columbia Rifles, and who had begun drilling under Guy C. Pierce, their elected captain. Mustered in June, the Columbia Rifles became Company D of the 4th Wisconsin Infantry Regiment. Joseph was formally mustered in on June 2, and Isaac entered the Union service three weeks later, on June 24. William, the third Earl brother, waited until August 10 before joining the 7th Wisconsin Infantry. (On November 28, 1861, he was detached from the infantry to serve in Battery B of the 4th United States Artillery.)

At the time of his enlistment, Isaac Earl conformed to the physical average for Union soldiers. He was 5 feet 8 inches tall and weighed about 150 pounds. Photographs show a young man with a square, firmly set jaw and thick, unruly hair. His service record says that he had hazel eyes and dark brown hair. Colonel Halbert Paine, who commanded the 4th Wisconsin, described him as "a straight, slender, handsome youngster, a reckless resourceful daredevil."[4]

Camp Utley

Wisconsin had two troop depots and training camps in the summer of 1861. In addition to Camp Randall in Madison, the state opened a camp in Racine, roughly twenty-five miles south of Milwaukee. Named in honor of Wisconsin's adjutant general, William Utley, Camp Utley was located in an expanse of open farmland, on a bluff about forty feet above Lake Michigan. New arrivals in camp generally came by trains via Milwaukee, and then routing south to Racine. For the Earl boys, the Chicago and Northwestern Railroad, which had come to Kilbourn in 1858, ending Adams County's isolation, provided a quick and direct route to Milwaukee and the world beyond.[5]

4. Culver, "Brevet Major Isaac N. Earl," pp. 308-9; Compiled Military Service Records of Lt. Isaac N. Earl, Pvt. Joseph Earl, Pvt. William Earl, National Archives Microfilm Publication M 559, Roll 8; Adams County, Wisconsin WiGenWeb site, Columbia Rifles Civil War Veterans: http://www.wiroots.org/wiadams/index.html (accessed Jan. 15, 2012); *Muster and Descriptive Roll of Company D of the Fourth Regiment of Wisconsin Volunteers*, Wisconsin Adjutant General's Office, Regimental muster and descriptive rolls (Red Book), 1861-1865, Wisconsin Historical Society Archives Series 1144; Samuel C. Hyde Jr., ed., *Halbert Eleazar Paine: A Wisconsin Yankee in Confederate Bayou Country* (Baton Rouge: Louisiana State University Press, 2009), p. 152.

5. "Early Days in Adams County as Told by Mrs. S. W. Ferris," *Adams County Times*,

Camp Utley offered few amenities. New arrivals first stopped at the quartermaster, where they received a blanket, a towel, a wash basin, and soap. Later they also received grey state military uniforms. Jerry Flint, who arrived from River Falls in western Wisconsin at about the same time as the Earls did, wrote his parents that "sleeping apartments consisted of oak trees and a clear sky," ventilated by a wind that "blew like fury" off Lake Michigan. Constructed in little more than two weeks, the camp was, in the words of a visiting Racine reporter, "very simple and economical," with several hundred soldiers' tents laid out along "streets" and dominated near its center by a 218-foot-long, three-section main building. The structure consisted of two buildings connected at its north end, one for food storage, the other a kitchen; those were adjoined to a 100-by-75-foot dining hall that featured ten long serving tables, each having the capacity to seat one hundred men at a time. Shielding the central building from the elements were six parallel seventeen-foot-high gabled roofs set on posts, with exterior windowed walls — but no interior walls. When it rained, one-foot-wide troughs under the eaves between the pitched roofs kept the diners reasonably dry as they drained the rainwater into cisterns to be used for washing. Cooking took place in three large brick fireplaces covered with heavy iron sheets to create a large cooking surface.[6]

Isaac and Joseph Earl and their comrades were introduced to "the mysteries of Hayfoot, Strawfoot, and U" — or "left face," "right face," and "about face" — as soon as they arrived in camp. Knute Nelson, who later served as governor of Minnesota and then as its U.S. senator, outlined a typical day at Camp Utley to his friend Gullick Thompson: "Morning: 4:30 reveille; 5:00–6:00 drill; 6:00 breakfast; 8:00–9:00 drill; 10:00–12:00 drill. Afternoon and evening: 12:30 dinner; 2:00–3:00 drill; 4:00–5:30 drill; 5:30 supper; 7:00–7:30 drill." He concluded: "It is a beautiful sight to see so many men together drilling." That opinion was not likely shared by all of Nelson's contemporaries; even the most enthusiastic volunteer could not have helped but find seven hours of drill per day tedious and wearisome.

Sept. 20, 1929, p. 1. Adams County, Wisconsin WiGenWeb site: http://www.wiroots.org/wiadams/index.html#news (accessed Feb. 25, 2012).

6. Jerry Flint to his brother, June 16, 1861, Jerry Flint Papers, Area Research Center, University of Wisconsin, River Falls; E. B. Quiner, *Correspondence of Wisconsin Volunteers, 1861-1865* (10 scrapbook volumes of Wisconsin Civil War newspaper clippings of soldier correspondence) (Madison: State Historical Society of Wisconsin), vol. 1, pp. 187-88. Hereafter cited as Quiner, *Correspondence*, with name of correspondent, newspaper, volume, and page number.

Regular deliveries of supplies and food sustained the nearly 1,000 volunteers of the 4th Wisconsin Infantry. Knute Nelson thought the food he received was "fairly good. Mess . . . is like what is found in American hotels except for cake and pie. Our utensils are all of tin except the knives and forks, which are part iron and part steel." Even sleeping on the ground did not seem to weigh heavily on Nelson, who had been attending Albion Academy when the war began. "We are billeted in big canvas tents with six men living in each tent," he reported. "One puts a little hay on the ground inside the tent and when we go to bed we wrap ourselves in big, thick woolen quilts or blankets. This is our bed." Perhaps because it was new, Utley was a clean, healthy camp. With Lake Michigan a short distance away, and three wells on the grounds, Nelson reported, "great emphasis is placed on cleanliness, so we must wash our feet every morning and our whole bodies once a week."[7]

On Duty in Maryland

For those who did not share Nelson's rosy perspective, life in camp was tiresome and unproductive. Therefore, few of the enlistees complained when, little more than two weeks after they had arrived at Camp Utley, the 4th Wisconsin received orders to pack their bags and prepare to travel. Their destination was Baltimore, Maryland, the seat of the war — farther from home than most of them had ever been. President Lincoln and his generals wanted a greater troop presence around the nation's capital, and hence they called the most recent volunteers east. At 2:00 on the afternoon of July 15, 1861, their haversacks stuffed with food, including freshly baked pastries provided by the ladies of Racine, the men of the 4th Wisconsin boarded railroad cars for their journey. The fact that they had not yet been issued weapons created some anxious moments as they headed toward the epicenter of conflict.[8]

On its way to Baltimore, their train stopped several times: first in Toledo, then in Cleveland, before it pushed onward to the cities of Buffalo, Elmira, and Corning in New York State, and finally, to Harrisburg,

7. Bennett, "Sketch of Military Service," p. 1; Knute Nelson to Gullick Thompson in Millard L. Gieske, "Some Civil War Letters of Knute Nelson," *Norwegian American Studies* 23 (1967): 17-18.

8. George Rankin, *William Dempster Hoard* (Madison, WI: W. D. Hoard and Sons, 1925), pp. 26-36.

Pennsylvania. At each of those stops they received meat, bread, pastries, and rousing cheers from the local citizens. Finally, in Pennsylvania, they received their first weapons. Upon learning that they had not yet been armed, Governor Andrew Curtin pulled some antiquated smoothbore muskets and ball-and-powder ammunition from the state's arsenal and issued what he had on hand to the Wisconsin regiment. Many of the men remained unarmed, but until they received army-issued rifles, Pennsylvania muskets would have to do.[9]

Eight days after they left Camp Utley, on July 23, the regiment rolled into Baltimore, a border city where tensions ran high. On April 19, Massachusetts soldiers marching through the city had received a violent reception from a secessionist mob. Four soldiers and twelve civilians had been killed before order was established. With that incident as his justification, President Lincoln, on May 13, had ordered the Union Army to arrest the city's secessionist-sympathizing mayor, city council, and police commissioner — orders that were later declared unconstitutional — and place the city under martial law. Two months later, the 4th Wisconsin, armed with their Pennsylvania muskets, passed through the city without incident. For the next week they settled at Camp Carroll, in an area known as Mount Clare, on the southwest edge of the city. There they were finally issued the Model 1842 .69 caliber Springfield rifled muskets with bayonets that they had been promised when they left Wisconsin. They also received their first official U.S. Army blue uniforms. Thus armed and uniformed properly, the regiment was assigned to relieve the 6th Massachusetts Infantry and guard the railroad and bridges leading twenty miles west from Baltimore. With their regimental headquarters located at Relay House, about nine miles from the city, the 4th Wisconsin spent the next three months engaged in a mixed routine of drilling and guard duty.[10]

From the beginning of the war, President Lincoln and members of his cabinet were determined to keep the Union's four border states — Delaware, Kentucky, Maryland, and Missouri (all of which allowed slavery)

9. Theodore Gillette, *Reminiscences* (Port Hudson State Historical Site, Zachary, Louisiana), cited in Martin, *History of Fourth Wisconsin Infantry*, p. 22.

10. Mount Clare was the property of the Carroll family. Today the 1760 colonial Georgian home, built by Charles Carroll, remains as a museum house in the center of Baltimore's Carroll Park. Mount Clare Museum House: www.Mountclare.org (accessed Feb. 16, 2012); Maj. Gen. John Dix to Maj. Gen. George B. McClellan, August 19, 1861; O.R., I, 5, pp. 569-71; O.R., 1, 51, p. 431.

Union troops at the Relay House station in 1861. Earl and his 4th Wisconsin Infantry comrades saw their first action guarding the B & O railroad west of Baltimore. (B&O Railroad Museum)

— from joining the Confederacy. In the fall of 1861, they were especially worried that pro-Confederate legislators in Maryland would lead the state's secession from the Union when the state legislature met in mid-September. Based on sketchy intelligence provided to him by General George McClellan, Lincoln ordered the arrest and imprisonment of more than two dozen pro-Confederate members of the Maryland legislature, along with the mayor of Baltimore and several other local officials — offering no legal justification for their arrest. McClellan, for his part, was seeking to curry favor with the president and was ambitious to replace the aged and ailing general-in-chief of the U.S. Army, Winfield Scott. Hence McClellan carried out the order and supported the President's plan for the Union Army's occupation of Maryland.

The thirty-four-year-old McClellan achieved his goal to head the entire Union Army on November 1, 1861, the day Lincoln accepted Scott's request to retire and made "little Mac" the youngest general-in-chief in U.S. Army history. Three days later, McClellan authorized Major General John Dix, military commander of Maryland, to gather in Baltimore the 4th Wisconsin, the 2nd Massachusetts Light Artillery, and a Pennsylvania cavalry company for a campaign down the east side of Chesapeake Bay, known as Maryland's Eastern Shore. Maryland's gubernatorial and legislative election was scheduled for November 6, and Gen. Dix's assignment was to assure that the Eastern Shore's elections be protected from Rebel interference and safe for Unionist candidates.

The southern half of the Eastern Shore featured rich farmland and a strongly secessionist, pro-slavery population. According to newspaper reports, Rebel groups were holding secret meetings and were concocting plans to deny polling access to Unionists — and thus to steal the election. To counteract those efforts, Gen. Dix ordered his Wisconsin, Massachusetts, and Pennsylvania units to march down the peninsula to the Virginia border to "give protection to the Union men . . . [and] prevent the migration or importation of [secessionist] voters . . . with a view to carry the election . . . [and] aid the United States marshal and deputies in putting down any open demonstration of hostility to the Government or resistance to its authority."[11]

After several hours of loading men, equipment, and supplies aboard the steamer *Adelaide*, the Wisconsin, Pennsylvania, and Massachusetts soldiers got underway at 9:00 p.m. on November 4, 1861, moving quietly through the darkness to the Wicomico River, across from the mouth of the Potomac. They then steamed carefully up that smaller river about three miles to the village of Whitehaven, arriving early the next day. Disembarking as soon as the *Adelaide* docked, they immediately set out for Princess Anne, a small community about thirteen miles to the south, where they arrived at 10:00 p.m. — tired, hungry, and soaked by a nighttime rain. By morning, that rain had turned their campgrounds and surrounding roads into mud and standing water. Nonetheless, the officers of the 4th Wisconsin had their troops on the road at daybreak; they were headed for Snow Hill, about twenty-five miles further south.

Marching through persistent rain, with mud oozing over the tops of their shoes, each man carried his "musket, knapsack, haversack, canteen and cartridge box" — about thirty pounds. By the time they reached their destination on November 6, "their shoulders ached . . . and their feet were blistered and bleeding." During the trek, the regiment subsisted on hard tack and uncured ham while marching. Their commanding officer, Colonel Halbert E. Paine, shared his men's discomfort. Writing home, one soldier spoke approvingly of Paine's performance: "Seeing him sitting on his horse with bread in one hand and pork in the other," he wrote, "was a sight that will not be forgotten." Fortunately for the men of the 4th, Unionists at Snow Hill had food and coffee waiting when they arrived,

11. *New York Times*, Nov. 1, 1861; O.R., I, 5, pp. 641-42.

Colonel Halbert E. Paine
(Quiner, *Military History of Wisconsin*)

and the Unionists had also placed public buildings, churches, barns, and homes at the regiment's disposal, so all the Wisconsin soldiers spent the night warm and dry.

The 4th Wisconsin's arrival on the Eastern Shore had the desired effect for Lincoln and the Union. The election went smoothly and the Union candidates prevailed. Confirming the importance of the Union forces' presence, community leaders informed regimental officers that "a large [Confederate] military force was on the march for that part of the country the day previous, but learning of our approach, at once beat a retreat." The three Union units remained at Snow Hill for several days waiting for their tents, baggage, and equipment to catch up. It was not until November 11 that their remaining equipment and supplies arrived over the muddy, rutted roads, and by that time they had cleaned and dried their clothes, shoes, and rifles.[12]

12. Halbert Paine was an Ohio native and graduate of Western Reserve College who had established a legal practice in Milwaukee in 1857 with German expatriate and union

Once again ready to be on the move, the 4th Wisconsin and its supporting cavalry and artillery units proceeded to Newtown, about fifteen miles south of Snow Hill, to join the 5th New York Volunteer Infantry (Duryée's Zouaves), the 21st Indiana, the 6th Michigan, the 17th Massachusetts, and Purnell's Legion of recently recruited Maryland Unionist volunteers, a total of 4,000 effectives. The combined force, now commanded by General Henry Hayes Lockwood, had information that the Confederates that they had initially pushed back from Snow Hill were now at Oak Hall, Virginia, about eight miles further south, where Virginia's northern border cuts across the southern tip of the Delmarva Peninsula. The combined Union force set out after them, which meant that the Wisconsin soldiers were entering the Old Dominion State at the end of their march. As they crossed the state line into Virginia — and for the first time, entered the Confederacy — a "prolonged cheer burst forth from each regiment."

Upon reaching the reported Rebel campsite, they found that the Confederates had fled in the face of the larger Union force, leaving a deserted, partially finished earthwork, several abandoned cannons, and five hundred muskets. The area's remaining residents, both black and white, avoided the Yankees, who, they had been told, had come "to murder, ravage, plunder, and . . . sell them [slaves and free blacks] into bondage." When they saw that that was not the case, they became friendlier and told questioners that, at the first sign of Union soldiers, the Rebels had "beat a hasty and disgraceful retreat, spiking their guns and flying in all directions." Correspondents from the Wisconsin regiment were struck by the "suffering and squalid poverty of the inhabitants." A letter from "B," which was printed in the Oconto *Pioneer,* blamed the area's fleeing leaders for leaving behind residents with "no communication, either by land or water, with[out] any ports of trade, and . . . utterly destitute of everything."[13]

Lockwood's brigade remained in the Oak Hall area for three days, searching the surrounding area and interviewing residents, and then it

---

general Carl Schurz. Several members of the 4th Wisconsin wrote home telling of their march down Maryland's eastern shore, and a number of their letters were reprinted in Wisconsin newspapers. Quiner, *Correspondence,* vol. 1, "B to Friend Ginty," Nov. 23, 1861, printed in the Oconto *Pioneer,* pp. 193-95; "Unidentified letter writer to Editors," *Patriot,* Nov. 7, 1861, p. 195, and Dec. 15, 1861, pp. 196-97; "Beloit to *Journal and Courier,*" Nov. 15, 1861, pp. 195-96; "Correspondence of the *State Journal,*" Dec. 15, 1861, p. 196; Dec. 30, p. 197.

13. Quiner, *Correspondence,* vol. 1, "B to Friend Ginty," printed in Oconto *Pioneer,* Nov. 23, 1861, pp. 193-95; Correspondence of the *State Journal,* Dec. 15, 1861, p. 196.

continued further into Virginia. On November 20, advance scouts came upon a group of Rebels attempting to load artillery pieces into a fishing "smack" (sailboat) to be shipped to the Virginia mainland. Seeing the Union men, the Rebels abandoned their cannons, along with a large number of muskets, and fled. Hitching horses to the cannons' caissons, the Union soldiers continued on to Drummondtown (now Accomac), near the southern tip of the Eastern Shore peninsula. There they camped on the plantation of Confederate general — and former Virginia governor — Henry H. Wise, availing themselves of meat, fruits, and vegetables in his cellars before moving on to the village of Pungoteague to meet steamers sent to take them back to Baltimore. By Tuesday, December 10, the regiment was back where their expedition had begun five weeks earlier, and were ensconced in hastily built barracks in Baltimore's Patterson Park, which were intended for their use for the remainder of the winter. During their time on the Eastern Shore, they had provided security for Maryland's state election, had driven an estimated group of 800 Rebels across the Chesapeake Bay to mainland Virginia, and had seized thirteen cannons and several hundred muskets.[14]

Their time in Maryland introduced Isaac and Joseph Earl, and their 4th Wisconsin comrades, to a complex society of slaves and free blacks, slaveholders, secessionists, and Southern Unionists. They discovered that in occupied areas they had to deal with angry Confederates, while they were providing protection to Unionists, freedom-seeking slaves, and free blacks. In Baltimore they saw blacks, slave and free, forced to show deference to whites. In the tobacco counties of southern Maryland and the eastern shore of the Chesapeake, they encountered large farms dependent on slave labor. They saw for the first time the appalling conditions of slaves' lives. And they learned that blacks could be an important source of information in their pursuit of Rebels.

Isaac Earl left no personal explanation for his decision to volunteer for military service. However, an incident that occurred during the Eastern Shore campaign testifies to his loyalty to the Union and President Lincoln. At some point during the campaign, a local resident with Southern sympathies drove his carriage past a group of soldiers and said or did

14. Quiner, *Correspondence,* "Chaplain A. C. Barry, *The Accomac Expedition,*" vol. 1, pp. 197-203. In April 1968, over a century later, Patterson Park was used once again as a military encampment for troops sent to Baltimore after the murder of Martin Luther King triggered rioting.

something provocative. There is no report of what he did, but there is no doubt what happened next: Isaac Earl leaped forward and began shaking the carriage, demanding that its occupant "hurrah for Lincoln," and he didn't stop until the man complied. It is a single, simple incident, and it should not be overemphasized; but Earl's prompt and decisive response suggests a young patriot with strongly held beliefs that were to underpin his later military performance.[15]

To New Orleans

The 4th Wisconsin remained in their Patterson Park quarters until February 17, 1862, when General McClellan designated the regiment to join Gen. Benjamin Butler's New Orleans expedition. Within four days of receiving the notice, the regiment moved out, traveling from Baltimore to Newport News, Virginia, at the mouth of Chesapeake Bay. There they joined twelve other regiments that were waiting to board ocean vessels bound for Louisiana to be part of the southern half of a great Mississippi River pincer action that was intended to grasp the entire river out of Confederate control.[16] After eight months of daily drills and guard duty — and their first encounters with the Southern economic and social system — most of the men of the 4th Wisconsin were fully prepared to assume the more active role portended by McClellan's order.

On Tuesday, March 4, the 4th Wisconsin Infantry, together with the 6th Michigan and the 21st Indiana, boarded the steamship *Constitution* — a total of 2,700 men — and were crammed so tightly together that the 4th Wisconsin's second in command, Lieutenant Colonel Sidney Bean, complained bitterly that they were "packed away, just like any other part of the ship's cargo, and in places which you would not dream could be made to receive human beings." The *Constitution* got underway on March 5, with

15. Newton Culver, "Brevet Major Isaac N. Earl: A Noted Scout of the Department of the Gulf," *Proceedings of the Historical Society of Wisconsin* (1917): 308-9.

16. Gen. Winfield Scott originally devised the plan to seize the Mississippi. In 1862, Gen. McClellan placed Gen. Butler at the head of an estimated 18,000 soldiers comprising the land portion of a joint army-navy campaign that was to travel up the Mississippi River past Confederate-held Forts St. Philip and Jackson and seize control of New Orleans and continue upriver to Baton Rouge and beyond, ultimately joining with troops who were headed downstream, placing the entire river under Union control. McClellan's orders to Butler can be found in O.R., I, 6, pp. 694-95.

Major General Benjamin Butler
(Library of Congress)

a booming sendoff from Rebel batteries at the mouth of the James River. Rebel cannon balls flew overhead and landed around the vessel but did little damage. For the three regiments aboard, the heavy seas they encountered at Hampton Roads were more menacing than the Confederate cannon fire. New to ocean travel, nearly all of the soldiers became seasick. The fortunate were able to get to the rail, while the less agile befouled decks and passageways. It took several days for the passengers to adjust to life at sea.

Past Hampton Roads and out on open water, the voyage turned calm and uneventful. The speedy *Constitution* delivered her passengers to Ship Island, on the Gulf Coast midway between Mobile, Alabama, and the mouth of the Mississippi, on March 12, and began unloading men, equipment, and food provisions the next day. Twelve miles off the Mississippi shore, Ship Island, as one soldier told his family, "is a narrow, low strip of sand, about ten miles in length, and, with the exception of a small portion of the eastern end, is as barren as the Great Desert of Sahara. The eastern — or, as we call it, the upper, end — of the island is chiefly noted for the alligators, wild boars, and snakes which infest the sloughs and canebrakes in the vicinity." With upwards of 20,000 infantry, cavalry, and artillery troops already on the island jockeying for space — and more arriving — Ship Island seemed as though it might sink under the weight of its new occupants. Union vessels encircled much of the island: anchored offshore were about twenty vessels of U.S. Navy Commander David Dixon Porter's mortar fleet, together with numerous prizes of war ensnared by the Union blockade. Gen. Butler and his naval counterpart, Flag Officer David G. Farragut, were assembling a formidable land and sea force for their grand assault on New Orleans and the lower Mississippi, and the men of the 4th Wisconsin, who had yet to see combat, were eager to prove their mettle.[17]

Their opportunity came a month later, on Monday, April 14, when — after several false starts due to bad weather and changed plans — the assault flotilla got underway. The 4th Wisconsin joined the 6th Michigan and the 21st Indiana aboard the steamer *Great Republic*, and headed for the mouth of the Mississippi. Four days later, at their destination, the regiments transferred to the frigate *Colorado*, whose shallower draft enabled her to pass over the shoal at the mouth of the river. Once the *Colorado* was on the river, Fort Jackson and Fort St. Philip stood guard — heavily armed and fortified, with seemingly impenetrable walls. The 4th Wisconsin was to be part of the assault force attacking those two forts, but the assault proved unnecessary when, following a heavy bombardment, Farragut ran his fleet past the forts and continued upriver. No longer defensible, New Orleans surrendered on April 29, and the forts, after a second heavy bombardment, surrendered when the isolated troops inside began to mutiny.[18]

Shortly after arriving in New Orleans, Isaac Earl received news from Ship Island that tempered his satisfaction over the successful trip up the Mississippi and the surrender of New Orleans. While his regiment was making its way to New Orleans, Earl's brother Joseph, who had been too ill

17. The *Constitution* was a new vessel, commissioned in Nov. 1861. At the time she was launched, *The New York Times* described her as over 350 feet in length and 45 feet at her greatest breadth. To produce steam, she had four main boilers that were 32 feet long and 13 feet in diameter. The diameter of her paddlewheels was 40 feet. *New York Times*, Nov. 16, 1861; Quiner, *Correspondence*, vol. 3, "Unidentified letter writer," p. 79; "2nd Lt. Henry B. Lighthizer to editor of *Patriot*," p. 87; "High Private to Friend Mills," April 3, 1862, p. 90; Bennett, "Sketch of Military Service," p. 4.

18. For the most recent account of the mutinies at Fort St. Philip and Fort Jackson, see Michael D. Pierson, *Mutiny at Fort Jackson* (Chapel Hill: University of North Carolina Press, 2008).

When Gen. Butler's army left Ship Island for New Orleans, it abandoned several vessels and mounds of debris at their training site in the Gulf of Mexico.
(*Harper's Weekly*, May 3, 1862)

to travel, had died back on Ship Island. Before the war, the island had been a healthy location, with soft Gulf breezes making it an attractive summer resort; but the polluted water and standing sewage produced by 20,000 Union troops had turned the island into a disease incubator. Captain Webster P. Moore of the 4th Wisconsin's Company E reported one death, serious illness, and "a good bit of debility" on the island. Another writer told of "more colds, sore throats and rheumatism than they had had during the winter in Maryland. In drilling, the men would often fall down from dizziness caused by biliousness." By the time the regiment prepared to leave for New Orleans, deaths had become a regular part of daily reports, and "34 men had been discharged sick and sent home. Nearly 100 were left ill on the island, and some 75 who went with the regiment . . . were unfit for duty."[19]

Joseph Earl's condition had continued to deteriorate after the regi-

19. Quiner, *Correspondence*, vol. 3 "Letter of Capt. W. P. Moore," p. 83; "'S' to editor of *Patriot*, March 21, 1862," p. 87; "High Private to Friend Mills," Apr. 3, 1862, p. 90; "The 4th Regiment at New Orleans," p. 98; Service Record of Pvt. Joseph Earl, Washington, DC: National Archives Microfilm Publication M 559, Roll 8.

ment left, and on June 21, 1862, he died in Ship Island's military hospital. It is not known when Isaac last spoke with his brother before leaving for New Orleans with the 4th Wisconsin, and there is no indication he was ever able to visit his brother's grave. With Joseph's death and their parents gone a dozen years earlier, Isaac Earl had few remaining close family members. Only his brother William, serving with the 7th Wisconsin Infantry in the Army of the Potomac, and the cousins in Wisconsin remained.

CHAPTER TWO

On the Mississippi

T HE 4TH WISCONSIN HAD BRUSHED UP AGAINST THE COMPLEX POL-
itics of disunion and slavery in Maryland, but little in their first year
of service in the Union Army prepared Isaac Earl and his comrades for
their arrival in New Orleans on May 1, 1862. As they disembarked, they
found themselves in the midst of a dyspeptic population. Belligerent Confederates hissed and shouted angry epithets in their frustrated and futile
resistance to the Union forces, who were now asserting control over the
nearly 170,000 residents of the largest city in the Confederacy, while the
men and women who supported the Union held back.[1]

Social and Political Complexities

They came as invaders and occupiers into a complex society of secessionists, capitalists, laborers, slaves, and owners — an economy built on
cotton production and river commerce. Thinly settled and economically
unimportant until cotton-growing was introduced in the 1790s, the region
from Memphis south to New Orleans had grown rapidly thereafter. Taking advantage of the fertile loam of the river delta, entrepreneurs drained,
cleared, and planted the land, and by 1800, they were harvesting an esti-

1. Chester G. Hearn, *When the Devil Came Down to Dixie: Ben Butler in New Orleans*
(Baton Rouge: Louisiana State University Press, 1997), pp. 71-75; Quiner, *Correspondence*,
vol. 3, "High Private to Friend Mills," May 1, 1862, pp. 102-4; "Frank Ferris to Parents and
Friends," May 10, 1862, p. 104; "W.P.W. [William P. Ward] to a Friend," May 4, 1862, pp.
101-2.

mated annual 2,500 bales of cotton (weighing 500 pounds each). During the first sixty years of the nineteenth century, abundant cotton grown on cheap land produced remarkable wealth for the region's agricultural entrepreneurs. Their production had reached well over 400,000 bales by 1860. A slave labor force bound to their will for life underpinned a system dominated by a group of fewer than a thousand successful elites who owned fifty or more slaves and at least a thousand acres of the richest agricultural soil in North America. The most successful of these planters, men with strong ties to the North, such as Stephen Duncan and Haller Nutt, had operations worth well over $1 million, owned as many as 800 slaves, and controlled thousands of acres. In addition to their wealth, their lifestyle distinguished these cotton grandees of the deep South. They had few qualms about displaying their wealth. Most had fine country homes as well as grand mansions in Natchez or other river cities, and many traveled to cooler northern and European climes during the summer heat. They were known for their lavish, tailored clothing, large libraries, and stables of well-bred horses — all of which impressed their peers, if not always the less successful growers and merchants. In addition to their opulent lifestyle, their role as government, religious, and cultural leaders further set them apart. By 1860 they were a small, tight-knit group who socialized and married within their class — and permitted few outsiders to penetrate that circle.[2]

Supporting those at the top were middle-class merchants and traders, small farmers, tradesmen and laborers, free blacks, and the largest concentrated slave population in Mississippi and Louisiana. The region's emergence as a cotton-growing center and the opportunity for quick gain drew scores of speculators and entrepreneurs; all soon discovered that, although highly profitable, cotton-growing was labor intensive. It required a dependable supply of field workers to prepare the soil, tend the growing plants, pick and gin the crop, and then begin the cyclical process again. Slaves who could be purchased and controlled for life proved to be the most manageable labor pool; their numbers grew quickly in the first half of the nineteenth century. By 1860, an estimated 3,000 slaves, individually

2. The value of Nutt's property 150 years later would be in the range of $30-60 million. "Measuring Worth": http://www.measuringworth.com/uscompare/relativevalue.php (accessed Apr. 10, 2013). Michael Wayne, *The Reshaping of Plantation Society: The Natchez District, 1860-80* (Baton Rouge: Louisiana State University Press, 1990), pp. 5-12; Morris Christopher, *Becoming Southern: The Evolution of a Way of Life; Warren County and Vicksburg, Mississippi, 1770-1860* (New York: Oxford University Press, 1995), pp. 29-41.

valued at as much as $2,000 each, labored on plantations in five Mississippi counties between Natchez and Vicksburg alone.

The great wealth created by cotton-growing, as well as its dependence on slavery, presented a political dilemma to midcentury plantation owners in the Natchez-Vicksburg region. Although they were concerned about the emerging power of the new Republican Party and the Northern abolitionists, most of the region's leaders were not convinced that secession was the way to protect their way of life. Economically and socially, the region depended on the continued free flow of river commerce. The region's economy tied plantations and farms to urban traders, merchants, and investors, most of whom wished to see slavery continued and sought to avoid a war's disruption of their prosperity. Improved agriculture techniques and the clearing of more land had increased the size of their plantations and cotton crops, while Congress's 1808 prohibition of the African slave trade had driven up the value of slaves already in the country. Furthermore, secession and the likely war to follow would cut them off from investments and acquaintances in the northern United States and in Europe.

Political tensions along the lower Mississippi grew increasingly volatile in the 1850s. Antisecessionists won the 1850 Mississippi gubernatorial election, finishing especially strong in the counties along the river; but that was their high point. Throughout the following decade, secessionists gained momentum. In the campaign before the 1860 presidential election, the *Vicksburg Whig* and the *Natchez Courier* still resisted secession, but most Mississippians were prepared to leave the Union, supporting the Democrats' presidential candidate, the secessionist John Breckenridge. Only the counties along the Mississippi directed a majority of their votes to the less extreme Constitutional Union Party candidate, John Bell.

On December 20, 1860, six weeks after Abraham Lincoln's electoral victory, but well before his inauguration, which was to occur on March 4, 1861, South Carolina began the secession parade. During the next forty days, Mississippi, Florida, Alabama, Georgia, Louisiana, and Texas followed; and in slightly more than four months, Virginia, Arkansas, North Carolina, and Tennessee completed the march away from the Union. Some in the lower Mississippi River valley openly opposed secession, while others sought to slow the process. One group of these "go-slower" moderates gathered at Raymond, Mississippi, about thirty miles east of Vicksburg, and concluded that, if secession must come, it should be led by men of education and talent (like themselves), not by "fire eaters." Similarly, prominent Natchez residents sought to send as many moderate delegates to the secession convention as possible. Members of the Surget, Brown, and Foote families, all prosperous landholders and businessmen, sponsored meetings and dinner gatherings; but they could not slow the secession momentum. In the end, the state seceded by a delegate vote of 84-15, with only seven counties along the Mississippi River failing to support the majority.[3]

In Louisiana similar sentiments brought a like result. In Baton Rouge, former U.S. Senator Pierre Soulé joined others seeking to slow the process. Joseph Rozier of New Orleans openly resisted the Louisiana ordinance of secession, arguing presciently that Europe would not recognize a separate Southern nation, and that economic ruin would follow. Charles Bienvenu, also of New Orleans, proposed that, rather than a vote of the delegates, secession should be done by a popular vote of all the Louisianans. Most pro-Union in his position was James Taliaferro of Catahoula Parish, across the Mississippi River from Natchez: he denied Louisiana's right to secede and predicted that secession would be followed by high taxes, property loss, and, ultimately, war and anarchy. Taliaferro had few statewide allies, but the mere fact that he had been elected a delegate to the secession convention shows that such sentiments were not his alone. However, when the time came, all but a small resistant minority of Louisiana delegates voted to secede from the Union. When a last-ditch February peace conference in Washington, D.C., failed to resolve the crisis, Mississippi, Louisiana, and five other original seceding states adopted a provisional constitution for the Confederate States of America and established their temporary capital at Montgomery, Alabama. The Confederacy's last four states joined in April and May. By then, Confederate troops had fired on Fort Sumter, the first salvos of a four-year Civil War that would claim at least 620,000 lives.[4]

Moving Upriver

Gen. Butler intended to occupy the Mississippi well north of New Orleans, and after a week on guard in that city, the 4th Wisconsin received orders to board the steamers *Burton* and *Ceres*, with seven companies from the 6th Michigan Infantry, and to head upriver. Commanded by Gen. Thomas

3. *Natchez Courier*, Nov. 29, 1860; William Banks Taylor, *King Cotton and Old Glory: Natchez, Mississippi in the Age of Sectional Controversy and Civil War* (Hattiesburg, MS: Fox Printing, 1977), pp. 7-19, 31-37; Wayne, *Natchez District*, pp. 8-11; John D. Winters, *The Civil War in Louisiana* (Baton Rouge: Louisiana State University Press, 1963), pp. 3-13.
4. Winters, *Civil War in Louisiana*, pp. 12-13.

Williams, they pushed cautiously north, assessing conditions and dealing with pockets of resistance as they went.

Their first destination was a levee about fifteen miles above New Orleans, where they were assigned to destroy two bridges and the connecting track of the New Orleans, Jackson, and Great Northern Railroad to prevent Confederate troops and materials from traveling between Jackson, Louisiana, and the Mississippi River. Arriving at the levee, the soldiers disembarked and began marching inland. The river was above flood stage, which forced the troops to hike through "a Cyprus swamp, in the water up to [their] armpits [where] alligators and soldiers were mixed up in general confusion, and . . . these interesting creatures outnumbered the soldiers." Upon reaching their destination and happy to be out of the water, the soldiers got to work. They burned the bridges and ripped up nearly twenty miles of track. One soldier described pulling up the rails with special tools: "[T]hen the ties, and those we piled up and placed the rails across them, and set fire to the heaps. The heat would cause the rails to bend, from their own weight, which made them forever useless."

Isaac Earl and his Company D comrades were sent to destroy several miles of trestle and track bordering Lake Pontchartrain. Heading down the track to begin their task, they heard a noise coming toward them. Soon a handcar with seven passengers hove into view. Despite their shouted orders of "Halt," the car kept coming. Repeated commands finally brought a shout from the car that to some sounded like "Let us run through them." Others could not understand what was said. Whatever the occupants shouted, the car kept coming at full speed until Major Frederick Boardman, leading Company D, gave the command to fire. The resulting barrage left three of the car's passengers dead, and one wounded. Only after the shooting stopped did Maj. Boardman learn that the handcar occupants were unarmed citizens "of the vicinity and of New Orleans," including the proprietor of the St. Charles Hotel in New Orleans, "who escaped unhurt." They were hoping to reach New Orleans, the survivors said, and they were traveling by handcar because guerrillas and partisans were known to be in the area, regularly sniping at passing vessels. Tension was high all along the river, and though they were troubled by the accidental shootings, Union authorities deemed the incident an accident and absolved Maj. Boardman of any blame for the deaths.[5]

5. Quiner, *Correspondence*, vol. 3, "Chaplain A. C. Barry to Editor, *Sentinel*," May 13, 1862, May 19, 1862, pp. 106-8; "High Private to Friend Mills," May 30, 1862, pp. 110-11.

**The Union river fleet depended on laborers on
Baton Rouge's riverfront to load the coal and wood to fuel its vessels.**
(Louisiana State University Library, G. H. Suydam Photograph Collection)

Following the shooting, members of Company D went further inland
to take out a bridge, and in the process got another taste of the difficulty of
operating among hostile residents in unknown terrain. As they continued
their march to the bridge, they encountered a second handcar. This time
they held their fire and captured its occupants. Leaving several of their
members to guard them while the remainder pressed on, they reached
the bridge (more like a long causeway). Rebels at the far end of the bridge
were preparing to fire a small cannon in the direction of the Union soldiers. The cannon misfired and the Rebels fled, leaving Company D to
complete its demolition without further disruption. When the destruction
of the railroad and its bridges was complete, the exhausted soldiers and
their prisoners pulled back to Ashland plantation, home of a wealthy sugar
planter, Duncan F. Kenner. There, on pleasant grassy grounds, with well-
stocked storehouses nearby, they rested for two days before returning to
the Mississippi River and continuing north.

The 4th Wisconsin and 6th Michigan regiments traveled all the way
up the river to Vicksburg, with stops at Baton Rouge, Natchez, and Warrenton to examine docks, roads, railroads, and warehouse facilities, and

to determine the mood of the residents. A quick look at Vicksburg, high on a bluff overlooking the Mississippi, convinced expedition leaders that it was too well defended to permit an assault, and they turned back. By the end of May they were back in Baton Rouge, and were based on the site of the former United States Arsenal.[6]

Occupation Duty

Their river expedition and time in Baton Rouge had given the 4th Wisconsin's leadership a firsthand look at the level of guerrilla activity along the river, prompting ideas for how to deal with the irregular groups that were harassing Union troops throughout the region. Lieutenant Colonel Sidney Bean, the 4th's second in command, wrote that "guerrilla bands infest the surrounding country. . . . These guerrilla parties are being organized everywhere . . . [and their goal] is to drive us from the country."[7]

Because they were on their home terrain, the guerrillas moved stealthily and quickly, and Union commanders understood that they needed intelligence about the numbers, preparedness, and location of these irregulars. Prompt and forceful responses to guerrilla strikes were needed to limit their effectiveness. Union leaders also realized that they needed to know the lay of the land wherever they went. Accurate information and maps about roads, trails, rivers, and creeks, and the location and occupants of plantations and farms, often meant the difference between an expedition's success and failure.

It was also in and around Baton Rouge that the Wisconsin soldiers first encountered large numbers of slaves, who had fled nearby plantations and come to Union lines seeking freedom, safety, and sustenance. Now free, these former slaves brought with them — and willingly shared — useful information about the swamps, forests, and fields along the river, as well as about the location and activities of guerrilla groups. Chaplain A. C. Barry of the 4th Wisconsin wrote to the *Milwaukee Sentinel*: "The negroes . . . [are] the only true friends of the country, a few whites excepted

6. Quiner, *Correspondence*, vol. 3, "Chaplain A. C. Barry to Editor, *Sentinel*," May 19, 1862, pp. 107-8; "Correspondence of the *Sentinel* from B," May 18, 1862, p. 108; "Pvt. Leon C. Bartlett to Friend Ross," May 30, 1862, pp. 109-10. Kenner's Ashland plantation is now on the National Register of Historic Places.

7. Quiner, *Correspondence*, vol. 3, "Lt. Col. Sidney A. Bean to Family," June 8, 1862, pp. 112, 115.

[and provide valuable information]." He cited an incident in which members of the 4th learned from former slaves where guerrillas were camped, and thus were able to avoid a deadly ambush. Later, as they pursued the guerrillas, additional information from the same blacks helped them set a surprise of their own in which they captured several of the enemy and wounded or killed others.[8]

For many members of the 4th Wisconsin, the more they saw of slavery and its consequences, the stronger their opposition became. Byron Kenyon of Osceola, Wisconsin, a small farming community near the state's western border with Minnesota, spoke for more than himself when he wrote home from Louisiana describing "the arch execrable institution of slavery" as "essentially, primarily, and eternally wrong, and not all the sophistry of satan nor his hell polluted tools of human form can make them appear right to a just mind and a true heart." Although many of his comrades did not have Kenyon's capacity for expression, they shared his distaste for slavery and were determined to see its elimination.[9]

The regard Earl and his contemporaries came to hold for former slaves began with their regimental commander, Colonel Halbert Paine. An attorney before the war, Paine turned to his legal training when his brigade commander, General Thomas Williams, issued an order banning freedom-seeking slaves from Union Army camps in Baton Rouge. Under the order, Williams's commanders were to "turn all such fugitives, in their camps and garrisons, out beyond the limits of their respective guards and sentinels." Paine challenged Williams's order, citing the 1861 Confiscation Act, which prohibited army officers from returning to their masters any slaves who had escaped. Paine realized that the legislation had been prompted by actions of his commanding general, Benjamin Butler, an attorney before the war, who the previous spring had defined escaping slaves who reached his lines in Virginia as "contraband of war," that is, property that could be used to aid the enemy and therefore property liable to seizure. Butler's case was carefully reviewed by President Lincoln and his cabinet, most of whom sanctioned the policy, helping push Congress to pass the Confiscation Act, which authorized the seizure of all property, including slaves, that could be used to aid the Rebellion. As more escaping slaves

8. Quiner, *Correspondence*, vol. 3, "Chaplain A. C. Barry to Editor, *Sentinel*," May 30, 1862, pp. 111-12.

9. Byron Kenyon to parents, 12-16-64, Kenyon Letters, Port Hudson State Historic Site.

Former slaves, known as "contrabands," left their owners and made their way
to Baton Rouge as soon as the Union troops arrived in 1862. This contraband
camp was located on the grounds of Baton Rouge's former Female Seminary.
(Louisiana State University Library, G. H. Suydam Collection)

made their way to Union lines, and some conservative generals refused
to accept them, Congress responded by prohibiting army officers from
returning slaves to their masters — even those loyal to the Union.[10]

Convinced that he was in the right legally, Col. Paine stood his ground,
declaring, "I am compelled to either disobey him [Williams] or defy the
sovereign power of the Republic," saying that he would not violate the
law of the land. Gen. Williams responded by ordering Paine's arrest. This
brought the 4th Wisconsin to the edge of mutiny, especially when Colonel Frederick Curtenius of the 9th Connecticut Infantry, a veteran of the
Mexican War, also refused the order. Even more might have come of the
incident if Paine had not ordered his men to cease further objection and
"obey your officers." Although they were under arrest, both Paine and
Curtenius remained with their regiments and continued to take charge
when they were in the field.[11]

10. James McPherson, *Tried by War: Abraham Lincoln as Commander in Chief* (New
York: Penguin Press, 2008), pp. 58-59, 85-86.
11. Quiner, *Correspondence*, "Undated Clippings from the *Evergreen City Times*, She-

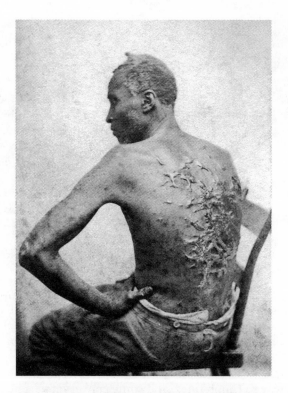

This former slave, known as "Peter" or "Gordon," made his way to Baton
Rouge in March 1863. The mass of scars on his back from beatings were made
well known by a photo taken of him during a medical examination. Earl and
the 4th Wisconsin were in Baton Rouge at the time, and they may very well
have seen him (or this photo) and heard his story. Peter/Gordon served Union
troops in Baton Rouge as a guide, and is said to have fought at Port Hudson.
(National Archives, John Taylor Cartes de Visite Collection, no. 165-JT-230)

Williams and Paine simply did not like each other. Gen. Williams
had made his feelings clear by arresting Paine, and the Wisconsin colonel, for his part, vented his anger in a letter to his wife, calling Williams
"an imbecile, juvenile, drunken, malignant, shallow, cowardly, traitorous,
incompetent, blockhead." But the dispute between Paine and Williams

---

boygan," vol. 3, p. 117; Michael J. Martin, *A History of the 4th Wisconsin Infantry and Cav-
alry in the Civil War* (El Dorado Hills, CA: Savas Beatie, 2006), pp. 77-79; Samuel C. Hyde
Jr., ed., *Halbert Eleazer Paine: A Wisconsin Yankee in Confederate Bayou Country* (Baton
Rouge: Louisiana State University Press, 2009), pp. 77-97.

also reflected a split within Union military leadership. Some generals, mainly those who held political appointments, favored a conciliatory policy toward everyone in occupied territory, hoping that would ease the way for the early return of seceding states. Military generals preferred a tougher approach that would keep everyone, including Unionists and former slaves, beyond their lines. At first the conciliatory policy seemed to be working, but as the occupation troops moved in and guerrilla and partisan raids — and smuggling — increased, more officers leaned toward tougher actions. For the most part their soldiers agreed.[12]

"Butler's Ditch"

The 4th Wisconsin spent nearly three weeks in Baton Rouge in late May and early June 1862, bivouacked at the arsenal as they patrolled in and around the city. When new orders came in mid-June for them to return to Vicksburg on the steamer *Ceres*, they expected to see more fighting, and they approached the assignment with the purposeful confidence of seasoned soldiers. Due to losses from disease and disability that were brought on by the summer heat, their time on Ship Island, and the swamps and bayous north of New Orleans, the regiment was mustering only about 300 effective soldiers, about one-third its full strength. Some men had been sent home, others were in hospital camps, and still others were simply too weak to travel.

Guerrilla activity and sniper fire from both banks of the Mississippi made the 4th Wisconsin's second trip north one of constant watchfulness. Particularly contentious was the area around Grand Gulf, Mississippi, about thirty-five miles south of Vicksburg. Gen. Williams learned of the existence of a guerrilla camp in the area, and he sent Col. Paine and the 4th Wisconsin to investigate. They had been fired on from Grand Gulf on their

12. Halbert Paine to My Lovely Wife, August 3, 1862, in Fred Benton Collection, Center for Southeast Louisiana Studies, Southeastern Louisiana University, quoted in Hyde, ed., *Halbert Eleazer Paine*, p. xiv. For a fuller discussion of the changing Union policy, see Grimsley, *The Hard Hand of War*. Sutherland, *A Savage Conflict*, is the best account of the importance and changing nature of guerrilla warfare in the west. Sutherland contends that the use of guerrillas worked against state and local governments because their unregulated behavior blurred the line between partisan and outlaw and diminished Confederate citizens' trust in government to protect them.

previous expedition to Vicksburg, losing a soldier of the 6th Michigan, and they remained angry about the incident.

Shortly after landing near Grand Gulf, Paine's men found a recently abandoned guerrilla camp, with pieces of broken equipment, and abandoned supplies scattered about. He ordered his men to destroy everything they couldn't carry, and move against the town itself. Soon enough, they discovered that most of its residents had fled inland, abandoning the town. Angered that his quarry had slipped away, Col. Paine ordered every building burned; that action prompted Gen. Williams to commend them for "doing good service." Captain Webster Moore added his approval, writing to a friend, "I hope every place in rebeldom, which offers the least resistance to our forces, will be treated in the same manner." Moore apparently got his wish. Writing at about the same time, Chap. Barry described an "uninterrupted scene of charred remains" all along the shore and "floating masses" of cotton in the river.[13]

With the 4th Wisconsin back aboard the *Ceres* after they had burned Grand Gulf, the 2nd Brigade moved slowly upstream for a second stop at Vicksburg; they arrived on June 25 and settled in to await further orders. When their orders arrived, they proved an unpleasant surprise. Expecting to engage in forays into the surrounding countryside, they instead learned that Gen. Williams, on orders from Gen. Butler, had assigned them to build a canal (popularly known as "Butler's Ditch") across the peninsula created by the horseshoe bend in the Mississippi River at Vicksburg. Butler's theory was that, if it was successful, this canal would enable Union vessels to bypass the city and avoid the heavy fire from Confederate cannons on the bluff. Captain Joseph Bailey of the 4th Wisconsin's Company D, a trained engineer with dam- and ditch-building experience in Wisconsin, directed the project. Isaac Earl and several other men of Company D had worked with Bailey in Wisconsin, and they now joined the other companies of the 4th Wisconsin, along with regiments from Vermont, Iowa, and Illinois, to redirect the course of the great river. They quickly concluded that it was a fool's errand.

Working with little more than shovels and horse-drawn wagons, they labored in mud and water to their waists, enduring oppressive heat, insects, and disease. Illness and mortality rates soared in the already depleted regiments. Having volunteered to fight, the infantrymen hated the work and were close to mutiny when Gen. Williams agreed to employ

13. Quiner, *Correspondence*, vol. 3, "Captain Webster P. Moore to W. W. Wood," June 28, 1862, pp. 122-23; "Chaplain A. C. Barry to Editor of *Sentinel*," May 18, 1862, p. 107.

**Black laborers replaced Union soldiers working on "Butler's Ditch" to
bypass Vicksburg through the fetid lowland opposite the city.**
(*Harper's Weekly*, August 2, 1862)

1,200 black laborers to complete the project. Although many believed the
former slaves were physiologically better suited to the climate and work,
disease and death continued at the same high rates, and they ended only
when caving canal walls convinced Williams and Butler to abandon the
project and remove the workers from the swamp.[14]

Relieved of the construction work, the 2nd Brigade left Vicksburg on
Friday morning, July 25, and hurried back to Baton Rouge, bivouacking

14. Ironically, an 1876 flood accomplished what the Union army could not, sealing
the river channel that ran below Vicksburg's bluffs with debris and forming a new channel
further west. The most complete account of the effort to construct the canal is David F.
Bastian, *Grant's Canal: The Union's Attempt to Bypass Vicksburg* (Shippensburg, PA: Burd
Street Press, 1995). In 1864, Butler tried another canal at Dutch Gap on the James River in
Virginia. Although not completed until after the war, it, too, eventually became the main
channel of that river.

again on the arsenal grounds. At this point, the Wisconsin volunteers had been in service for slightly more than a year, but they had yet to experience heavy fighting. That was about to change. Confederate troops under former presidential candidate John Breckenridge, now a general, were reported to be gathering northeast of the city, spoiling for a fight.[15]

Battle of Baton Rouge

When the 2nd Brigade headed downriver from Vicksburg, Gen. Breckenridge and a little over 3,000 Confederate troops had followed by land, intent on liberating Baton Rouge from Union control. Breckenridge's destination was Camp Moore (named for Louisiana Governor Thomas Overton Moore), about seventy miles east of Baton Rouge, in the Louisiana panhandle just below the Mississippi border. He and his soldiers arrived there at the same time that the 2nd Brigade returned to Baton Rouge, and within a week Gen. Williams had information about the location, numbers, and equipment of Breckenridge's troops. Based on this intelligence, Williams ordered the 4th Wisconsin and six other regiments to assemble in a defensive line along the eastern edge of the city. The 4th was on the left, or north, end of the perimeter, with the 14th Maine, 9th Connecticut, 7th Vermont, 30th Massachusetts, 6th Michigan, and 21st Indiana arrayed to their right. In all, Williams had seven infantry regiments, one cavalry company, and four artillery batteries, totaling about 2,500 men. Breckenridge had a slightly larger force, estimated at just over 3,000.[16]

Before daylight on August 5, with fog masking his movements, Breckenridge attacked the center of the Union defenses, driving the defenders back, but not managing a breakthrough. Heavy shelling by Union gunboats on the Mississippi halted his advance. The Confederate ironclad *Arkansas* was also on the Mississippi, assigned to neutralize the Union gunboats, but she was forced to withdraw when her engines failed. Unable to repair the damage, her crew scuttled and burned her the following day.[17]

15. Culver, Diary, July 26, 1862.

16. Report of Lt. Godfrey Weitzel, U.S. Corps of Engineers, Chief Engineer Department of the Gulf, August 7, 1862; O.R., I, 15, pp. 51-52; see Report of Maj. Gen. John C. Breckenridge, C.S. Army, Commanding Expedition, of the engagement at Baton Rouge and the occupation of Port Hudson; O.R., I, 15, pp. 75-76.

17. Report of Maj. Gen. Earl Van Dorn, C.S. Army, commanding district of Mississippi, of operations at Vicksburg and Baton Rouge, June 27–August 6 (including destruc-

In this newspaper artist's depiction of the battle of Baton Rouge, General Thomas Williams is leading Union troops. He was killed later that day.
(*Harper's Weekly*, September 6, 1862)

As the battle raged before them, the 4th Wisconsin and 9th Connecticut were held in reserve, with orders to lie down so that they would be less visible and wait until the enemy came closer or until they were called forward. Rifle and artillery fire flew all around them, but their order to advance and engage never came. By 10 a.m., Breckenridge's assault had been stopped. A brief artillery bombardment in the afternoon covered his withdrawal. At the end of the day Union forces had maintained their position — and would hold it for the remainder of the war. From time to time there would be rumors of new efforts, but Confederate forces would not again attempt to take Baton Rouge.

Both sides paid a heavy price. The Union lost Gen. Williams, who was killed while rallying the 21st Indiana to hold its heavily assaulted position. Colonel Thomas W. Cahill, of the 9th Connecticut, replaced him during the battle. After the battle, Gen. Butler lifted Williams's earlier arrest

tion of the *Arkansas*), with congratulatory orders; O.R., I, 15, pp. 14-19; Report of Maj. Gen. John C. Breckenridge, C.S. Army, Commanding Expedition, of the engagement at Baton Rouge and the occupation of Port Hudson; O.R., I, 15, p. 79.

The ironclad *Essex*, part of Admiral David Farragut's river fleet, provided
support to Union forces during the Battle of Baton Rouge.
(Louisiana State University Library, G. H. Suydam Collection)

order of the 4th Wisconsin's Col. Paine and assigned him to command
the 2nd Brigade.[18] Both sides suffered heavy casualties in their ranks. Official reports listed 383 Union killed, wounded, or missing, while Gen.
Breckenridge's commanders reported 446 killed, wounded, or missing.
Because they were held in reserve, the 4th Wisconsin had no casualties.
Nonetheless, the regiment received an introduction to the noise, carnage,
and losses of a full battle, and, in the words of Lt. Col. Bean, who succeeded
Col. Paine in commanding the 4th Wisconsin, "displayed the greatest eagerness to meet the enemy. . . ." Their time at the heart of a battle was yet
to come, but now they knew what to expect.

Following the battle of Baton Rouge, the 4th Wisconsin spent several
months moving back and forth between New Orleans and Baton Rouge.
Confederate leaders hoped to disrupt Union control of the lower Mississippi, and their Union counterparts were equally determined to keep the

18. Report of Col. Thomas Cahill, Commanding at Baton Rouge, August 9, 1862; O.R.,
I, 15, pp. 55-58; William DeLoss Love, *Wisconsin in the War of the Rebellion: A History of
Regiments and Batteries the State Has Sent to the Field* (Chicago: Church and Goodman,
1866), p. 536.

river open to boats carrying troops, passengers, and freight. In late August, anticipating another Confederate attack, Gen. Butler ordered Baton Rouge evacuated and burned. This upset Col. Paine, who believed the city was of limited strategic importance and placed little credence in the attack report. He withdrew his regiment to a camp outside New Orleans, and although several buildings were destroyed, he managed to convince Butler to rescind his order to burn the entire city, a decision that was justified when no Confederate attack materialized.[19]

Waller's Texas Cavalry and Port Hudson

Col. Paine established the 4th Wisconsin's New Orleans camp immediately north of the city in an orange grove, giving the Wisconsin boys access to a rare treat, and putting them in an unusually good humor at the end of their first summer in the South. With little to do other than daily drills, they also received regular passes into New Orleans, further elevating their mood.

On September 6, Gen. Butler interrupted the 4th Wisconsin's idyll with an order for them to join the 21st Indiana under Colonel James McMillan and steam about fifteen miles upriver to St. Charles in search of mounted guerrillas reported in the area. Cols. McMillan and Paine drew up a plan that called for Paine to land his force below the last known location of the Rebels, while McMillan's Hoosiers were to go north and land above, squeezing the guerrillas between the two regiments. The trap worked. Paine's forces landed and located a hidden trail running parallel to the river behind a heavy tree line and underbrush. Guerrillas regularly used the trail to ambush passing river vessels and flee pursuing Union forces. Pushing hard up the hidden trail, the 4th Wisconsin encountered a few stragglers and then an abandoned camp. Realizing the fleeing guerrillas had gotten above McMillan, Paine took his men back to the steamboat and hurried further north, forcing the Rebels — whom they subsequently learned were not guerrillas but Lt. Col. Edwin Waller's 13th Texas Cavalry Battalion — to leave the trail and flee into a bordering swamp.

Wading after them into water that became chest-deep in places, the pursuing 4th Wisconsin soldiers began encountering abandoned horses

---

19. Report of Lt. Col. Sidney A. Bean, 4th Wisconsin Infantry; O.R., I, 15, pp. 75-76; Love, *Wisconsin in the War of the Rebellion*, p. 538; Winters, *Civil War in Louisiana*, pp. 113-24; Martin, *History of 4th Wisconsin Infantry*, pp. 93-110.

After Confederate forces were pushed away from the lower Mississippi River by Union troops, guerrilla sharpshooters continued to harass Union vessels on the river. (*London Illustrated News*, May 14, 1862)

and fatigued Texans. They pushed deeper into the swamp until they concluded that further pursuit was futile, and then turned back, bringing with them their prisoners and horses. Together with the Wolverine and Hoosier regiments, the 4th Wisconsin captured fifty soldiers, more than three hundred horses, several battle flags, and a large quantity of abandoned equipment. As a participant in the attack on Waller's battalion, Isaac Earl observed firsthand the importance of accurate intelligence concerning backcountry trails and roads, as well as the use of a steamboat to move quickly and quietly on the river. Col. Paine used the hidden trail and his steamboat to pinch Waller's Texans between the two Union regiments and force them to flee into nearly impenetrable swamps. Following their St. Charles expedition, the 4th Wisconsin returned to New Orleans, where they remained until December, when concerns about another possible assault on Baton Rouge sent the regiment back upriver for a time to gather intelligence about Confederate troop movements.[20]

20. "Report of Col. James W. McMillan, 21st Indiana Infantry, Expedition from Carrollton to Vicinity of St. Charles Court-House, La. and Skirmish"; O.R., I, 15, pp. 135-38;

General Banks

President Lincoln, who had twice traveled the Mississippi to New Orleans as a young man, fully appreciated the river's importance, and in November 1862 he decided that the greatest opportunity for capturing the remaining outposts at Vicksburg and Port Hudson lay with a unified command. He gave that responsibility to a political colleague, General Nathaniel Banks. Complaints about Benjamin Butler's profiteering and harsh treatment of Southern civilians had convinced Lincoln and his advisors that a change was necessary, though Banks, like Butler, was a "political general," with little military knowledge or experience. However, he had volunteered for Union service prior to — and therefore outranked — West Point graduate Ulysses Grant, who had resigned from the army in the 1850s and reentered service in 1861 as a colonel of an Illinois volunteer regiment. With their armies separated by Confederate strongholds at Vicksburg and Port Hudson, the two generals agreed to operate independently unless their forces could be combined, in which case Banks would supersede Grant (now a general) by virtue of his earlier appointment, a situation neither Grant nor Lincoln desired.

In addition to sharing Lincoln's desire to control the Mississippi from Minnesota to the Gulf of Mexico, Gen. Banks supported the President's commitment to returning a nominally pro-Union Louisiana to the United States as quickly as was practicable. Initially, members of the 4th Wisconsin worried that Banks's desire for better relations with Louisianans would lead to a softer approach toward partisans and guerrillas. Soon enough, however, they discovered that Banks, a former Massachusetts governor and congressman, and a former Speaker of the House of Representatives who had White House aspirations, believed that if he captured Port Hudson before Gen. Grant took Vicksburg, it would cement his name in the minds of voters. That meant vigorously prosecuting his portion of the offensive to open the great river.[21]

Martin, *History of 4th Wisconsin Infantry,* pp. 117-18. The loss of more than fifty of his men, as well as horses and supplies in their initial engagement, was the low point of Waller's military career. The battalion remained in southern and western Louisiana until the end of the war. A farmer and merchant, Edwin Waller Jr. joined the 2nd Texas Cavalry Regiment when it was formed in 1861, and he served in West Texas and New Mexico. In 1862, he became lieutenant colonel and commander of the 13th Texas Cavalry Battalion and led them east to Louisiana. *Handbook of Texas Online:* http://www.tshaonline.org/handbook/online/articles/fwaas (accessed Jan. 26, 2012) (published by the Texas State Historical Association).

21. "General Orders No. 184"; O.R., I, 15, pp. 590-91; James G. Hollandsworth Jr.,

Banks's first effort to close the gap between his army and Grant's was to support Admiral David Farragut's effort to push several ironclads and gunboats past Port Hudson's guns and to seize control of the mouth of the Red River, thereby preventing its use as a supply route that carried western agricultural products and soldiers to the Mississippi River and up to Vicksburg. In their support of Farragut, the 4th Wisconsin was to approach Port Hudson by land, creating a distraction while his vessels steamed past the Confederate cannons. Banks and Farragut set the joint plan in motion on Friday, March 13, 1863, sending the 4th Wisconsin to a point four miles from Port Hudson and posting Farragut's seven vessels just out of sight around a bend in the river below Port Hudson. Shortly before midnight, Farragut began his run, and the 4th Wisconsin made a diversionary feint toward Port Hudson. The joint operation failed when only two of Farragut's seven vessels managed to pass Port Hudson's big cannons. Of the remaining five, one ran aground, another burned, and three others, heavily damaged by artillery fire, withdrew back downriver. Failure to get their vessels past Port Hudson convinced Banks and Grant that both Port Hudson and Vicksburg would have to be taken by assault if they were going to split the Confederate states and their military forces west of the Mississippi from their eastern counterparts.[22]

After Farragut's failure to get his vessels past Port Hudson, the 4th Wisconsin soldiers returned to Baton Rouge to clean and repair their equipment and uniforms and fill vacant leadership positions. The reorganization began when Col. Paine was promoted to brigadier general to lead the 2nd Brigade, setting off a chain of changes through the command structure. Lt. Col. Sidney Bean moved up to become the 4th Wisconsin regiment's new colonel; Frederick Boardman was made lieutenant colonel; and Cpt. Joseph Bailey, of Company D, was promoted to major. Further down in the ranks, the changes included Isaac Earl's promotion to corporal in Company D, responsible for leading small squads in pursuit of Confederate partisan and guerrilla units around Baton Rouge. Earl's future performance would prove this to be a savvy appointment.[23]

Pretense of Glory: The Life of General Nathaniel P. Banks (Baton Rouge: Louisiana State University Press, 1998), pp. 89-98.

22. Reports of Maj. Gen. Nathaniel P. Banks, U.S. Army, Commanding Department of the Gulf, of operations March 7-27, 1863; O.R., I, 15, pp. 251-56.

23. Martin, *History of 4th Wisconsin Infantry*, pp. 137-38; Military Service Record of

Campaigning in Southwest Louisiana

As 1863 began, the attention of Generals Grant and Banks remained fo-
cused on the nearly two-hundred-mile stretch of the Mississippi between
Vicksburg and Port Hudson that was still under Confederate control. The
Gulf of Mexico blockade and the occupation of New Orleans and Baton
Rouge had secured the southern end of the great river for the Union;
Grant's forces controlled the river above Vicksburg and, with the capture
of Forts Henry and Donelson, they controlled its tributaries, the Tennessee
and Cumberland Rivers. Following his own unsuccessful attempts to get
his troop vessels past Vicksburg, Grant moved his army down the west side
of the Mississippi into northeast Louisiana and then, once below Vicksburg, crossed back to the river's eastern shore and began an encircling
movement that was designed to cut off the city from outside aid. At the
same time, Gen. Banks began a campaign to push Confederate troops from
the Louisiana region across from Port Hudson. If the two efforts were to
succeed, Vicksburg and Port Hudson would be isolated and destined to
fall, placing the entire Mississippi in Union hands and cleaving the Confederacy in two.

The Confederates had heavily fortified Port Hudson following Gen.
Breckenridge's retreat from Baton Rouge, and Gen. Banks initially chose
to avoid a frontal assault. He and Brigadier General Godfrey Weitzel developed a plan to isolate the Confederate citadel by going around it through
Louisiana. Their plan was to march west from New Orleans to the Atchafalaya River, follow that inland waterway north to Alexandria, and then
take the Red River back to the Mississippi above Port Hudson.[24]

They began to implement their plan in late March and early April,
with troops traveling west from New Orleans and Baton Rouge, respectively, toward Bayou Teche, where they planned to meet and push on to the
Atchafalaya. Their first target was Fort Bisland, an earthworks fortification
on the west bank of Bayou Teche, about sixty miles southwest of Baton
Rouge near present-day Franklin, Louisiana. Bisland's 3,000 defenders,
under General Richard Taylor, son of former President Zachary Taylor

---

Lt. Isaac N. Earl, Record Group 94, National Archives and Records Service, Washington,
DC: National Archives Microfilm Publication M 559, Roll 8.

24. Gen. Banks's adjutant, Lt. Richard B. Irwin, describes the plan in Robert Under-
wood Johnson and Clarence Clough Buel, eds., *Battles and Leaders of the Civil War* (New
York: The Century Co., 1887-1888), vol. 3, pp. 589-90; Brig. Gen. Godfrey Weitzel to Maj.
Gen. C. C. Auger, Feb. 15, 1863; O.R., I, 15, pp. 676-77.

and brother-in-law of Jefferson Davis, included Col. Waller's Battalion of the Texas Cavalry, the group that the 4th Wisconsin had routed earlier along the Mississippi. Gen. Banks arrived from New Orleans by train on April 8, found his troops ready for the assault, and ordered them forward. While attackers in front of them kept Bisland's defenders occupied, General Cuvier Grover, whose 4th Division had made its way along the gulf coast and had landed further west, moved them toward a position behind Bisland to prevent a retreat.[25]

The assembled troops in front of Bisland who were awaiting Gen. Banks's order included Cpl. Isaac Earl and the 4th Wisconsin. This time, instead of being held in reserve, they spearheaded the assault, straight at the artillery pieces mounted on the Confederate breastworks. Initially, the assault was unsuccessful, with artillery and small-arms fire from within the fort keeping Union forces at bay. As night settled, the 4th Wisconsin, with Bayou Teche to their right and the 8th New Hampshire on their left, held the Union troops' right flank. In the darkness, they were sent forward to deploy around several slave cabins and other outbuildings that stood near the fortifications. There they spent a sleepless night with loaded rifles clutched in their arms and Confederate snipers keeping them constantly on edge. At morning's first light, Confederate General Henry Sibley, taking advantage of heavy morning fog, sent a cavalry probe against the 4th's forward skirmishers, and followed with an infantry foray. Soldiers poured out of the earthworks directly at Earl and his fellow skirmishers; but, despite a brief period of intense fighting, the status quo remained when the Confederates withdrew.[26]

In response to the Confederate offensive, Gen. Paine ordered Company D skirmishers to fan out across the front of the 4th regiment and maintain a steady fire. Earl's company returned the fire of Confederate sharpshooters, while a two-hour artillery bombardment took place over their heads. Taylor's cannons ceased firing at noon, and the 4th rose to lead an assault that was stopped by withering rifle fire before it reached Bisland's breastworks. Writing home after the battle, Lt. Leon Bartlett of Co. C spoke proudly of the 4th Wisconsin's performance: "At 12 AM . . . [we] advanced our line of battle about ½ a mile under a terrific shower of

25. Martin, *History of 4th Wisconsin Infantry*, p. 143. For the Confederate perspective of the campaign, see Report of Maj. Gen Richard Taylor, C.C. Army, commanding District of West Louisiana, of operation April 9-23; O.R., I, 15, pp. 388-96.

26. Quiner, *Correspondence*, vol. 8, "Col. Sidney A. Bean to a Friend," April 18, 1863, pp. 207-8.

Major General Edmund Kirby Smith
(Library of Congress)

shot, shell, grape and canister. We were now about 60 rods [about 1,000 feet] from their entrenchments. . . . We then lay down in a ditch about 3 feet wide and 1½ [feet] deep. . . . Co. D was deployed as skirmishers and did their duty nobly; they won the admiration of their comrades by their coolness and undaunted bravery. They kept one battery silenced by picking off the gunners with their long range rifles and engaged their sharpshooters." Company D's skirmishers continued to exchange fire with the Confederates, and were preparing for another assault when orders came from Gen. Banks for everyone to hold his position.

There would be no more fighting at Fort Bisland. Outnumbered on his front, and with Gen. Grover's 2nd Battalion moving into position at his rear, Taylor ordered his men to quietly abandon their positions during

Major General Richard Taylor (Library of Congress)

the night of April 13-14. Earl and the other skirmishers in front of the fort heard sounds of activity coming from inside Fort Bisland during the night and suspected a Confederate retreat, but they could not confirm their suspicions until daybreak, when they stormed the fort and found it empty. Gen. Taylor's retreating forces left in their wake forty Union soldiers killed, including five men from the 4th Wisconsin — the first from their unit to die in combat — and another 184 wounded, including eight from the 4th. No report of Confederate casualties is known to exist.

Once Taylor was away from Fort Bisland, he turned his troops northwest toward Franklin, with Banks in close pursuit. A grounded steamboat kept General Grover's forces from fully deploying as promptly as planned, but they managed to confront Taylor's forces on April 14 at Irish Bend, a loop in Bayou Teche near Franklin. Once again, Taylor managed to disengage after intense fighting and slip away from his foe, retreating further north. Grover's forces followed about twelve miles behind their quarry.

Grover and Taylor continued their fox-and-hound chase, while Banks, further behind, spread his forces out to sweep stragglers before them. By

April 19, the Atchafalaya was under Union control. At that point Banks and Grover paused and waited for their supply trains to catch up, while Taylor's forces moved on, arriving at Alexandria on April 24. Just prior to Taylor's arrival, his superior, Lieutenant General Edmund Kirby Smith, had pulled his headquarters back to Shreveport to evade the oncoming federals. Taylor followed.[27]

Mounted Infantry

The 4th Wisconsin pulled into Alexandria on May 7, just as stragglers from Taylor's forces were leaving the city. They followed the Texans for twenty-five more miles, capturing "large quantities of cotton, sugar and horses" as they went. The captures were important, but the short expedition to the northwest of Alexandria was even more significant in that it marked the first time that the 4th Wisconsin took to the field as a mounted infantry. Two weeks earlier, on April 20, Gen. Banks's infantry caught up with a mounted Confederate unit near Opelousas, Louisiana, but the horsemen easily raced away. Banks, who had been requesting more cavalry since the beginning of his command in Louisiana — and had been building a case for transferring the 4th Wisconsin from infantry to cavalry — was furious. Later, when he observed several members of the 4th Wisconsin riding captured horses, he took matters into his own hands, instructing Col. Bean to take his farmboys and mount the entire regiment on confiscated horses. Within a day, most of the men had horses and tack, and two days later, after scouring nearby farms and pastures, the entire regiment had horses.

To some, including their general, the 4th Wisconsin Mounted Infantry presented a comical sight. One soldier described Gen. Banks's reaction to the scene:

> I saw the general smiling, and suspected it was not our warlike appearance which pleased him. . . . There was every conceivable style of horse and rigging. There was the five hundred dollar horse rigged off with a mule's pack, saddle and ropes, and the rawboned, browse-fed filly,

27. Quiner, *Correspondence*, vol. 8, "Lt. Leon C. Bartlett to Friend Ross," April 21, 1863, 213; "Col. Sidney A. Bean to a Friend," April 18, 1863, pp. 207-8; "Return of Casualties in the Union Forces Engaged at Fort Bisland, La.," April 12-13, 1863"; O.R., I, 15, p. 319; CWSAC Battle Summaries, Irish Bend: http://www.nps.gov/history/hps/ABPP/BATTLES/la007 (accessed Jan. 31, 2012).

with a gentleman's saddle and bridle. There were little men mounted on great horses, and great men mounted on little horses. There were long legs hung up in short stirrups, and short legs that went dangling six inches above long stirrups. There were some men riding on side saddles and some on sheepskins. . . . But the object of the day was to let the general know that Western men knew how to ride a horse, and knew how to guide one.

Gen. Banks got the message. He petitioned Gen. Henry Halleck at Union headquarters in Washington to designate them the 4th Wisconsin Cavalry, and until Halleck acted they would be mounted infantry.[28]

Simultaneous with Banks's soldiers' move into Alexandria from the south, Admiral David Dixon Porter's gunboat fleet came up the Red River to Alexandria from the Mississippi. Their arrival completed the Union plan to control the Atchafalaya and establish a Port Hudson bypass. The Teche Campaign succeeded in driving the Confederate army away from southwestern Louisiana for the remainder of 1863. Gen. Banks proudly reported: "[W]e captured over 2,000 prisoners and twenty-two guns; destroyed three gunboats and eight steamers; captured large quantities of small arms ammunition, mails, and other public property, and the steamers *Ellen* and *Cornie*, which were of great service to us in the campaign." Banks also reported that his expedition deprived the Confederacy of valuable livestock and agricultural resources. He reported seizing "20,000 head of horses, cattle, and mules, 10,000 bales of cotton, and destroyed the enemy's salt-works at New Iberia. . . . The cattle, horses, mules, cotton, and other products of the country were sent to New Orleans, turned over to the quartermaster. . . ." Louisiana's Confederates could ill afford this loss of resources and the blow to citizen morale that the actions of Banks's troops delivered.[29]

The Teche campaign marked Isaac Earl's first time in the heat of battle, and his first experience as a squad leader; it came at the end of his first two years of service in the Union Army. As a corporal in Co. D, he

28. Love, *Wisconsin in the War of the Rebellion*, p. 542; Quiner, *Correspondence*, vol. 8, "G.W.B. to Editors of *Banner*," March 24, 1863, p. 203; "Lt. Leon C. Bartlett to Friend Ross," April 21, 1863, p. 213.

29. "Report of Maj. Gen. Nathaniel P. Banks to Hon. E. M. Stanton, Secretary of War, April 6, 1865"; O.R., I, 26, pp. 5, 11, 18; Louisiana's Military Heritage: Battles, Campaigns, and Maneuvers, The Teche Campaign (Jan.-May, 1863): http://www.usskidd.com/battles-teche.html (accessed Jan. 31, 2012).

Shallow-draft steamships brought supplies to General Banks's forces during his Bayou Teche campaign, and carried away captured horses, cattle, and seized cotton. (*Leslie's Illustrated Newspaper*, March 5, 1864)

led a squad of skirmishers at Fort Bisland, and later he was part of the successful mounted raid north and west of Alexandria. His promotion to corporal capped a year in which Earl gained valuable experience as part of the Union occupation forces along the lower Mississippi River. He learned firsthand the importance of steamboats for surprise raids and for outflanking irregular Confederate units active along the Mississippi and in the Louisiana bayous and swamps. When the 4th Wisconsin captured prisoners, equipment, and horses from Waller's Texas Cavalry, they used detailed knowledge of local back roads and paths to pursue and cut off the retreating Texans — another important lesson. Watching former slaves and Union sympathizers deliver valuable information to the Union officers, Earl also developed a good understanding of how to gather information in occupied areas. Soldiers of the 4th Wisconsin brought former slaves within their lines and listened to what they had to say about conditions in the surrounding countryside. As slaves, these people had learned how to be present but unnoticed, and now many of them used that talent to gather information for the army. The assistance of former slaves, together with the experience, knowledge, and skills he had gained during his initial two years as a soldier, served Earl in good stead during the remainder of his military career.

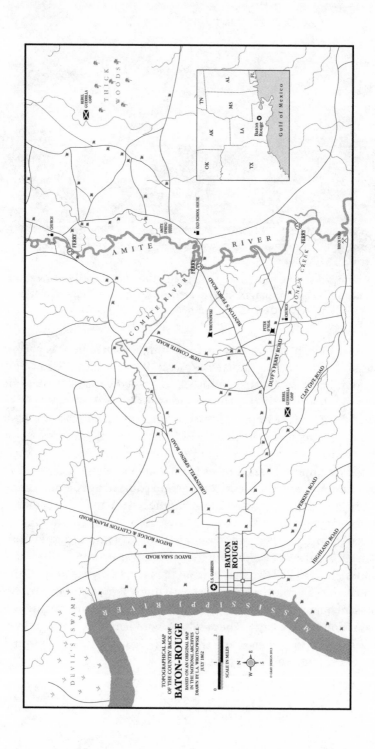

TOPOGRAPHICAL MAP
OF THE COUNTRY BACK OF
BATON-ROUGE
BASED ON AN ORIGINAL MAP
IN THE NATIONAL ARCHIVES
DRAWN BY L.A. WROTNOWSKI C.E.
JULY 1862

SCALE IN MILES
0   1   2

N
W   E
S

© GRAY DESIGN 2015

CHAPTER THREE

"Zeal, Daring, and Good Conduct"

TIRED, BUT PLEASED WITH THEIR SUCCESSFUL EXPEDITION UP THE Atchafalaya River and with their new status as mounted infantry, the 4th Wisconsin remained in Alexandria nearly a week, resting men and horses, and sorting and repairing their commandeered riding equipment. They took on their next assignment on May 14, when Gen. Banks sent them back to the Mississippi River to be part of the force assigned to attack Port Hudson. Two days earlier Banks had learned that Gen. Grant had crossed the Mississippi at Grand Gulf and was moving to encircle and lay siege to Vicksburg. Banks was determined to take Port Hudson before Grant succeeded at Vicksburg. The two generals had originally agreed to coordinate their efforts to seize Vicksburg and Port Hudson, but now circumstances had overtaken their planning. Grant had earlier indicated that he might spare as many as 20,000 men to help Banks take Port Hudson; now, however, as he tightened his noose around Vicksburg, he could no longer spare troops. Even without Grant's troops, Banks outnumbered Port Hudson's defenders by more than two to one, and he "concluded to move immediately . . . and to take my chances for the reduction of that post." Grant supported Banks's decision, and he agreed to send 5,000 men when he could — but warned that Banks "should not wait for them."[1]

A week after departing from Alexandria, Banks's troops reached Simsport on the Atchafalaya River, which ran adjacent and parallel to the Missis-

---

1. Report of Maj. Gen. Nathaniel P. Banks to Hon. E. M. Stanton, Secretary of War, April 6, 1865; O.R., I, 26, pp. 11-12; Howard C. Westwood, "The Vicksburg/Port Hudson Gap — the Pincers Never Pinched," *Military Affairs* 4, no. 3: 113-19.

sippi; they crossed the smaller stream, and on May 22 arrived at Morganza, on the west bank of the Mississippi. Steamers waited on the big river to ferry Banks's entire force across and a short distance downriver to Bayou Sara, Louisiana. Crossing such a large force required several trips, and the 4th Wisconsin spent all day and the evening of May 23 transporting men, horses, and equipment to the east side of the river. Instructed to report to Gen. Banks at Port Hudson as soon as possible, Gen. Paine had his entire 3rd Division, which included the 4th Wisconsin, across the river and on the road on the morning of Monday, May 25. Despite a heavy rainstorm, Paine pushed them hard toward their destination — twelve miles to the south. Soaked and tired, they arrived in late afternoon, tethered and cared for their horses as best they could, and camped for the night. The next morning they left their horses and moved forward to resume their role as infantrymen in Colonel Hawkes Fearing's Second Brigade of Halbert Paine's 4th Division on the right end of the Union forces facing Port Hudson's Rebel fortifications.[2]

Assaulting Port Hudson

It had been a long two months for Gen. Banks's tired forces. They had marched and skirmished, and had engaged in two heavy battles since early April, but their politically ambitious commander was determined to proceed against Port Hudson immediately. His adjutant, Lieutenant Colonel Richard Irwin, assured him that the men, "elated by their success in the Teche Campaign, were in the best of spirits for an immediate attack," an assessment not shared by all division commanders. When Banks called his staff together late on the evening of May 26 to lay out a coordinated frontal assault on Port Hudson for the next day, Gen. Weitzel, who had probably helped draft the plan, offered his support, while the other brigade commanders, Christopher C. Auger and Thomas W. Sherman, felt that the Confederates were too well entrenched and the Union troops too weary for a frontal assault. They argued for a siege, pointing out that the Confederate commander, Major General Frank Gardner, and his forces would be confined inside their fortifications and cut off from reinforcements and resupply.

Despite his divided commanders, Banks was determined to take Port Hudson before Grant captured Vicksburg; he pushed ahead with his plan.

2. O.R., I, 26, 1, pp. 67-69.

Left: **Major General Nathaniel P. Banks** (Library of Congress)

Above: **Major General Franklin Gardner** (Library of Congress)

He ended the meeting by sending his generals back to inform their subordinates that the assault would commence early the following morning with artillery fire announcing the offensive "at the earliest hour practicable . . . say at 6 a.m." Only similar broad directives — lacking timing and procedural specifics — indicated what would follow. After the cannonade, Gens. Auger and Sherman were to "force the enemy's works at the earliest moment," and Gen. Weitzel was to "take advantage of the attacks on other parts of the line to endeavor to force his way into the enemy's works on our right."

At about 11:00 p.m., Col. Bean relayed Banks's plan to the 4th Wisconsin, and company commanders began preparing all available men to fall in line at 4:00 a.m. and join the attack when signaled. They faced an enemy that was dug in and fully prepared. Defending the fort, Gen. Gardner had twenty-two heavy guns aimed west to cover the Mississippi and another fifty artillery pieces facing east along a 4.5-mile-long earthwork, fronted by a nearly impenetrable jumble of trenches, felled trees, and, in several places, thick magnolia groves and heavy brush undergrowth. Advancing

Hastily constructed cabins had provided housing for members of Port Hudson's Confederate garrison. (Library of Congress)

soldiers complained that trunks and branches of felled trees were so entangled "that it was difficult not only to move but even to see. . . ."[3]

The 4th Wisconsin was positioned at the far north of the Union line, on Gen. Weitzel's right wing, below the point where the Big Sandy River ran into the Mississippi. Gen. Auger's brigade covered the Union front's center, and Gen. Thomas W. Sherman's wing continued the line back to the Mississippi on the south. In the dark before sunrise, Banks's forces began drawing up side by side in regimental battle lines, waiting for the opening blasts of artillery to signal the beginning of the assault. The shelling began at 6:30 a.m. and an hour later the 4th Wisconsin troops moved out. With the sun at their back, they stepped into the open. As they began to move forward, their advance drew heavy defensive fire from an artillery battery that poured deadly "grape and canister" all along their line. Despite the heavy fire of what Lt. Col. Irwin would later call "a gigantic bush-whack," Weitzel's brigade managed to drive Rebel skirmishers back inside their fortifications; the Union brigade moved within 300 yards of its objective, but got no further.

3. James G. Hollandsworth Jr., *Pretense of Glory: The Life of General Nathaniel P. Banks* (Baton Rouge: Louisiana State University Press, 1998), pp. 118-33; Richard B. Irwin, "The Capture of Port Hudson," *Battles and Leaders of the Civil War* (New York: The Century Company, 1887), vol. 3, p. 593; George W. Carter, "The Fourth Wisconsin at Port Hudson," *War Papers Read Before the Commandery of the State of Wisconsin, Military Order of the Loyal Legion of the United States*, vol. 3 (Milwaukee: Burdick and Allen, 1903), p. 228; Special Orders, No. 123, May 26, 1863; O.R., I, 26, 1, pp. 508-9.

This newspaper artist's depiction of the May 27, 1863, Port Hudson assault by Major General Christopher Auger's division shows the tangle of tree limbs and ditches that confronted Union troops. (*Harper's Weekly,* June 27, 1863)

Banks's assault began to break down after first contact with the enemy. Instead of coordinated attacks from the center and left drawing defenders away from Weitzel, tangled trees and brush stopped Auger short, and Sherman's forces did not start as planned. When Banks rode up shortly after noon to see what was detaining Sherman, he claimed to have found him "at dinner, his staff officers all with their horses unsaddled, and none knowing where to find their command." Banks threatened to replace Sherman on the spot unless he attacked immediately, and Sherman agreed to launch his assault. At about 2:15 p.m., he got his forces underway. Despite a determined effort, his men could not breach their well-fortified foe's defenses. Inside the fortifications, Gen. Gardner moved troops from the stalled north end of his defensive line to the south and stopped Sherman's assault cold. By evening, all three segments of Banks's assault had been stopped short of the enemy fortifications; none had broken through. Auger's men were "close up to the works"; a storming party under Gen. Grover had "reached and retain[ed] a position against the parapet"; and Gen. Weitzel's right wing, which included the 4th Wisconsin, had "carried the heights before them," and also held a position close to the defensive works. But the three brigades had not acted in concert, and Port Hudson's outmanned defenders had managed to stop each assault short of its goal by moving quickly from one threatened point to another.

Banks's subsequent report told of his soldiers' determined effort, but failed to mention the lack of coordination and the heavy losses his forces had suffered. He also neglected to mention the tangled obstructions and difficult terrain they encountered. The 4th Wisconsin had marched forward that morning under orders not to fire their rifles because they were directly behind the 8th New Hampshire and 131st New York. They followed that order until they realized that the 8th New Hampshire had veered to their left as they slid right, placing the two regiments side by side. At this point the Wisconsin boys were below the crest of a small ridge, about 100 yards from the enemy breastworks, and when they ventured over the top, fire from within the fortification drove them back to cover. Col. Bean ordered his men to dig in and fire a heavy fusillade at the artillerists who were causing them heavy damage. Their marksmanship produced "excellent results," making it "extremely hazardous for Confederate gunners to operate their pieces." Relative quiet, occasionally interrupted by cannon and gunfire, began to settle over the battlefield.[4]

What occurred next prompted stories that would be repeated by veterans, both Union and Confederate, for decades after the battle. In the late afternoon, someone in the 4th Wisconsin began waving a white flag, leading the combatants to assume a truce had been declared. A lull followed, and men on opposing sides began calling to each other. From their shouted conversations, the men of the 4th concluded they were facing the 1st Alabama and 12th Arkansas. They also confirmed that the Confederates were running short of staples such as beef and coffee, and one soldier later reported trading Confederate corn cake for Yankee coffee. The quiet interlude did not last long. As soon as regimental officers learned of the white flag, they spread word that there was no truce, bringing communications between the lines to a halt. With a final warning from the 4th that "you Johnnies better take care of yourselves now," and a reply from the Rebels, "All right, Yanks, you'uns better do so, too," hostilities resumed.

4. Maj. Gen. N. P. Banks to Col. S. B. Holabird, Chief Quartermaster, May 27, 1863; O.R., I, 26, 1, pp. 510-11; Carter, "The Fourth at Port Hudson," pp. 228-31; Irwin, "Capture of Port Hudson," p. 593; Lawrence L. Hewitt, *Port Hudson: Confederate Bastion on the Mississippi* (Baton Rouge: Louisiana State University Press, 1987), p. 146.

At the end of the day, the 4th Wisconsin was settled just below the ridge where, supplied with picks and spades, they began digging rifle pits "like true badgers." The crest of the ridge afforded them a line of sight to the enemy entrenchments, as well as some protection from Rebel sharpshooters and artillery. There the two forces remained, locked in a deadly embrace.

The 4th Wisconsin losses from the assault were high, and some of the dead and wounded were still lying in the open field between the lines. Their comrades had managed to take some of the wounded from the field during the false truce — and after nightfall — but others had to wait until the following day, when Banks and Gardner arranged a truce for the purpose of recovering the dead and treating the wounded. The 4th Wisconsin suffered fifteen dead and fifty-four wounded on that May 27 battle, leaving the regiment with fewer than 300 men available for duty.[5]

Leading the 4th Wisconsin sharpshooters was Cpl. Isaac Earl, whose stalking and shooting skills, which he learned while growing up in the woods of central Wisconsin, served him well. Earl slowly worked his way as far forward as he could, then dug a shallow rifle pit that gave him protection and a line of sight, across the open field, of the enemy breastworks over a hundred yards away. At some earlier point, he had acquired a breechloading rifle, probably a Sharps, the preferred weapon of Union sharpshooters, which was accurate up to a thousand yards and used paper or linen cartridges, which seldom misfired. Quiet and motionless in his rifle pit, Earl watched for careless enemy targets and then, in the words of Pvt. Newton Culver, "made good use of the weapon." Culver was not the only one who knew of Earl's prowess with his rifle; Gen. Paine had witnessed Earl's marksmanship firsthand at Fort Bisland, when the Wisconsin corporal led a group of skirmishers positioned in front of the fort's earthworks. Recalling that earlier performance, Paine selected Earl to be a sniper during the siege of Port Hudson.

---

5. Carter, "The Fourth at Port Hudson," p. 231. A different interpretation of the episode appears in official correspondence between Gen. Banks and Gen. Gardner, as discussed in an official truce to remove dead and wounded from the field. Banks referred to a white flag "improperly used . . . by an inexperienced officer," and assured Gardner that he had "taken great pains to enforce the observance of the usages of war in regard to such flags within my command." No record can be found describing those "great pains," or the name of the "inexperienced young officer" on whom they were enforced. Maj. Gen. N. P. Banks to Maj. Gen. Frank Gardner; O.R., I, 26, 1, pp. 513-18; Quiner, *Correspondence*, vol. 8, "Killed and Wounded of the 4th Wisconsin," June 4, 1863, p. 224.

Writing after the war, Gen. Paine recalled the trouble Confederate sharpshooters were causing and the need for good Union marksmen to retaliate. They had "lashed themselves in trees overlooking our positions and killed and wounded our men." Resolving to "abate this nuisance if possible," Paine assigned Earl and other Wisconsin shooters to "locate and disable these sharpshooters." Earl, he recalled, "eagerly undertook the task assigned him. He messed at my headquarters and remained there when not engaged in his work, and soon acquired the sobriquet of 'our squirrel hunter.' Watching for the puffs of smoke which disclosed the position of the sharpshooter he crawled along sometimes for many hours until able to see his man and then fired on him often bringing him down dangling dead or wounded in the rope by which he was lashed to the tree." It was dangerous business, and Earl was as much hunted as hunter. Paine recalled one instance in which "a [Confederate] sharpshooter got the better of him and [fired a shot that] ploughed a cruel furrow down through his cheek." Earl suffered no lasting effect from the facial wound.[6]

Fighting had been even more intense to the right of the 4th Wisconsin, at the very northern tip of the Union line, where two black regiments, the 1st Louisiana Native Guards (consisting mainly of free blacks from New Orleans) and the 3rd Louisiana Native Guards (a recently formed unit of mostly former slaves), faced even greater odds and rougher terrain. They faced two willow-lined creeks, Little Sandy and Big Sandy, and a high bluff along the top of which the Confederates had built defensive earthworks. Further west was a large swamp, which was full of water because the Mississippi was unusually high.

An earlier offensive against the bluff's defenders had failed, and Gen. William Dwight, commanding the division, ordered the two black regiments forward at midmorning for a new effort. The two Louisiana regiments emerged from the willows along the Little Sandy, crossed on a hastily constructed pontoon bridge and charged toward the bluff while artillery pieces shelled them with canister and grape, and riflemen sent bullets rak-

6. Newton Culver, "Brevet Major Isaac N. Earl: A Noted Scout of the Department of the Gulf," *Proceedings of the Historical Society of Wisconsin* (1917): 310; Samuel C. Hyde Jr., ed., *Halbert Eleazer Paine: A Wisconsin Yankee in Confederate Bayou Country* (Baton Rouge: Louisiana State University Press, 2009), p. 152. Neither Culver nor Paine mention how Earl obtained his rifle or its manufacturer and model. By 1863, several manufacturers were producing limited numbers of easy-to-use, quick-loading, clean-firing breechloading rifles. Less likely to misfire when wet, breechloaders became popular during the last two years of the war.

Colonel Sidney Bean
(Quiner, *Military History of Wisconsin*)

ing through their ranks. In just fifteen minutes the black troops had been forced back to their starting point, their casualties as high as 50 percent. Although it was purchased at a great price, the assault earned the respect of doubters who had earlier questioned black soldiers' willingness to fight.[7]

For the next five days the two sides faced each other, sharpshooters from both sides shooting at and often hitting anyone foolish enough to make himself a target. One of those who fell to a sharpshooter's bullet was the 4th Wisconsin's commander, Col. Sidney Bean. At the front on May 29, Bean learned of Cpl. Earl's rifle pit and decided to check it out for himself. Crawling into the small depression, he asked Earl if he might give the breechloader a try. The corporal handed over his prized weapon and Bean began scanning the earthwork in front of them for a target. Seeking a better view, he began to stand, but Earl jerked him back, warning that the Confederates were deadly accurate. Twice more Bean recklessly rose above the pit searching for a target. The third time, he had barely risen up when a Confederate marksman hit his mark with a shot that entered Bean's

7. "Map of Port Hudson, La. and Vicinity," vol. 40, pt. 1, plate 38, *Atlas to Accompany the Official Records of the War of the Rebellion* (Washington, DC, 1890) (hereafter cited as O.R. Atlas, with volume, part, and plate numbers); Hewitt, *Port Hudson*, pp. 147-50.

side and passed through his lungs, killing him in a matter of minutes. Bean had disregarded Earl's warnings, and now he lay dead in his sharpshooter's arms in the shallow rifle pit. Because Bean was well regarded by his men for the bravery and concern that he showed leading the regiment (they had given him the affectionate nickname "Little Napoleon"), his death was a hard blow to his weary soldiers. With Lieutenant Colonel Frederick Boardman ill in New Orleans, and Major Joseph Bailey on detached duty as an engineer, Captain Webster Moore of Company E temporarily assumed command.[8]

Driving Confederates from Clinton

The 4th Wisconsin maintained their position in front of Port Hudson's breastworks for five days, until they were relieved by the 53rd Massachusetts on the evening of June 1. As the Massachusetts soldiers took their place, the men of the 4th expected to rest and visit wounded comrades. But Gen. Banks had other plans. One of his greatest concerns was a Rebel attack from the east that would be intended to relieve the pressure he was putting on Port Hudson. Confederate Colonel John Logan, with a force of over 1,000 cavalry and mounted infantry, was nearly twenty-five miles to the northeast, using the railroad town of Clinton, Louisiana, as a base depot and departure point to jab at Gen. Banks's rear guard. Logan's force was not large enough to displace Banks, but the presence of his cavalrymen tied down troops that could be better used for offensive operations. One day after the 4th Wisconsin troops had been sent to the rear, Cpt. Moore received orders for his regiment to join Colonel Benjamin Grierson, together with the 6th and 7th Illinois and the 2nd Massachusetts cavalry regiments, plus the black 1st Louisiana Native Guard and Nims's Light Artillery Battery, for a fast raid on Clinton to "scatter the troublesome Rebels in our rear and flanks." Grierson, who had recently led a 600-mile raid from southern Tennessee to Baton Rouge, tearing up railroads, burning buildings, supplies, and equipment, and leaving confusion as he went, seemed the ideal man for the task.

Very early on the morning of June 3, Grierson led his combined force of 1,200 away from Port Hudson toward Clinton. They got all the way to

8. Culver, "Brevet Major Isaac N. Earl," p. 310; "Letter from New Orleans," *Milwaukee Sentinel*, June 19, 1861: www.genealogybank.com (accessed Sept. 19, 2013).

the Comite River, within a mile of the town, before they met resistance. A contingent of Logan's men were hiding in the marshy lowlands beside the narrow road leading to the bridge over the Comite, and a larger group was deployed on the far side of the bridge. With the 4th Wisconsin in the lead, the Union troops rode over the bridge; but Logan's cavalry prevented them from going further. A three-and-a-half-hour firefight ensued, with the 4th Wisconsin holding the bridge, aided by the 2nd Massachusetts on their left and the 6th Illinois and part of the 1st Louisiana on the right. Stopped from going forward, with Logan's forces threatening both flanks, and with his own forces stretched in a thin line over the swampy road that brought his troops to the bridge, Grierson had no choice but to withdraw before Rebel sharpshooters and skirmishers turned his only way out into a gauntlet of small-arms fire.

On the road's tight confines, the Union troops' withdrawal quickly turned into chaos. Broken and overturned wagons created bottlenecks as the Union cavalrymen attempted to reverse course. Pushing the no longer useful wagons aside, Grierson's main force moved as rapidly as possible down the road, depending on the 4th Wisconsin, which was running low on ammunition, to protect its rear. At one point Cpt. Moore bought extra time by ordering the 4th's Company B to turn and charge the Confederates, shouting and firing their few remaining rounds. The feint succeeded in slowing the Rebels; and, together with a pair of two-pound guns firing canister and grape and the covering fire by the 6th Illinois Cavalry with their Sharps carbines, Grierson managed to extricate his force from the tight fix it had gotten into. Once disengaged, the Union forces returned to Port Hudson where Grierson, while reporting eight killed, twenty-eight wounded, and fifteen missing (including three killed and eight wounded from the 4th Wisconsin), tried to portray the episode as a victory by claiming that the Clinton Confederates had lost twice as many killed and wounded.

If the Clinton affair was a victory, it was a hollow one. Cpt. Carter of the 4th Wisconsin's Company B bitterly remembered that the regiment "returned to Port Hudson after midnight, tired and disgusted, having ridden fifty miles and fought a sharp battle, suffered considerable loss, with no advantage to our cause." He laid blame squarely on Grierson. "This misfortune," he concluded, "was the result of the utter failure of Colonel Grierson to comprehend the situation and make any advantageous disposition of forces. . . ."

Isaac Earl was in the heavy fighting at the bridge and drew two im-

Constructed in 1840, the East Feliciana Courthouse, a still functioning courthouse, remains at the center of Clinton, Louisiana. It was there when Earl
and members of the 4th Wisconsin arrived to drive the Confederate forces of
Colonel John Logan from the town. (Gordon Olson)

portant lessons from the experience. First, the need to know the size of
the force ahead before rushing headlong into combat; second, never get
pulled into an area that provides little opportunity to maneuver and only
a single avenue for withdrawal. And Earl learned another bit of important
information that day. Personally armed with a Sharps rifle, he witnessed
the heavy fire that a cavalry unit, in this case the 6th Illinois, could generate when armed with rapid-firing Sharps breechloading carbines rather
than the longer, more awkward muzzle-loading rifles the men of the 4th
Wisconsin were still using. Later, as leader of the Special Scouts, he requested — and received — similar weapons.

Grierson's failure meant that Banks's concern about Confederates at
his back remained, and he responded by deciding to send a second, larger
expedition to deal with Col. Logan at Clinton. On the morning of June 5,
the 4th Wisconsin mounted infantry and four regular infantry regiments,
two artillery batteries, and Grierson's cavalry, a total of over 2,000 men —
now led by Gen. Paine — made a return trip to Clinton. Traveling into the
night, they rested on the outskirts of the town for a few hours and then

entered in the early morning. Grierson's cavalry led the way into the town, only to discover that Col. Logan's troops had withdrawn further east toward Jackson. Grierson allowed his men to destroy everything in Clinton that they thought might be useful to the enemy, including the railroad depot, machine shops, "a locomotive, woolen and cartridge factories, a large quantity of ammunition, several hundred hides, and much other government property. . . ." They then joined the rest of the expedition for the trek back to Port Hudson. The 4th Wisconsin and the other regiments had traveled almost a hundred miles during "the hottest [three days] of the season." Weary to their bones, the 4th Wisconsin arrived back at Port Hudson on June 8.[9]

Second Port Hudson Assault

After their second trip to Clinton, the 4th Wisconsin had only a single day to rest before General Banks called his division commanders together to lay out the details for another frontal assault on the Confederate bastion of Port Hudson. Mindful of his previous plan's shortcomings, he prepared the second assault more carefully. He organized his army into several 2,000-man "columns of assault," each led by 300 skirmishers, followed by groups of pioneers (combat engineers) equipped with picks, shovels, saws, and axes with which to clear the way through the fallen trees and ditches that had successfully obstructed the first assault. Then, storming parties were to rush forward, with cotton bags and pontoons to fill ditches and ford streams ahead of the main assaulting column.[10]

Upon receiving the plan, Gen. Paine selected the 4th Wisconsin and the 8th New Hampshire to lead his division's advance, which was to begin on the morning of June 13, when the skirmishers and pioneers moved into place just out of range of the Confederate sharpshooters. At 11:00 a.m., an hour-long artillery bombardment announced the impending assault. But just before the Union soldiers were to move forward, Gen. Banks surprised everyone by suspending the operation while he sent a message to Gen.

9. Carter, "The Fourth at Port Hudson," pp. 231, 234-35; Maj. Gen. U. S. Grant to Maj. Gen. H. W. Halleck, May 8, 1863; O.R., I, 24, 1, p. 34; Reports of Col. Benjamin H. Grierson, Sixth Illinois Cavalry, Commanding Cavalry Brigade, of operations June 3-7, 1863; O.R., I, 26, part 1, pp. 134-37.

10. Also known as "sappers," pioneers performed tasks such as tunneling, removing obstructions in the path of infantry, and in-the-field construction and repair of fortifications, bridges, and roads.

Union dead and wounded were carried from the battlefield under a flag of
truce following the June 14, 1863, assault on Port Hudson.
(*Harper's Weekly*, June 18, 1863)

Gardner inviting him to surrender. Gardner responded that he was duty
bound to defend his position, and Banks decided to begin the assault anew
the next morning.[11]

Union forces went into the second assault with what seemed to be
overwhelming advantages in numbers and weapons. They had nearly
three times as many effective, experienced combatants, more artillery,
and more support equipment than did their opponents. For his part,
Gardner had determined defenders and a strong, fortified defensive position. Banks had an additional advantage that he chose to ignore: time.
He needed only to be patient. Gardner, with his forces extremely short of
food, would soon have been compelled to surrender.

Banks's second Port Hudson assault began before sunrise on Sunday,
June 14, with an artillery barrage. An hour later the guns quieted and signal rockets announced that the assault was underway. The 4th Wiscon-

11. Abstract from Trimonthly Report of the Department of the Gulf, correspondence
between Maj. Gen. N. P. Banks and Maj. Gen. Franklin Gardner, June 13, 1863; O.R., I, 26,
1, pp. 527-28, 552-53.

**Isaac Earl and other Union prisoners were held inside the
Port Hudson fortifications at the former hotel building.**
(National Archives, John Taylor Cartes de Visite Collection, no. 165 JT 432)

sin and 8th New Hampshire skirmishers moved forward into the face of heavy canister and grape fire. Cpt. Moore described the scene in front of the Confederate lines: "Men struck with rebel bullets and grape fell . . . in every direction. . . . No one halted but the dead and the wounded."

The skirmishers who advanced farthest, including Isaac Earl, reached the base of the enemy earthworks, where about thirty of their number managed to punch an opening in the line of defenders and fight their way inside. But before others could follow, Port Hudson's defenders closed the gap, sealing inside those who had broken through, leaving them no choice but to surrender. While the battle continued outside the Confederate fortifications, the prisoners were taken to Port Hudson's hotel, which was now serving as a prison building.[12]

12. Quiner, *Correspondence*, vol. 8, "Correspondence of the *Sentinel* from Peme," July 3, 1863, p. 241; "Correspondence of the *Times* from L. C. Bartlett," July 15, 1863, p. 242; Michael J. Martin, *A History of the 4th Wisconsin Infantry and Cavalry in the Civil War* (El Dorado Hills, CA: Savas Beatie, 2006), p. 193.

The 4th Wisconsin's momentary breach of the Confederate lines represented the farthest extent of the Union advance. Gen. Banks and some of his supporters would later maintain that the assault would have succeeded if others had followed Earl's group. However, as they encountered the damage and death in front of them, oncoming ranks faltered, the attack stalled, and men sought cover wherever they could find it. On the field in front of the Confederate earthworks, dead and wounded soldiers lay on the sunbaked earth for the remainder of the day, their comrades facing deadly accurate sharpshooter fire if they tried to reach them. Gen. Paine, who had gone forward to rally his men, lay among the wounded, his leg shattered by two bullets. He was unable to walk or crawl, but had managed to slide on his back to relative safety behind a log, where he lay until the battle ended at sunset and rescue parties could begin retrieving the wounded under the shroud of darkness.

Banks's second assault had ended like his first — with heavy losses and no change. Among all regiments, the 4th Wisconsin and the 8th New Hampshire suffered the greatest losses. One report placed the 4th's casualties at thirteen dead, seventy wounded, and fifty-two missing, nearly 60 percent of the men who had marched forward on that fateful morning of June 14. With his second frontal assault repelled, Banks finally adopted the slower, more certain tactic of a siege, and he tightened his perimeter around Port Hudson.[13]

Escape

Meanwhile, inside the Port Hudson fortifications, Earl and the other captured skirmishers had been taken to a two-story prewar hotel building

13. Quiner, *Correspondence*, vol. 8, "Correspondence of the *Times*," n.d., p. 226; "Correspondence of the *Sheboygan Times*," June 16, 1863, pp. 226, 229; "From the 4th Regiment, W. P. M. [Webster P. Moore]," June 16, 1863; "Gen. Paine Seriously Wounded — Interesting Particulars — Noble Conduct of Negro Troops, from *Madison Journal*," June 18, 1863, p. 230; "Harrison from Friend Ross," June 19, 1863, pp. 230-31; "Correspondence of the *Sentinel* from High Private," June 19, 1863, p. 231; "Sparta Eagle from Olio," June 29, 1863, p. 232; "Incidents of the Siege of Port Hudson," n.d., pp. 235-41; "Incidents of Banks' Late Campaign," "Correspondence of the Sentinel from Publico," July 25, 1863, pp. 246-51; "Interesting from the Fourth Wisconsin," *Milwaukee Sentinel*, July 3, 1863: www.Genealogybank.com (accessed Sept. 19, 2013); Trimonthly Report of Maj. Gen. Nathaniel P. Banks of operations in the Department of the Gulf, Dec. 16, 1862, to Dec. 31, 1863; O.R., I, 26, 1, p. 14.

"Quaker guns" were made of pine logs and mounted on gun carriages to fool Union officers into believing that the Confederates were better armed at Port Hudson. (*The Photographic History of The Civil War*, vol. 2)

and confined under close guard. Nonetheless, Earl set about doing what he could to take stock of conditions among Port Hudson's defenders. He estimated that there were about 3,000 Confederate defenders, whom Gen. Gardner moved regularly so that there would appear to be more, concentrating "where the assault was to be made, leaving a man here and there on the parapet to fire as rapidly as possible, 'changing the base' continually, so as to leave the impression . . . that they had the whole line well defended." Earl also noted that Port Hudson's defenders did not have as many big guns as it appeared. Some were, he later reported, "honest old Quakers," fake cannons made from large logs painted black. As the ranking prisoner, Cpl. Earl was summoned by Gen. Gardner, who was at a parapet observing the action. Gardner realized he could not hold out much longer without resupply and reinforcements, and he asked Earl "if he [Earl] thought he [Gardner] could cut his way out?" Earl thought the possibility "rather insignificant," and claimed to have told Gardner as much.

Prisoners inside Port Hudson received minimal daily rations — an ear of corn, molasses, and a small amount of meat — and had to do their own cooking. Isaac Earl volunteered to serve as cook, seeing it as an opportunity to conduct reconnaissance of Port Hudson's defenses. Each day he left the prison building to gather firewood, and to count the number of Confederate defenders and assess their available food and weapons. He also explored possible escape routes. After a few days he concluded that his best chance would be to flee across Big Sandy Creek at the north end of the fortifications. His plan was simple: while gathering wood, he would edge away from his guards, get as close as possible to the stream, and then dash for freedom. The first opportunity to try his plan came on the morning of June 20, when inattentive guards permitted him to wander farther afield than usual. Suddenly, with the creek within reach, he dropped his armload of wood and sprinted away. In front of him, the Louisiana Native Guards rushed to provide covering fire, and with Confederate shots splashing around him (one soldier said he counted eleven) Earl waded and swam to the Big Sandy's opposite bank, finding safety in the surrounding underbrush. Back within Union lines, Earl was taken to Gen. Banks and his staff to give a detailed description of the situation inside Port Hudson.[14]

"Food is growing scarcer," Earl told Banks, "and the garrison [is] greatly reduced by sickness, by constant fatigue and fighting. . . ." Even more important, "they [are] discontented, and heartily [wish] us success." Earl's news of Port Hudson's demoralization and hunger spread quickly through the camp. Soldiers needing good news latched onto his adventures and spread them to the regiments in front of Port Hudson. As 2nd Lt. Leon Bartlett wrote home, "This was all important; it was worth more than a battle." Everyone was talking about Earl, the "Wisconsin boy that got out of the fort." His story, which seemed to grow with each retelling, "was in everybody's mouth." He was, in Bartlett's words, "a ten times greater personage than Gen. Banks. It electrified the whole army, to think that a prisoner confined in that fortress, should ever manage to escape." The information he brought gave everyone confidence in the final outcome of their siege of the fort, "that one more attack would bring success, that they could not withstand the siege but a short time."

Two days after Earl's escape, two more prisoners fled the Port Hudson fortress. They corroborated his information, as did another Wisconsin man who, together with two Confederate deserters, managed to get away the following night. Earl's initial assessment was accurate. The men

14. Quiner, *Correspondence*, vol. 8, "Correspondence to the Sentinel from Peme," July 3, 1863, p. 241.

inside Port Hudson's fortifications were dispirited and wanted the siege to end. In fact, they seemed to be aiding the prisoners' escapes, and a few, feeling like prisoners themselves, joined the escapees. Bartlett reported that "each day now brought another escaped prisoner till Gen. Gardner ordered every Wis. prisoner confined to a closely guarded underground cell, well secured by lock and key." But even this was not sufficient. The next night a man dug his way out of the cell using his plate as a shovel, and "then the whole [remaining group] got away, so there was not a Wis. man left in the fort, excepting the wounded." The last escapees reported that the garrison could not hold out much longer: provisions were gone, and the Confederates had begun to kill their draft mules.

The escapes from Port Hudson begun by Isaac Earl drew a great deal of favorable attention to the 4th Wisconsin. "Wisconsin men," wrote Lt. Bartlett, "had become quite famous; it was found that they were as hard to keep as they were to take." Men of the regiment, exhausted from hard use a few days earlier, walked with a lighter step as they moved throughout the camp," Bartlett continued. "Any man might well feel proud of belonging to that Regiment at that time. [It] was a sure passport to commanding attention and respect."[15]

On June 22, Gen. Banks, confronted with "fifteen vacancies in the field, staff and line of the 4th Wisconsin," and impressed by Isaac Earl's escape and the respect he enjoyed among his peers, appointed him first lieutenant in Company D, in place of his fellow Dell Prairie townsman Guy C. Pierce, who had been severely wounded in his ankle during the second assault. In announcing the promotion, Banks cited Earl's "conspicuous gallantry in the assault upon the enemy's lines . . . and for his subsequent zeal, daring, and good conduct."[16]

Despite signs of the siege's success, Banks refused to abandon the idea of another assault. Even as he instructed his generals to continue the siege, he issued a call for volunteers to lead a third offensive against the center of Port Hudson's defenses. Given the weakened and demoralized state of the Confederate garrison, he was confident of success. However, before he could mobilize his latest assault, news came that Vicksburg had surrendered.

15. Quiner, *Correspondence*, vol. 8, "Correspondence of the *Times* from L. C. Bartlett," July 15, 1863, pp. 242, 245.

16. Quiner, *Correspondence*, vol. 8, "General Order No. 51 by Maj. Gen. Banks," June 22, 1863, p. 241.

Surrender

Five days in early July 1863 changed the course of the Civil War. On July 3-5, General Robert E. Lee's thrust into Pennsylvania was turned back at Gettysburg. On the afternoon of July 3, 1863, beneath the ineffective shade of a battered oak tree outside Vicksburg, Mississippi, Confederate General John Pemberton agreed to surrender the city to Union General Ulysses S. Grant, whose troops had besieged the Confederate soldiers and townspeople for six weeks. With their food and ammunition nearly gone, they could hold out no longer.[17] After initially considering a demand for unconditional surrender, Grant agreed to a surrender and parole that sent Pemberton's troops home and his officers to prisoner-of-war camps, avoiding the logistical nightmare of feeding and transporting more than 30,000 Confederate prisoners. (Within two months, most of the officers were exchanged, and they, along with many enlisted men, returned to the Confederate Army. Others stayed closer to home, joining state partisan units or becoming guerrillas operating along the lower Mississippi.) The formal surrender at Vicksburg took place on July 4.

By the time it was over, Vicksburg's encirclement and siege had cost both sides dearly. Union casualties numbered nearly 5,000, while Confederates counted more than 3,200. In addition, Pemberton turned over to Grant 172 cannons and 50,000 rifles. Five days after Lee was stopped at Gettysburg, and Pemberton met with Grant, Port Hudson, the last remaining Confederate defensive emplacement on the Mississippi River, surrendered.[18]

17. Shortly after the historic meeting of Pemberton and Grant, the tree was gone. In his memoirs, Gen. Grant wrote: "It was but a short time before the last vestige of its body, root and limb had disappeared, the fragments taken as trophies. Since then the same tree has furnished as many cords of wood, in the shape of trophies, as 'The True Cross.'" Ulysses S. Grant, *Personal Memoirs of U. S. Grant* (New York: Charles L. Webster, 1885-86), vol. 1, p. 268.

18. Although always overshadowed by the Union triumph at Gettysburg, the Vicksburg siege and surrender has been covered in numerous volumes. Best known and most detailed is Edwin C. Bearss, *The Campaign for Vicksburg*, 3 vols. (Dayton, OH: Morningside House, 1995); Winston Groom, *Vicksburg, 1863* (New York: Knopf, 2009); William L. Shea and Terrence J. Winschel, *Vicksburg Is the Key: The Struggle for the Mississippi River* (Lincoln: University of Nebraska Press, 2005); Terrence J. Winschel, *Triumph & Defeat: The Vicksburg Campaign* (Campbell, CA: Savas Publishing Company, 1999); Terrence J. Winschel, *Triumph & Defeat: The Vicksburg Campaign*, vol. 2 (New York: Savas Beatie, 2006); Terrence J. Winschel, *Vicksburg: Fall of the Confederate Gibraltar* (Abilene, TX: McWhiney

Word of Vicksburg's surrender reached the Union camp at Port Hudson late in the evening of July 7; but, despite the hour, word spread quickly, and men immediately began to stir. In a matter of minutes, quiet conversation turned to shouts, and then shouts to a roar. Banks's men knew that with Vicksburg in Union hands, Gen. Gardner could no longer hold out. They did not know that even before he received word of General Pemberton's surrender, Gardner had assessed the condition of his troops, and the amount of food remaining, and had begun to prepare for surrender. Now, after learning the cause of the noise in the Union camp, he sent a formal message to Banks asking for "official assurance" that what he had been told was true. He went on to say that if it was, then he wished to suspend hostilities with an eye toward surrendering. Banks responded that the rumor was indeed true, and as proof sent a copy of Grant's announcement of the Vicksburg garrison's capitulation. At 6:00 a.m. on July 8, Banks reported to Adm. Farragut that he had received Gardner's written surrender, and that staff officers would meet that morning at 9:00 to negotiate details. Those discussions lasted until 2:30 p.m., and in the end the surrender contained four terms:

1. The enemy surrenders everything.
2. We respect private property.
3. Officers and soldiers not paroled. [This was changed to include only officers.]
4. We take care of the sick.[19]

Port Hudson's surrender also came at a dear price. Union casualties in and near Port Hudson from the beginning of May through early July were reported to be 4,363. Of that number, 45 officers and 663 enlisted men had died. The wounded totaled 3,336, and missing numbered 319. Fourth Wisconsin casualties were reported at 219, included three officers and 46 enlisted men killed, 117 officers and enlisted men wounded, and 53 missing. Adding earlier losses, two years of service had taken their toll on the more than 1,100 men who left Camp Utley in July 1861. In addition to the 219 men lost at Port Hudson, they had been losing men to wounds, illness, and battle from the moment they began their initial training. There had been casualties in Maryland and on Ship Island, during Gen. Banks's Fort

---

Foundation Press, 1999); Michael B. Ballard, *Vicksburg: The Campaign That Opened the Mississippi* (Chapel Hill: University of North Carolina Press, 2004).

19. Correspondence of Maj. Gen. N. P. Banks, July 8, 1863; O.R., I, 26, 1, pp. 622-27.

Following Port Hudson's surrender, Confederate soldiers laid down their arms in front of Union troops. (*Harper's Weekly*, August 8, 1863)

Bisland and Alexandria campaign, in the ill-fated effort to cut a channel through the peninsula across from Vicksburg, and in the many patrols around Baton Rouge. Even though many sick and wounded had returned to its ranks after Port Hudson, the 4th Wisconsin still reported fewer than 300 available men.[20]

Because of their strong defensive positions, Confederates reported significantly fewer losses at Port Hudson. Incomplete returns enumerated 671 casualties, with commissioned and non-commissioned officers accounting for 46 killed and 104 wounded. Losses among enlisted men were 142 killed and 379 wounded. When the surrender was complete, 5,953 enlisted men and noncommissioned officers laid down their arms and received parole, and 451 officers were detained as prisoners of war. An undetermined number of officers and enlisted men had slipped away before the surrender. In addition to the prisoners, Gen. Gardner turned over 51 artillery pieces, 5,000 stands of small arms, 25 tons of gunpowder, 150,000 rounds of ammunition, and two river steamers.[21]

20. Quiner, *Correspondence*, vol. 8, "Correspondence to the *Sentinel* from Peme," July 3, 1863, p. 241.

21. Hewitt, *Port Hudson*, p. 181; Maj. Gen. N. P. Banks to Maj. Gen. Henry Halleck,

Banks's and Gardner's staffs arranged the formal surrender for 7:00 a.m., July 9, and at the appointed time, the 13th Connecticut band struck up "Yankee Doodle" as Union troops marched in to take possession of Port Hudson. Its Confederate defenders stood at attention facing the Union men until Gen. Gardner commanded them to lay down their weapons and offered his saber to Brigadier General George L. Andrews, designated by General Banks to receive the surrender. The band then played the "Star-Spangled Banner" and "Dixie" as the American flag was run up the flagpole. It was a somber and reflective moment, with little celebration by the Union troops thinking of their lost comrades. Later, in a mid-July 1863 letter to his Illinois friend James Conkling, President Lincoln famously declared, "The Father of Waters again goes unvexed to the sea."[22]

Back to Baton Rouge

Shortly after Isaac Earl's escape and return to the Union lines, the 4th Wisconsin had been withdrawn from the front lines and sent to the rear. From there they were sent on patrols into the area east of Port Hudson, where John Logan was once again conducting surprise raids, seizing prisoners, horses, wagons, and provisions. The regiment had continued to look for Logan until July 4, when they received a new assignment. Logan's forces had hit the Union troops guarding Springfield Landing, about seven miles south of Port Hudson on July 2, and the 4th Wisconsin was sent to reinforce the small post. They remained there during the week preceding Port Hudson's surrender.

Weary, pleased by the cessation of fighting, but subdued and saddened by the losses they had suffered, Isaac Earl and his 4th Wisconsin comrades marched away from Port Hudson and back to Baton Rouge on July 11. At their head was Joseph Bailey, promoted to colonel by Gen. Banks, based on his "indefatigable and enterprising" services during the siege of Port

---

July 10, 1863; Returns of Casualties in the Union Forces, May 23 to July 8, 1863; Report of Capt. C. M. Jackson, of the surrender of Port Hudson, July 9, 1863; O.R., I, 26, 1, pp. 55, 69-72, 144.

22. Special Orders no. 164, July 8, 1863; O.R., I, 26, 1, pp. 626-27; Bearss, *Campaign for Vicksburg*, vol. 3, pp. 1309-11; Hollandsworth, *Pretense of Glory*, p. 132; Jean Edward Smith, *Grant* (New York: Simon and Shuster, 2001), pp. 254-55; Ballard, *Vicksburg*, pp. 398-99; Roy P. Basler, ed., *Collected Works of Abraham Lincoln* (New Brunswick, NJ: Rutgers University Press, 1953), vol. 6, p. 409.

Hudson. However, Bailey's promotion and new appointment created a dilemma. Wisconsin's governor, Edward Salomon, maintained that the 4th Wisconsin was a state volunteer unit and, because it was, responsibility for appointing their commanding colonel rested with him. He promoted the regiment's lieutenant colonel, thirty-year-old Frederick Boardman, a graduate of the United States Naval Academy, to the position. Boardman was away on sick leave in Wisconsin, and Bailey was to take over until the former returned to Baton Rouge. While Boardman was traveling south, Gen. Banks resolved the situation by giving Bailey an engineering assignment — for which he would prove extremely well qualified — to begin when Boardman arrived to assume leadership of the regiment.

During his short tenure at its head, Bailey continued the effort to have the 4th Wisconsin Infantry officially recognized as a cavalry unit. Gen. Banks endorsed his request and forwarded it to Army headquarters. It was a sound idea. Nearly all the men of the 4th Wisconsin were farmboys who had grown up on horseback, they knew how to train and care for their horses, and they had experience riding long distances. Having horses for transport was preferable to the long marches infantrymen had to endure, not to mention that, with their mounts and flashy yellow-trimmed uniforms, cavalrymen were the most romanticized members of the army. Finally officials in Washington approved the new designation for the 4th Wisconsin on September 1, with appropriate uniforms, equipment, and arms distributed to the men who, in the eyes of L. C. Bartlett, "cut quite a dash."

With enthusiasm in the North running high after the Union successes at Gettysburg, Vicksburg, and Port Hudson, Union recruiters moved into high gear in the fall of 1863. In late August, eight officers from the 4th Wisconsin headed north, intending to use its battlefield reputation and its new cavalry designation to attract volunteers to fill its vacancies. Meanwhile, veterans in Baton Rouge developed a confident feeling that their service along the Mississippi was entering its final phases. Pvt. L. C. Bartlett wrote home: "The Union cause is progressing finely in this region, rebellion is gone up, completely squelched."[23]

---

23. E. B. Quiner, *The Military History of Wisconsin: A Record of the Civil and Military Patriotism of the State in the War for the Union* (Chicago: Clarke and Company, 1866), p. 507; Quiner, *Correspondence*, vol. 8, "Correspondence of the *Times* from L. C. Bartlett," July 15, 1863, p. 242; August 27, 1863, p. 253.

CHAPTER FOUR

"Rusticating, Foraging, and Scouting"

A S THE 4TH WISCONSIN SETTLED BACK INTO ITS QUARTERS AT BA-ton Rouge, Isaac Earl received distressing news: his brother William had been arrested for desertion at Gettysburg and sent to Wisconsin. Even worse, William had been killed while attempting to escape from an army prison in Madison. In an instant, the excitement over his promotion to lieutenant and the prospect of the 4th Wisconsin's designation as cavalry were gone. After their parents had died, the Earl brothers had depended on each other and their uncles' families. Now Isaac was the lone survivor of his immediate family. His brothers, both of whom were Union soldiers, were now dead, and the Crosbys were far away in Wisconsin. Joseph and Isaac had enlisted in the 4th Wisconsin together, but William had waited and volunteered later in the summer. Joseph died alone in a hospital on Ship Island, and it had been several days before Isaac learned of his death. Now William was dead, and no one could explain to Isaac what had happened.

While Isaac battled heroically at Port Hudson, William had been en-gaged in three days of equally intense combat on Cemetery Hill at Get-tysburg as a member of Battery B of the 4th U.S. Artillery. Despite de-termined Confederate onslaughts, his unit had held its position, losing a total of thirty-two men killed, wounded, and missing. William was among the survivors, but several days later he inexplicably left his unit. He was located several miles away from his unit and arrested for desertion; he was then sent home to be imprisoned at Madison's Camp Randall. Soon after he arrived in Wisconsin, William's life took a final tragic turn: as he attempted to escape, he was shot and killed by his guards. No explanation of what went wrong in William's life can be found. His service record notes only that he was shot while trying to escape, an escape attempt that occurred almost simultaneously with his brother Isaac's escape from the Confederates at Port Hudson.

William had soldiered steadfastly at Second Bull Run, Antietam, Fredericksburg, and Chancellorsville. Perhaps he had seen too much fighting, heard too many loud artillery shots, seen too many men die. Newton Culver, who had seen his share of battle stress while serving with Isaac Earl, offered the most succinct statement of what happened when he wrote that William "had always been a good soldier. . . . [In] the absence of any known reason for his desertion it may be supposed that he was suffering at the time from some temporary lapse of reason." Terms such as "shell shock" and "combat fatigue" — or the more recent, more analytical "acute combat stress reaction" or "posttraumatic stress disorder" — did not exist when William walked away from his unit and later attempted to escape confinement at Camp Randall. But his behavior does seem to reflect the fact that he simply could face war no longer.[1]

By mid-1863, Isaac Earl was painfully familiar with death and the loss of friends and loved ones. In addition to his loss of family members, several of his Adams County friends had fallen in the deadly frontal assaults at Fort Bisland and Port Hudson. His regimental colonel, Sidney Bean, had died in his arms in front of enemy earthworks at Port Hudson. Isaac himself had successfully faced down death at close range on several occasions. Known to his comrades as brave to the point of recklessness, Earl had several times charged headlong toward death and lived. While others had fallen, he had emerged unscathed (except for his slight facial wound). With each battle experience his confidence grew, and those around him became more willing to follow. He left no explanation for his aggressive behavior. Perhaps he sought to avenge the loss of his brothers and friends.

1. Theophilus F. Rodenbough and William L. Haskin, eds., *The Army of the United States Historical Sketches of Staff and Line with Portraits of Generals-in-Chief* (New York: Maynard, Merrill, and Co., 1896), p. 361. U.S. Army Center of Military History website, Books and Research Materials: http://www.history.army.mil/books/R&H/R&H-FM.htm (accessed Mar. 21, 2012); Newton Culver, "Brevet Major Isaac N. Earl: A Noted Scout of the Department of the Gulf," *Proceedings of the Historical Society of Wisconsin* (1917): 308-9. For more on the effect of traumatic war experiences in the Civil War, see Judith Pizzaro, Roxane Cohen Silver, and Joann Prause, "Physical and Mental Health Care of Traumatic Experiences among Civil War Veterans," NIH Public Access: www.ncbi.nlm.nih.gov/pmc/articles/PMC1586122/.

He may have concluded that only a thoroughgoing defeat would bring rebellious Southerners back into the Union. It is also possible that experience led him to the conclusion that aggressiveness was the best action when facing enemy soldiers. Whatever his motivation, he was closest to those with whom he shared the experiences of war, men who had seen his behavior and were prepared to follow his lead.

When he volunteered at the beginning of the Civil War, Isaac Newton Earl was an uneducated young man who was barely out of his teens and knew little of America outside his central Wisconsin home. The events that swirled around him in his first two years as a soldier greatly broadened his horizons. He had traveled east by railroad to the seat of the national government and the first sites of war, seeing for the first time the immense size and richness of the nation, from lush rural farmland to crowded city streets. By way of comparison, Adams County, home to most of the 4th Wisconsin's Company D, had a total population of 6,497 in 1860, with no town having more inhabitants than Dell Prairie's 650.

Although they may have encountered African Americans prior to their first excursion outside Adams County, it was in Maryland that Isaac and Joseph Earl and most of the men of the 4th Wisconsin had their initial encounters with slaves and slavery. In 1860, census takers identified four families of "black" or "mixed" settlers farming in central Adams County near the Wisconsin River, within a few miles of Elisha Crosby's farm. These may have been free blacks from the East or freed or escaped slaves living in remote isolation in south central Wisconsin. Isaac Earl could have first learned of slavery from these neighbors, and even if he had not, he first knew African Americans as free people, a fact to remember when we consider his later encounters with slavery and escaped slaves in Louisiana.[2]

More than being an introduction to the world beyond Adams County, Earl's first two years as a soldier changed who he was, how he thought of himself, and how he interacted with those around him. Before enlisting, he had held no positions of leadership, had never faced war's unimaginable violence, nor been responsible for the death of a fellow human being. Two years later, he had seen many men die in battle, and he had learned that his comrades would follow where he led. Acclamation from his peers had rung in his ears, and superiors had offered recognition and promotion. Finally, he had discovered that the South was a complex place, filled with

2. Michael Goc, ed., *From Past to Present: The History of Adams County* (Friendship, WI: Adams County Historical Society, New Past Press, 1999), p. 28.

a population that varied from totally committed Confederates to loyal Unionists, and with a large population of slaves who looked for freedom and sustenance to the Union soldiers they encountered, and joined with them in common cause.

By mid-1863, Isaac Earl had a clear sense of who he was and what he believed. He was an anti-slavery Unionist whose closest companions were like-minded members of the 4th Wisconsin. Most shared his experiences, political beliefs, and personal philosophy. From this point forward, he would call on them to follow him against the men — and women — he saw as enemies of his government, and thus his own personal enemies.

On Patrol around Baton Rouge

Back in Baton Rouge, the 4th Wisconsin spent the last days of July in camp near the buildings of the former Louisiana Deaf, Dumb, and Blind Asylum — on the southern boundary of the city, close to the Mississippi River. Able to muster only about 20 percent of their authorized strength, they were limited to short scouting forays into the surrounding countryside while they awaited new recruits to replace those lost through death, wounds, illness, and desertion.

The regiment's manpower limitations came at a time when replacements were greatly needed to counteract increasing guerrilla activity around Baton Rouge. While many of the more than 35,000 paroled defenders of Vicksburg and Port Hudson rejoined regular Confederate forces, others remained closer to their homes in Louisiana and Mississippi, where they joined up with state militias, partisan rangers, or guerrilla bands. During the last eighteen months of the war, actions against these guerrillas, partisans, and outlaws became an increasingly important responsibility of the federal army in the West.

After more than a year along the lower Mississippi, the 4th Wisconsin's soldiers knew its surrounding roads, trails, bayous, and swamps well, making them determined and forceful adversaries of the Confederate irregulars. They were especially familiar with Baton Rouge and its environs. Besides the big river, a web of roads and trails radiated north, south, and east out of Baton Rouge. Highland Road followed the river southward; along the southern border of the city, Government Street became Clay Gut Road as it headed out of town to the east; North Street, which became Greenwell Springs Road, formed Baton Rouge's northern border;

straight north from the city, the Clinton-Jackson Road forked, becoming the Bayou Sara Road to the northwest and the Clinton-Jackson Road to the northeast.[3]

After several weeks of recuperation following their ordeal at Port Hudson, the 4th Wisconsin men who were available for duty began scouting forays around Baton Rouge. In addition to preventing guerrilla activities along the river, small company-sized groups regularly went on twenty-to-thirty-mile patrols into the backcountry, scouting, foraging, and tracking — then reporting back on the location of both regular and irregular Confederate units. Secessionists had grown more antagonistic, while Unionists seeing an increased Union Army presence became more outspoken, thus pitting community members and even family members against one another in destructive conflict.

By early August, the 4th Wisconsin was back in action, sent out to investigate the presence of two hundred guerrillas reported near a plantation about twenty miles south of Baton Rouge. Fearing that the guerrillas intended to disrupt traffic on the river, the command gave the 4th Wisconsin simple instructions: capture as many as you can, and drive the others away. An easy ride through a quiet countryside brought the cavalrymen to their destination, where they found that the guerrillas had departed. With no enemy in sight and time on their hands, they bivouacked at the plantation and "rusticated, foraged, scouted, etc., and had a good time generally." They "were anticipating a fine season of repose" when orders came to move a short distance back upriver to Placquemine, on the west bank of the Mississippi, about twelve miles south of Baton Rouge, where half of the regiment set up a new camp and stayed from October 1863 until February 1864. The remainder of the regiment continued on to Baton Rouge. Those at Placquemine regularly encountered men they suspected of being guerrilla scouts, but they got no closer than a few long-distance rifle shots away, which "had the desired effect [of] sending them scurrying away."[4]

Even before the Union's military successes in mid-1863, the growth in the number of irregular soldiers and the increases in guerrilla activity in many parts of the occupied South had caused the Union high command to start grappling with the legal issues involved in irregular warfare. Presi-

3. Michael J. Martin, *A History of the 4th Wisconsin Infantry and Cavalry in the Civil War* (El Dorado Hills, CA: Savas Beatie, 2006), p. 213.

4. Quiner, *Correspondence*, vol. 8, "Correspondence of the *Times* from L. C. Bartlett," August 27, 1863, p. 253; Col. Richard B. Irwin, Assistant Adjutant General to Commanding Officer, Baton Rouge, August 1, 1863; O.R., I, 26, 1, pp. 666-67.

dent Lincoln's general-in-chief, the legalistically minded Henry W. Halleck, asked Dr. Francis Lieber of Columbia College for a careful review of the definitions and legality of guerrilla war. By the summer of 1863, Lieber had completed a lengthy essay entitled "Guerrilla Parties Considered with Reference to the Laws and Usages of War," in which he answered Halleck's questions about how to define different types of insurrectionaries. He identified several categories of combatants, which included partisans, bushwhackers, "guerrillamen," assassins, and armed prowlers. According to Lieber, the term one used to describe them did not matter as much as how they behaved. To him, only those who engaged in "fair fight[s] and open warfare" deserved to be called partisans and to be treated as soldiers. Those others who did not follow "peaceful habits," but engaged in "occasional fighting," were "brigands" and should be treated accordingly. Halleck distributed Lieber's essay to his generals and soon thereafter issued General Order Number 100 in August 1863. Also known as the "Lieber Code," it was intended to define the army's wartime authority to retaliate against guerrillas and other irregular combatants. Southerners railed against Lieber's portrayal of "irregulars," but most Union generals saw the code as a useful step in defining and justifying their increasingly strong response to insurrectionaries.[5]

In addition to defining "guerrillas" and "guerrilla warfare," Leiber also commented on the military's treatment of civilians and their property in the context of the necessities of war. He offered the opinion that "modern" warfare permitted destruction or seizure of public property, such as the means of travel and communications, and seizure of the resources necessary for the "subsistence and safety" of the army. Loyal citizens who avoided the conflict were to be left alone, as was their personal property. Although the army was not to engage in "wanton violence" against civilians, citizens who gave support to enemy troops or engaged in crimes or offenses against occupying soldiers could expect to see their homes and other buildings entered and searched, their property seized, and they might even be arrested for their actions. As the war continued and anger toward local residents grew, officers like Isaac Earl began to interpret rules toward civilians more broadly, making seizures and destroying property with less and less provocation.[6]

5. Daniel E. Sutherland, *A Savage Conflict: The Decisive Role of Guerrillas in the American Civil War* (Chapel Hill: University of North Carolina Press, 2009), pp. 126-29.

6. Mark Grimsley, *The Hard Hand of War: Union Military Policy toward Southern Civilians, 1861-1865* (New York: Cambridge University Press, 1995), pp. 149-52.

**Skirmishes between Union troops and local irregulars were regular occur-
rences around Baton Rouge as the 4th Wisconsin and other units patrolled
the region in search of guerrilla and partisan groups.**
(*Leslie's Illustrated History of the Civil War*)

In September 1863, buoyed by the return of several of their members who had been wounded or sick in the wake of the siege of Port Hudson, the 4th Wisconsin's officers began to organize systematic searches
and pursuits of guerrillas and outlaws around Baton Rouge. Most often,
Union forays were limited to daily and overnight patrols, but on occasion
company-sized — or larger — groups went out for longer, independent
operations. For example, in 1863 and 1864, several companies from the
4th Wisconsin served on detached duty "to prevent contraband trade, protect navigation and telegraphic communications, carry dispatches, etc.,"
occasionally staying at a location in the field for a month or more. In one
instance, a group led by Captain Nelson Craigue of F Company established
an outpost on the river where they remained from early October to the
following spring. They built their own stockade to defend their post and
captured eighty-five Confederates, along with "large quantities of goods
intended for the enemy" before finally being recalled to Baton Rouge.[7]

7. William DeLoss Love, *Wisconsin in the War of the Rebellion: A History of Regiments*

On September 8, a group of Rebel guerrillas who had somehow acquired Union uniforms rode up on D Company pickets stationed on the Greenwell Springs Road at the northeast corner of Baton Rouge city limits and opened fire, killing two men and capturing two others before galloping away. The entire regiment turned out in response, but the raiders were well away before a pursuit could be organized. For the men of the 4th it was a sharp warning about dealing with irregular units: the usual conventions of war did not pertain to them, and rapid response was crucial.[8]

Mindful of the time it took the 200-plus men of the 4th Wisconsin to respond to a guerrilla raid, Isaac Earl and other company leaders concluded that their best response was to take the fight to their enemy with small independent forays, "scouring the surrounding country, familiarizing [themselves] with the roads and streams, fords, bridges, and ferries." In one instance, the 4th Wisconsin's Luther Struthers and a companion ventured out on a successful two-man raid. They rode toward Clinton until they encountered the outlying pickets of Colonel John Logan, whose troops were still in the area, captured three of Logan's men, and returned with them to Baton Rouge before Logan could respond.

At about that same time, Col. Frederick Boardman arrived to take command of the regiment, and he decided to familiarize himself with the country his men were assigned to patrol. He arrived on September 24, and a day later he led the 4th Wisconsin on a long reconnaissance east past the Amite River, then north and west in a large arc to the Comite River, before turning south and back to Baton Rouge. The ride produced no contact with the enemy, but it enabled Boardman to get a good look at the surrounding terrain while observing how his new regiment operated in the field.[9]

During this period, as one of the regular leaders of these patrols, Isaac

and Batteries the State Has Sent to the Field (Chicago: Church and Goodman, 1866), p. 901; E. B. Quiner, Military History of Wisconsin (Chicago, 1866), p. 922.

8. This episode is described by Newton Culver in his diary entries for Sept. 8-9, 1863, State Historical Society of Wisconsin. Confirmation of the men killed and captured is found in Roster of Wisconsin Volunteers: War of the Rebellion, 1861-1865, an online digital book from the Wisconsin Historical Society Library. Two volumes were compiled in 1886 (Madison: Democratic Printing Co.). The alphabetical index was published in 1914 (Madison: Democratic Printing Co.), pp. 165, 171, 183.

9. Quiner, Correspondence, vol. 8, "Correspondence to the Evergreen City Times from L. C. Bartlett," November 31, 1862, p. 183.

Union patrols used local guides and the cover of darkness to locate and surprise guerrilla and partisan camps. (*Harper's Weekly*, April 4, 1863)

Earl added to his reputation as a quick-thinking and aggressive fighter. On September 29 he led a smaller group on a nighttime patrol east of the Amite River region; they were guided by "two Negro boys who knew every person and all the roads for miles up and down that side of the river." Quietly, they moved from house to house, picking up Confederates who were home spending time with their families. In the course of the evening they surprised and arrested an officer identified as Captain James Pinney, along with thirteen other Confederates. Earl's return with his prisoners caused excitement throughout the regiment.

The regiment's mood improved further in mid-October, when the first contingent of fresh Wisconsin recruits arrived. Smaller groups continued to report throughout the fall and early winter until, by January 1864, the 4th had reached a strength of more than 650 men. At its core were more than 400 "old members," to whom were added "new recruits from Wisconsin." Another 80 or more were still sick in hospital or in camp, and 19 were listed as "prisoners in the hands of the enemy." Observing the high percentage of veterans who had extended their time of service during the army's reenlistment campaign, a justifiably proud Newton Culver wrote to the editor of the *Milwaukee Sentinel*: "If we may judge by the number who are re-enlisting in the regiment, the boys are not going to desert 'Uncle Sam' yet awhile."[10]

More Scouting Patrols

Scouting patrols continued throughout the fall of 1863. The nearly daily patrols were authorized by Col. Boardman and led by one of the regiment's company lieutenants. In some cases, entire companies would go out; in other instances a smaller group of volunteers would be selected from one or more companies. Always ready to head such a group — and with a growing reputation for success — Isaac Earl led many of these patrols. Designated to head such a group on the night of September 28-29, Earl called for volunteers. Among those who responded were Newton Culver and Luther Struthers of Sheboygan Falls, Wisconsin, both of whom would later become members of Earl's Special Scouts. Culver was skeptical of some of the stories he had heard about Earl's scouting successes, and he wondered whether it was "due more to luck than to fitness. . . . [I was] desirous of going with him so as to judge of it for myself." After sunset, while most of the members of the 4th settled down for the evening, Earl quietly led his group east on the Greenwell Springs Road toward the Comite River, turned southeast to Benton's Ferry, crossed over the Comite and shortly thereafter apprehended the son of Confederate Colonel Samuel Hunter and a man identified only as "Captain Penny." Turning back to the southwest, they recrossed the Comite at Duff's Ferry and began their return to Baton Rouge. Their nighttime ride convinced Culver and Struthers of Earl's abilities as a leader, and thereafter they joined him whenever they could, often riding as his advance scouts.[11]

10. Culver, "Brevet Major Isaac N. Earl," p. 311; Quiner, *Correspondence*, vol. 8, "Correspondence to the *Sentinel* from Newton H. Culver," Jan. 14, 1864, p. 110.

11. Culver, "Brevet Major Isaac N. Earl," p. 311. The prisoner was the son of Col. Samuel E. Hunter of the 4th Louisiana Volunteer Infantry. Organized at Camp Moore, Louisiana, in May 1861, it served along the gulf for the remainder of the year. The following year the regiment participated in the battles of Baton Rouge and Shiloh, and the defense of Vicksburg and Port Hudson. Col. Hunter's roots were in Louisiana's Florida Parishes, and his regiment remained in the region for much of the war. Arthur W. Bergeron Jr., *Guide to Louisiana Confederate Military Units, 1861-1865* (Baton Rouge: Louisiana State University Press, 1989), pp. 79-82; Arcadians in Gray Web site: http://www.acadiansingray .com/4th%20Regt.%20Inf.htm (accessed June 28, 2012). Newton Culver was writing forty

Meeting Jane O'Neal

As they returned to Baton Rouge along Duff's Ferry Road in the early morning, Earl and his patrol noticed a farmyard with a flock of chickens and decided to seize a few as contraband and turn them into a good meal. According to a recollection published many years later, they were stopped before catching the chickens by an irate young woman who stormed out of her house and up to Earl, "lambasting the Yankees." Guerrillas and outlaws could not intimidate Earl, but this strong-willed woman was more than a match. He backed away from the confrontation, apologized, and ordered his men to move on without the chickens.

The young woman who stopped Lt. Earl so abruptly was Anna Jane O'Neal, the oldest daughter of Martha O'Neal, the widow of Peter O'Neal who, with her daughter and younger children, operated the farm. As sometimes happens in such cases, each of the young people came away from the incident impressed with the other and hoping their paths might cross again. Thereafter, Earl watched for Jane O'Neal when his patrols took him past her farm, or when she came to Baton Rouge. She seemed to be equally interested in him. During the remainder of the fall, they met several more times, turning their initial confrontation into romance.[12]

Locating and actively pursuing nearby guerrillas meant that the soldiers of the 4th Wisconsin needed friendly relationships with some local residents. Even though Baton Rouge had been the antebellum state capital, there were Union sympathizers among its slightly more than 5,000 residents, men and women who had opposed secession — some of whom favored ending slavery. Union control of the Mississippi River emboldened them and other commercially oriented residents to sign oaths of allegiance in order to do business with the Union Army quartermasters. As they became accustomed to the presence of the occupying troops, many residents openly socialized with officers and enlisted men, on occasion providing information about guerrilla movement and Confederate troop activity in the area.

Sometime in the fall of 1863, Jane O'Neal became one of the informants whom Isaac Earl turned to when he planned nighttime patrols around Baton Rouge. Before the war, the O'Neals had been a successful

years later, and his memory appears to be inaccurate by a month. Report of Col. Oliver P. Gooding to Maj. Gen. N. P. Banks, Sept. 29, 1863; O.R., I, 26, 1, p. 320.

12. *Baton Rouge Advocate*, July 23, 1984, p. 12.

middle-class farming family who had lived in the region for three generations. They were descended from families that came into Mississippi and Louisiana in the late eighteenth and early nineteenth centuries, the last years of Spanish governance and the beginning of American settlement in the region. Peter O'Neal's father, also named Peter, first appears in the records of the old Natchez District in 1814. Shortly thereafter, the senior O'Neal and his wife, Nancy, moved downriver to a small farm in East Baton Rouge Parish, where his family's fortunes improved with the region's growing agricultural economy. Peter O'Neal Sr. died in 1822, leaving his wife and seven-year-old son to tend the farm. Four years later, Nancy O'Neal married William Oates and had two more children, Henry and Samuel. When William Oates died, in about 1830, Nancy and her fourteen-year-old son, Peter, were left to manage their farm, now with two additional small children. As he grew older, Peter took on increased responsibility, and by the time he had reached his twentieth birthday in 1836, he had married Martha Susan Capers and taken over the farm. His mother, Nancy, continued to live on the farm with Peter and Martha until her death in 1852.[13]

In the two decades after their marriage, Peter and Martha Capers O'Neal became the parents of fourteen children, five of whom died in early childhood, and nine of whom still resided with them in 1860. At twenty-three, Anna Jane (usually called "Jane," but later sometimes referred to as "Jennie" by Lt. Earl and other Wisconsin soldiers) was the oldest, followed by Henry (17), Mary (14), Melchisedek (12), Melchina (11), Beverly (7), twins Susannah and Peter (5), and Ada (3). With such a large

13. In 1815, at age 35, the elder Peter O'Neal had married 29-year-old Nancy Bonnell Shelton, following the death of her husband, Lewis Shelton. Nancy Bonnell's roots in the Natchez District were as deep as Peter's. Her father, Elias Bonnell, had been banished with his family from Georgia as loyalists in 1782. By 1790 they were living in the Natchez District. Martha Capers's family had moved to the Baton Rouge region in the mid-1820s from South Carolina. The family traced its American roots to the seventeenth century, and members of the family had fought with Robert Marion, the "Swamp Fox," in the American Revolution. James Cornelius Capers, son of one of those men and an ordained Methodist minister, chose to head west. His wife, Eleanor, died in childbirth, in 1825, and two years later, he and his second wife, whose last name, "Lee," is the only name that is known, had moved to East Baton Rouge Parish, Louisiana, with his six children, perhaps in quest of opportunity and income that eluded him as a minister. He worked as a teacher until he acquired sufficient land to support his family as a farmer. By 1830, James Capers, his second wife, and nine surviving children by two wives all lived near Baton Rouge, where several descendants still live. Gary O'Neal, *The O'Neals of East Baton Rouge Parish: The Early Years* (Richmond, VA: Old Favorites Bookshop, 2005), pp. 5-8, 15, 17-19, 53-63, 76-81, 84.

family to support, Peter added to his farm whenever he could. By 1860 he owned nearly 200 acres, with a total assessed value of $6,000, and he employed two farmhands. Earlier, his mother had owned as many as six slaves, and in the 1850s she and Peter jointly owned a woman named Harriet and her eight-year-old son, Barton; but by 1860, they appear to have no longer owned slaves. There is little indication of the crops or livestock Peter O'Neal raised, but with two hired laborers and his young sons and daughters to help, he had options. He lived in an area of cleared fields, cattle farms, and sugar-cane plantations, and most likely he raised vegetable crops and animals, together with fields of cane that he could harvest and sell to Baton Rouge refineries.[14]

Contentious politics kept public discourse lively throughout the 1850s for Peter O'Neal and his neighbors. Voters split over issues ranging from the national Know-Nothing Party's opposition to Catholics and foreign immigrants (whom Southerners saw as more likely to oppose slavery), to the Florida Parishes' underrepresentation in state government, to the character of various candidates, to the political power of planter-politicians. Perhaps nothing upset life in the Florida Parishes as much as the state-supported construction of the New Orleans–Jackson Railroad, promoted by those who wanted closer commercial ties with New Orleans. The railroad brought in outside merchants and investors, disrupting the relationship between planters and "plain folk," destabilizing the isolated, independent lifestyle central to life in the piney woods. When yellow fever epidemics invaded the woods in the 1850s, they were seen as a sure sign that the railroad and city influences would portend little good for its inhabitants' lives.[15]

Further complicating political and social matters in the Florida Par-

14. According to *Measuring Worth*, $6,000 has a modern purchasing power of $162,000: http://www.measuringworth.com/uscompare/relativevalue.php (accessed Apr. 27, 2013); Sixth Census of the United States, 1840, NARA microfilm publication M 704, roll 129, p. 93; Seventh Census of the United States, 1850 NARA microfilm publication M 432, roll 229, p. 218B; Eighth Census of the United States, 1860 NARA microfilm publication M 653, roll 408; O'Neal, *The O'Neals of East Baton Rouge Parish*, pp. 17-19.

15. At one time part of French Louisiana, the Florida Parishes include eastern Louisiana from the Mississippi border on its eastern and northern borders, to the Mississippi River on its west, and Lake Pontchartrain to the south. The largest city in the region is Baton Rouge, the state capital. Prewar and wartime conditions in the Florida Parishes are discussed in Samuel Hyde Jr., *Pistols and Politics: The Dilemma of Democracy in Louisiana's Florida Parishes, 1810-1899* (Baton Rouge: Louisiana State University Press, 1996), pp. 72-91, 103-38.

ishes were a few strident Unionists who were determined to make their views known. Peter O'Neal's nearest neighbor, Polish emigré Stanislas Wrotnowski, was an outspoken Union man and abolitionist who ran a 300-acre farm where he raised cattle and crops including sugar cane, and he operated a sugar refinery in Baton Rouge — all with paid laborers, no slaves. Abraham Lincoln's election in 1860 and the lower South's attendant move toward secession added new spice to the Florida Parishes' political and social mix. Majorities in East Baton Rouge Parish who had believed moderation was the best way to preserve their property and fortunes supported the cooperationist candidate, John Bell, and resisted the secession movement that followed Lincoln's win. But nearly everyone accepted the popular will when secession convention delegates voted to leave the Union.[16]

A few residents, including the Wrotnowski family, remained steadfast Unionists throughout the war. Wrotnowski's son Louis, "a fine engineer, thoroughly acquainted with the topography of the country," joined the Union army as an engineer and cartographer as soon as Gen. Butler arrived in New Orleans. Louis began producing detailed maps of the Mississippi from Baton Rouge to Vicksburg, showing rivers and streams, terrain and vegetation, roads and pathways, the location of plantations, farms, fords, and ferries. Two of his maps of the region east of Baton Rouge show the Wrotnowski farm, ten miles east of Baton Rouge, and the O'Neal farm, about three miles to its south. Most important for Isaac Earl, they showed the location of two "guerrilla camps," one near Baton Rouge and another east of the Amite River. Earl met Louis Wrotnowski when the 4th Wisconsin came to Baton Rouge, and he served with him during the siege of Port Hudson, where Louis was killed by a sharpshooter while in front of the Confederate ramparts. After Port Hudson fell and the 4th Wisconsin returned to Baton Rouge, Union officers continued to use Wrotnowski's maps as they engaged in regular patrols east of the city. In 1864, Stanislas Wrotnowski was elected secretary of state in the Union Army–supervised election of a "free state" Louisiana government; this was mandated by President Lincoln's 1864 order calling for an election when 10 percent of the voters of 1860 swore allegiance to the United States. This move got Wrotnowski "disowned" as a Baton Rouge resident by the *Baton Rouge Weekly Advocate* two years later.[17]

16. Hyde, *Pistols and Politics*, pp. 104-5.
17. *New York Times*, April 26, 1864; Henry A. Willis, *The Fifty-third Regiment Massachusetts Volunteers. Comprising Also a History of the Siege of Port Hudson* (Fitchburg, MA:

The O'Neal family's feelings about Louisiana's secession after the election of 1860 are not known. There are no letters or diaries setting forth Peter and Martha's — or Jane's — thoughts about secession, slavery, Unionism, or abolition. They doubtless would have taken part in residents' discussions of the approaching secession, and later the arrival of the Union Army. As a successful farmer with a large family, Peter O'Neal would have been concerned about the disruptive potential of secession and the very real possibility that it would bring war. He had a son of military service age, and that alone may have been enough for him to support the position of former U.S. Senator Pierre Soule and others who sought to slow the secession process.[18]

In 1862, the question of whether Peter O'Neal supported immediate secession or a "go slower" approach had become moot. The war came to him. Following secession, their son Henry Cornelius, along with his cousin Sosthene Capers, enlisted in G Company of the Confederate Army's 9th Louisiana Infantry in March 1862 at the nearby hamlet of Amite Springs (now Denham Springs) and went to serve in Virginia. Within the first few months, Henry became a number in one of the war's largest and most depressing statistics: soldiers who died of disease. Although his service record contains confusing entries, it is clear that he died in Virginia in the early summer of 1862. He was reported "absent, sick at Charlottesville," on the regiment's June 18, 1862, muster roll. Another document indicates that he was admitted to Winchester C.S.A. Hospital on May 27, 1862, suffering from pneumonia. He continued to be listed on muster rolls as absent and sick until January 12, 1863, when his status changed to: "Dead; left the reg't very ill, has not been heard from since." A separate billing record of undertaker J. W. Saterwait indicates that he had died eight months earlier near Richmond and was buried there on May 9, 1862. (Sosthene Capers survived the war and returned home.)[19]

Press of Blanchard and Brown, 1889), p. 125; Topographical map of the Country Back of Baton Rouge, drawn by L. A. Wrotnowski C.E., July 1862; National Archives and Records Service, Record Group 23. "The Free State Government of Louisiana," *New York Times*, April 26, 1864; Frank J. Wetta, *The Louisiana Scalawags: Politics, Race, and Terrorism during the Civil War* (Baton Rouge: Louisiana State University Press, 2012), pp. 68-70. The impact of the Civil War on Louisiana's sugar industry is described in Charles P. Roland, *Louisiana Sugar Plantations during the Civil War* (Baton Rouge: Louisiana State University Press, 1997); *Baton Rouge Weekly Advocate*, July 30, 1866.

18. O'Neal, *The O'Neals of East Baton Rouge Parish*, pp. 26-28.

19. Compiled Service Records of Confederate Soldiers Who Served in Organizations

By the time they learned of Henry's disappearance, the O'Neal family was also mourning Peter's death, which was even more of a mystery than was his son's. According to O'Neal family sources, Peter had left home one day during the late summer of 1862; he was walking south and west toward Jones Creek, and was never seen alive again. His body was later found along the bank of that creek, which flows east into the Comite River. He had been buried in a shallow grave "near a gully just off Jones Creek," leaving his family with no clues about exactly when or how he had died. He may have been killed by robbers or in a confrontation with some of the area's guerrillas; the latter were known to prey on local civilians as well as on Union Soldiers. On the other hand, he may have been killed by Union soldiers.[20]

For the O'Neal family, the deaths of Peter and Henry meant that the mother, Martha, and her first daughter, Jane, were left to manage the farm with the help of teenagers Melchisedek (14) and Melchina (13), and five children under ten. In stable times that situation would have been difficult, but surrounded by guerrillas and outlaws, with a large occupying army a few miles away, it meant that their determination and farming skills were strained to the limit as they sought to generate sufficient income to support their family. One indication of their success through to the end of the war is an 1865 memorandum of agreement signed by U.S. Treasury agent G. W. Breckenridge that registered their "plantation" and authorized it to operate under federal occupation rules and regulations. In other words, Martha managed to hold her farm throughout the war, and she continued to operate it after the war. Another document from that same period indicates that she managed to retain the farm following Peter's death and ultimately settled his estate by paying state and local taxes of $14.65.[21]

As Jane and her mother worked to hold their family together, they may have found the Union Army payments for information an important

---

from the State of Louisiana, National Archives and Records Administration, Record Group 109, Microfilm Publication M320, Roll 210, Henry O'Neal Service Record, J. W. Satterwaite Burial Record, May 1862; *Louisiana Confederate Soldiers Online Database*, Provo, UT, USA: Ancestry.com (accessed Apr. 22, 2013). Original data from Andrew B. Booth, *Records of Louisiana Confederate Soldiers & Confederate Commands*, vols. 1-3, New Orleans, La., 1920; O'Neal, *The O'Neals of East Baton Rouge Parish*, pp. 27-29.

20. Hyde Jr., *Pistols and Politics*, pp. 102-38.

21. O'Neal, *The O'Neals of East Baton Rouge Parish*, p. 29. The tax payment had a value of $175.00 in 2010. *Measuring Worth* website: http://www.measuringworth.com/uscompare/relativevalue.php (accessed Apr. 25, 2013).

source of needed income. In the one month for which records survive, Jane received $70 from Lt. Earl for "information." Of that amount, $30 was for "services rendered," and $40 for "travelling expenses." As they continued working together, romance blossomed between these two young people from decidedly different backgrounds: dark-haired Jane O'Neal, independent and attractive, and the dynamic Isaac Earl, handsome and daring.[22]

Earl and his fellow members of the 4th Wisconsin continued scouting activities east of Baton Rouge throughout November and December 1863. On November 25, his group brought in eleven prisoners after several days in the field, and Earl paused only long enough to turn over his captives and change horses before joining a group led by Col. Boardman, who wanted to visit G. M. Pierce's plantation just north of Baton Rouge, a well-known stopping place for guerrillas. Pierce himself was suspected of gathering information for guerrillas. He always had plenty of whisky and cigars "freely set out" for passing Union soldiers, and "drunkenness inevitably followed." Boardman's party left Baton Rouge as sunset approached, joined by a detachment under Lt. James Farnsworth of Company A. They had information that Rebel guerrillas had stopped at Pierce's plantation, and their plan was to surround the plantation house and arrest them. Unfortunately, someone warned the guerrillas of the approaching federal troops, and the former were able to escape. According to Newton Culver, Isaac Earl and Col. Boardman surveyed the scene and — perhaps to the disappointment of some in their party — brought their group back to Baton Rouge "without being obliged to visit Captain Pierce."[23]

On December 4, Lt. Earl was placed in charge of another nighttime operation, and he made his way through the 4th Wisconsin camp, seeking volunteers. As soon as they heard about the planned ride, Newton Culver and Luther Struthers joined twenty-one others, and all of them prepared to depart shortly after the sun had set. Earl's route took them east of Baton Rouge on the Greenwell Springs Road and across the Amite River. Once

22. Abstract of Expenditures on Account of Special Services for the month of October 1864, Trimonthly Report of Lt. Earl, Oct. 20-30, 1864; Records of the Provost Marshall General's Bureau (Civil War) Record Group 110, Washington, DC: National Archives and Records Service.

23. Culver, "Brevet Major Isaac N. Earl," p. 312. G. M. Pierce is listed in the 1860 census for East Baton Rouge Parish with a farm valued at $12,000, and personal property, quite likely including several slaves, worth another $60,500. U.S. 1860 census, population schedule, East Baton Rouge Parish, Louisiana, National Archives and Records Administration, microfilm publication M 653, roll 408, p. 599, image 157.

across the river, they began a house-to-house search — probably aided, as they often were, by a former slave — arresting men suspected of being guerrillas who they found visiting their families. In short order, Earl's group took fourteen members of the 9th Louisiana Infantry, including their captain, B. F. Burnett, into custody.

The night's most exciting moment came when Burnett, an experienced horseman, managed a daring escape. Newton Culver observed the entire incident and later wrote about it in his journal. Sitting quietly in the saddle, Burnett had casually turned his mount up the trail — and then dug in his spurs. He disappeared into the darkness in a matter of seconds. Culver had been concerned about Burnett's "familiarity" with those watching him, and about his knowledge of the region's back roads and trails. In fact, he had even warned Burnett's guards to watch their prisoner closely, that he was likely to flee. As he turned and walked away, Culver heard the clatter of hoofs and a revolver shot; he turned around just in time to see the frustrated guards pointing into the darkness.

Earl saw a lesson in Burnett's escape. He later told Newton Culver that he "would never allow a prisoner to ride his own horse even if he had to let him have the best horse in the command." On their way back to Benton's Ferry, Earl's group picked up five more men who were hiding on the edge of a woodlot. It was a full night's work, and they did not arrive back in Baton Rouge with their eighteen prisoners until after dawn the next morning.[24]

Captured Again

After a quiet interlude during the Christmas and New Year holidays, which offered Earl more time than usual to call on Jane O'Neal, he resumed his forays into the region back of Baton Rouge on Sunday, January 10. Acting on information that Confederate troops under Brigadier General Wirt Adams had moved closer to Baton Rouge, he organized a detail of seventeen men, including Newton Culver, for a probing ride northeast on the Clinton Road toward the Amite River.

The squad was joined by a local guide, and Earl led them away from Baton Rouge just as the sun was setting. They rode about twenty miles, to the small community of Olive Branch, where they rested for a time at the

24. Culver, "Brevet Major Isaac N. Earl," pp. 312-13.

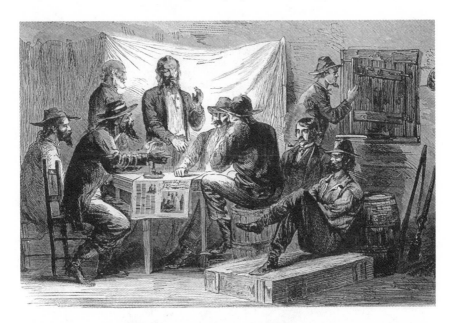

Unpopular, outnumbered, and vulnerable to harassment by guerrillas and partisans, Union sympathizers were often forced to gather in secret locations.
(*Harper's Weekly*, August 4, 1866)

home of a known Union sympathizer and friend of their guide. From their host they learned that they were near a camp of about fifty guerrillas, with Gen. Adams's Confederate encampment of several hundred soldiers only a few miles further northeast. While his men and horses rested, Earl decided on a risky maneuver. He would stay clear of the larger camp, but would strike the guerrilla encampment, seizing as many prisoners as possible. He would then turn and race back to Baton Rouge ahead of any pursuers.

Just before sunrise the next morning, he and his men began their attack by heading further north on the Clinton Road. After traveling only a short distance, they encountered three men on horseback, who immediately turned and fled. Earl ordered his guide and four of his men to pursue the horsemen, while he and the remainder of the force attempted to cut off their flight by following a little-traveled trail that intersected with the Clinton Road as it headed northeast. At a small bridge over the Olive Branch, a tributary of the Amite, Earl and his group came upon another Rebel picket. Earl gave the order to charge, but this time his squad came under fire just as they crossed the bridge. They had unwittingly ridden

Confederate General Wirt Adams
(Library of Congress)

into the guerrilla camp, and the guerrillas were shooting as they fled. Fearful of encountering Adams's much larger force, Earl and his men chased the Rebels only a short distance and then returned to the guerrilla camp, where his remaining squad members were waiting with their captives — the ones they had surprised before they could get to their horses.

At this point it appeared that Lt. Earl had led another successful raid. His squad held fourteen prisoners, plus several horses, with no losses of their own. However, they were about to learn from their captives that Adams's regular army force was only about two miles away, and that they needed to leave the area immediately. After taking a few minutes to destroy the guerrillas' abandoned equipment, Earl's squad hurriedly left, retracing their route toward Baton Rouge. But they had traveled no more than three miles when they found themselves about to be pinched between two large groups of Confederate soldiers. Ahead of them on the road was a force of about a hundred Confederate cavalrymen, while coming up behind them was a large contingent of Adams's soldiers.

Most members of Earl's group were quickly surrounded and captured, while Earl and four others eluded capture and galloped through the woods for Baton Rouge. They crossed several small creeks and got as far as the deeper and wider Comite River before Pvt. Miles Stanford of Company I was captured at its bank. Earl and Company D's Sergeant George Bailey managed to cross the river. But in that effort they lost their horses and were soon captured in the nearby woods. Only Pvts. Pharus Parker and Charles Bush, also from Company D, managed to elude their pursuers and return to Baton Rouge with news of the group's fate. Subsequent unconfirmed reports claimed six Confederates killed and five wounded.[25]

Leading their captors was Lt. E. B. Golden, who took Earl and his men back to Gen. Adams's Confederate camp near Clinton, Louisiana. There they were "stripped and abused" and threatened by Golden with being hanged as horse thieves. Earl asserted their rights as prisoners of war, and Golden chose not to carry out his threat. Instead, while Union leaders sent messages attempting to learn the captives' whereabouts and secure their parole, Confederate leaders made plans to transport Earl, as the officer in charge, to a prisoner-of-war camp in Alabama.[26]

25. Culver, "Brevet Major Isaac N. Earl," pp. 313-14; Quiner, *Correspondence*, vol. 10, "Army Correspondence from Volunteer," Jan. 20, 1864, p. 107.

26. O.R. Series I, vol. 34, part 2; Brig. Gen. Philip St. George Cooke to Brig. Gen. C. P. Stone, Jan. 11, 1864, p. 56; Jan. 12, 1864, p. 62; Jan. 16, 1864, p. 91; Feb. 10, 1864, p. 284.

CHAPTER FIVE

"Organize a Corps of Mounted Scouts"

I SAAC EARL WAS, BY ANY STANDARD, A DIFFICULT PRISONER. WHEN captured, he saw it as his duty to escape and return to his mates. He had escaped after being taken prisoner at Port Hudson and now, once again in Confederate hands, he began plotting a way out. As senior Confederate officer in the area, Gen. Wirt Adams declared that Earl and his men were prisoners of war; until shortly before Earl was captured, this would have meant a few weeks of captivity and then exchange or parole. However, the federal government had begun enlisting large numbers of former slaves, and Confederate leaders responded by refusing to recognize captured black soldiers as prisoners of war; instead, they declared that those blacks would be treated as escaped slaves, and their white officers would be executed. A Union threat to execute Confederate officers in retaliation prevented the Confederacy from carrying out any such executions; but a stalemate over exchanges ensued. On several occasions, the Southern states, needing soldiers, asked to resume the exchanges, but Gen. Grant refused.

Escape from Cahaba Prison

Because he was an officer, Earl was sent to Cahaba Prison near Selma, Alabama. Knowing how hard Earl had fought, and perhaps aware of his earlier escape at Port Hudson (and maybe in need of decent footwear himself), the capturing officer, Lt. Golden, took his boots, leaving Earl barefooted and shackled for transport to Cahaba. Those cautionary moves proved wise. According to accounts from men who later served with him, Earl at-

**"Castle Morgan," a former tobacco warehouse in Cahaba, Alabama, held
Union prisoners of war from 1863 to 1865, including Isaac Earl in early 1864.**
(Hawes, *Cahaba: A Story of Captive Boys in Blue*)

tempted at least two escapes during his trip to Alabama. On one occasion,
he managed to acquire a small knife, which he used to "sever the fetters
from his limbs," and nearly escaped in a nearby swamp. But his pursuers'
bloodhounds tracked him down and he was recaptured.[1]

Tightly constrained and carefully watched from that point on, Earl was
delivered to Cahaba without further incident. Unofficially called "Castle
Morgan" by Confederates wanting to recognize Colonel John Hunt Morgan, who had escaped from Union confinement in Ohio, Cahaba Prison
was located on the west bank of the Alabama River, near its confluence
with the Cahaba River. An important early water transportation depot,
Cahaba had flourished in the 1820s and had briefly served as the state's
capital. It fell on hard times after the railroad's arrival in Selma made that
city the region's transportation center, leaving Cahaba an isolated settlement of a few residences and commercial buildings. Shortly thereafter,
when Confederate authorities came looking for a prisoner-of-war prison

---

1. William DeLoss Love, *Wisconsin in the War of the Rebellion: A History of Regiments
and Batteries the State Has Sent to the Field* (Chicago: Church and Goodman, 1866), p. 908.

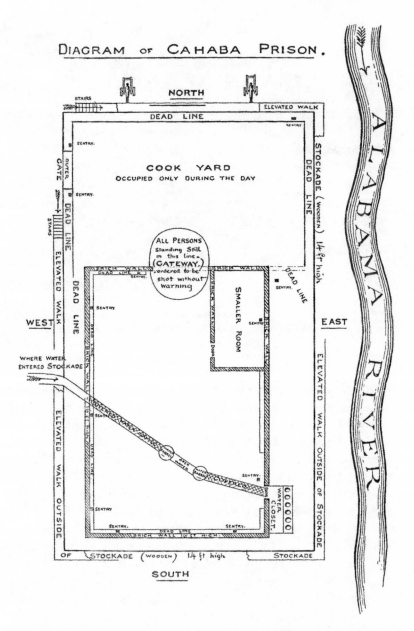

Former prisoner Jesse Hawes drew this diagram of Castle Morgan, which shows the "dead line" near the walls, the warehouse for sleeping, the cook yard, and the ditch that provided the prison's only source of water.

(Hawes, *Cahaba: A Story of Captive Boys in Blue*)

site, Cahaba's isolation and vacant buildings made it an ideal location. In June 1863, workers had begun to turn the brick walls of a partially completed cotton warehouse into a prison, surrounded by a twelve-foot-high wooden stockade.[2]

Cahaba's crowded and unsanitary interior may have added to Isaac Earl's desire to get away. In early 1864, at the time of his confinement, its overworked surgeon, R. H. Whitfield, complained that Cahaba housed over 650 prisoners in a 15,000-square-foot enclosure under a partially finished "leaky roof with 1,600 feet of open space in its center." Wooden bunks "of rough lumber, without straw or bedding of any kind" provided sleeping space for 432 men. The remaining prisoners slept on the ground. Sanitation was Whitfield's greatest concern. Water for drinking, cooking, and bathing came from an artesian well and flowed "along an open street gutter for 200 yards, thence under the street into the prison, in its course subjected to . . . filth of all kinds from the streets and other sources." The camp's single privy added another concern. It "accommodates but four men at once," he wrote near the end of his report, "with but one wheelbarrow to remove filth and other rubbish." The prison's location in the river's floodplain further compounded Whitfield's problems. More than once, the river's floodwaters forced prisoners to stand in water, sit together on their bunks, or climb onto woodpiles.[3]

Although he was far from the familiar roads and streams of Louisiana and Mississippi, Isaac Earl continued attempting to escape. On one occasion he took advantage of a decision by the camp's commandant, Captain H. A. M. Henderson, to move captive officers to quarters in nearby town buildings. Shortly after being moved, Earl escaped from the house in which he was confined and fled into the surrounding countryside through heavy underbrush and swampy lowlands. But he was tracked down by guards with a pack of bloodhounds and returned to the prison.[4]

2. Special Agent A. S. Gaines to George S. Randolph, Secretary of War, April 24, 1862; O.R., VI, vol. 1, pp. 1089-91; Lonnie Speer, *Portals to Hell: Military Prisons of the Civil War* (Mechanicsburg, PA: Stackpole Books, 1997), pp. 255-59; William O. Bryant, *Cahaba Prison and the Sultana Disaster* (Tuscaloosa: University of Alabama Press, 1990), pp. 16-25; Jesse Hawes, *Cahaba: A Story of Captive Boys in Blue* (1888), pp. 13-14; William Best Hasseltine, *Civil War Prisons: A Study in War Psychology* (1930); *Old Cahawba, Alabama's First State Capitol, 1820-1826:* http://www.cahawba.com (accessed Apr. 7, 2012).

3. Surgeon R. H. Whitfield to Medical Director P. B. Scott, March 31, 1864; O.R., II, 6, p. 1124.

4. Speer, *Portals to Hell*, p. 258. The Confederates' use of bloodhounds caused Earl

Isaac Earl was chased by bloodhounds on more than one occasion, leaving him with a bitter hatred for the animals. (*Harper's Weekly*, November 21, 1863)

His failed attempt only hardened Earl's resolve. Although he was free for only a short time, he had learned something about the surrounding region and about the tactics he would need to make a successful escape. In his next attempt he resorted to a greater level of violence and took steps to elude the bloodhounds that he knew would soon be on his trail. With an axe that had been carelessly left on the cooking woodpile as his weapon, he attacked his guards with blows that seriously injured one and may have killed the other. He had to know, of course, that given the violence of his acts, if he were to be recaptured this time, he would face the very real possibility of execution. Racing into the same swamps that he had reached in his earlier escape attempt, Earl "waded up and down streams so that the dogs could not track him." Traveling at night and hiding during the day, he avoided well-worn roads and trails and stayed away from villages, subsisting by stealing food from isolated farm gardens and fields. At length he came out at the Gulf of Mexico.

---

to hate the dogs. Newton Culver recounted that Earl tried to kill the animals whenever he encountered them (Newton Culver, "Brevet Major Isaac N. Earl: A Noted Scout of the Department of the Gulf," *Proceedings of the Historical Society of Wisconsin* [1917]: 314).

Bad luck had thwarted Earl's earlier escape attempts from Cahaba, but this time better fortune guided his steps. Rather than heading back to Baton Rouge, he turned his face east toward Pensacola, Florida, which was not only closer to his location but had remained in Union hands, its harbor and navy yard essential for docking, coaling, and refitting Union blockade vessels. When he reached Pensacola, Earl found a Union gunboat bound for New Orleans and boarded it for the last stage of his journey back to Louisiana. On April 28, 1864, after three-and-a-half months in enemy hands, and after traveling over a thousand miles, much of it on foot, he showed up in New Orleans to provide a report of the intelligence he had gathered behind enemy lines. A few days later he was back with the 4th Wisconsin Cavalry in Baton Rouge.[5]

The Awkward Squad

Back with the 4th Wisconsin, Isaac Earl resumed leading scouting parties east of Baton Rouge. On May 2 he led twenty advance scouts as part of a combined force of the 42nd Ohio Infantry, the 4th Wisconsin Cavalry, and the 18th New York Artillery Battery as they reconnoitered west and north of Baton Rouge toward Clinton. Colonel Lionel Sheldon of the 42nd Ohio led the force, and Col. Boardman commanded the 4th Wisconsin. Dubbing themselves the "Awkward Squad," slang for a group of raw, undisciplined recruits, Earl's handpicked advance guard consisted mostly of seasoned veterans who had scouted with him before and now stepped forward to ride with him again.

Col. Sheldon's force bivouacked for the night on the northern edge of Baton Rouge before getting underway at dawn the next morning — with the Awkward Squad leading the way. They were barely beyond sight of the city when the excitement started. Four skirmishers, including Newton Culver, took positions on either flank of the main expedition, pushing their way through heavy underbrush that grew along the Clinton Road.

5. Accounts of this and Earl's other escape attempts are understandably vague. Dates and locations of specific attempts are not known. In fact, it is not entirely clear whether he escaped alone or with Henry Stafford, with whom he had been captured. One account mentions both men, while others mention only Earl. This account is based on Culver, "Brevet Major Isaac N. Earl," pp. 313-14; Love, *Wisconsin in the War of the Rebellion*, p. 908; George F. Pearce, *Pensacola during the Civil War: A Thorn in the Side of the Confederacy* (Gainesville: University Press of Florida, 2000), p. 237.

Like the man in this *Harper's Weekly* illustration, Newton Culver served as advance skirmisher for the corps of experienced veterans led by Earl. (*Harper's Weekly*, May 7, 1864)

They had gone no more than two miles when they came upon three Confederate pickets in the woods watching the main Union body. Culver and his companions drove off the Rebels so quickly that they left behind "their boots, arms, and two horses." Culver and his companions chased the fleeing Rebels until a Confederate artillery battery that was concealed in a growth of small pines opened fire, sending them scurrying for protection behind a low hill. Sneaking up to the hill's crest, Culver peeked "through the dead weeds that covered the brow of the hill and shielded me from view," and observed infantrymen emerging from the pines no more than one hundred yards away. He was sitting quietly on his horse, waiting until the entire line of infantry was exposed so that he could estimate their number, when his horse jumped, giving away his presence. The infantrymen ran to the hill's front slope as Culver galloped down its back and made his getaway, his horse leaping a fence and a wide gulch as he raced across the field. Despite what he estimated as "over a hundred shots" fired in his direction, Culver returned unscathed to Earl and his friends in the Awkward Squad.

No sooner had Culver rejoined his comrades than Earl heard barking dogs making a racket on his left, which sent him to determine the cause of the commotion. Carefully working his way "thirty or forty rods" (perhaps 500 feet) into the heavy woods, Culver saw in the distance the backs of "200 or more cavalry" leaving the area. He reported his discovery, and as soon as the 4th Wisconsin arrived on the scene, Col. Boardman ordered Earl and the Awkward Squad, together with Company E, led by Cpt. Charles Wooster, and Company G, headed by Lt. Warren P. Knowles, to pursue the Confederates.

Culver once again went forward as an advance scout. This time he managed to capture a prisoner who turned out to hold special interest for Lt. Earl. Quietly riding through dense woods and leaning low over his saddle to peer beneath branches, Culver glimpsed the legs of a grey horse ahead. At the same time, the horse's rider saw Culver. Drawing his carbine, Culver aimed at the horse and rider, hitting the animal, which reared and fell. The rider was just getting disentangled from his injured mount when Culver rode up and placed him under arrest. Taking the man's navy revolver and saber, Culver was preparing to return with his prisoner when Earl arrived. As Culver looked on, a quick expression of recognition came over his prisoner's face, followed by a brief exchange with Earl.

"For God's sake, Earl, don't kill me," Culver remembered the prisoner saying, and Earl melodramatically responded: "Lieutenant Golden, brave men treat prisoners like brothers." Afterward, Culver, who had not been present at the raid in which Earl had been captured, asked what the conversation meant. "When that man had me a prisoner a few months ago," Earl told him, "he took the boots from my feet and marched me barefoot a hundred miles or more."[6]

---

6. Culver, "Brevet Major Isaac N. Earl," pp. 314-25. Lt. Golden is not further identified. It is most likely that he was Lt. E. Golden of the Fire Battalion of the Louisiana Militia. According to a *Louisiana in the Civil War Message Board* (http://history-sites.com/cgi-bin/bbs53x/lacwmb/webbbs_config.pl?noframes;read=12744#Responses [accessed July 11, 2012]), there were two fire battalions (regiments) in the Louisiana Militia. The Orleans Fire Battalion became the Orleans Fire Regiment in early 1862. It consisted of volunteer militia companies associated with the New Orleans Fire Department. The Louisiana Fire Battalion, comprised of volunteer militia companies associated with the fire departments from the area surrounding New Orleans, existed at the same time. The latter became the Louisiana Fire Regiment in late 1861 or early 1862.

Colonel Frederick Boardman
(Quiner, *Military History of Wisconsin*)

With their prisoner in tow, and realizing that Rebel units patrolled the woods around them, the 4th Wisconsin advance companies began making their way back toward the main Union force. After going only a short distance, they encountered a Confederate cavalry contingent that was twice their size and aligned two deep across their front. Sitting astride their horses facing the Rebels, Earl, Wooster, and Knowles exchanged a few hurried words about their options. Earl advocated a frontal charge, while the other two thought they should withdraw. Finally, Wooster, as the ranking officer, gave the order for his soldiers to turn at a gallop and head toward the nearby woods. The enemy cavalry followed, but Culver believed that they were firing high to avoid hitting Lt. Golden. The 4th Wisconsin companies made the woods, and their pursuers stopped, unwilling to charge the strong defensive position provided by the trees.

After the scouts reunited with the main Union force, the expedition set off again to find the Rebels. Approaching the Comite River, Col. Boardman halted the 4th Wisconsin and, not realizing Rebel sharpshooters were hiding on the river's far bank, rode forward to examine the crossing. Discovering that the Rebels had burned the bridge, Boardman rode to the water's edge to see how badly it was damaged. As he was about to turn back, bullets from several Rebel sharpshooters found their mark. Boardman fell from his horse, dead in full view of many of his men. Soon afterward, Earl, who had ridden downriver with the Awkward Squad, returned without finding another place to cross. Told of Boardman's death, he called for volunteers to retrieve their colonel's body, and he led a small group through the woods to a spot near where Boardman lay. Dashing on to the road, he and his men picked up Boardman's body and galloped back up the road as the sharpshooters resumed firing. With no way to cross the Comite River, Col. Sheldon decided to return to Baton Rouge. It had been a difficult trip, though both sides, in their reports, claimed victory. The Confederates reported stopping the larger Union force, while Sheldon claimed to have driven the Rebel cavalrymen back to within five miles of Clinton. The 4th Wisconsin and Lt. Earl's Awkward Squad had performed well, having captured Earl's nemesis, Lt. Golden. But the regiment had lost its colonel.[7]

Red River Disaster

After Vicksburg and Port Hudson fell, the Union Army's primary responsibility along the lower Mississippi shifted from offensive operations to occupation duty. Confederate armies were still active inland on both sides of the river, but the Union Army's responsibility along the great waterway was to keep it open to transportation and commerce. This occupation duty depended heavily on regular patrols, and whenever Confederate forces were detected moving toward the river, Union generals mounted campaigns to keep them at bay and prevent them from reestablishing links across the river. For example, in mid-1864, a year after being driven from Alexandria by Gen. Banks's forces, Confederate General Richard Taylor had moved his troops back into northwest Louisiana, and the Union general-in-chief, Ulysses Grant, wanted the area cleared again. The plan called for Banks's army, accompanied by Porter's gunboats, to drive up the Red River through Alexandria and on toward Shreveport, pushing Taylor's army before them. The plan's purposes were to seize cotton from the

---

7. Culver, "Brevet Major Isaac N. Earl," pp. 314-18. More than fifty years after Golden's capture, Culver wrote that the lieutenant's revolver and belt were still in the Culver family's possession. "Letter from the Fourth Cavalry," *Milwaukee Sentinel*, May 21, 1864: www.Genealogybank.com (accessed Sept. 19, 2013). Report of Brig. Gen. Henry W. Birge to Asst. Adj. Gen., Maj. John Levering, May 3, 1864; O.R., I, 34, 1, pp. 906-7; Report of Col. John S. Scott, 1st Louisiana Cavalry to Lt. Gen. Leonidas Polk, May 3, 1864; O.R., II, 34, p. 851.

region's plantations, to eliminate Texas as a source of food and supplies for the Rebel army, and to keep the western Confederate generals, Taylor and Edmund Kirby Smith, from crossing the Mississippi and uniting with forces further to the east.

Grant had given Gen. Banks a tall order, but Banks had more than 30,000 well-supplied and experienced troops at his disposal, as opposed to fewer than half that number of Confederates in the region. Just as important, Banks had support at the highest levels in Washington. However, his ignorance of military strategy, along with his quest for the political advantage he thought he would gain via military success, resulted in poor organization and bad decisions that doomed the expedition.[8]

The federal offensive began with a glitch and continued with a lurch. Porter's fleet came up the Red River to Alexandria on March 15 and 16, planning to join forces with Banks's forces coming from the south, and General Frederick Steele coming down from Arkansas. Unfortunately, Banks was late, and Steele was even later. Nearly two weeks passed before Banks and Porter were ready to push on toward Shreveport without Steele, who still had not arrived from Arkansas. Banks and Porter were under pressure to move quickly, in part because Gen. Grant had informed Banks that, after April 25, troops in his force that had been supplied by General William T. Sherman would return to Mississippi. Just as important, the Red River's level was unusually low, and it was falling, threatening to stop Porter's fleet and leave Banks's army without their support.[9]

On April 8, the armies of Union Gen. Banks and Confederate Gen. Taylor clashed at Mansfield, below Shreveport, with Taylor turning Banks's men back downriver. Taylor's men pursued and continued the fight the next day at Pleasant Hill, but this time it was the Confederates who were stopped, leaving both sides exhausted and needing to regroup. In the battles over two days, each side suffered about 4,000 casualties. More important, the battles ended any chance of success for Banks's Red River expedition. Having to retreat to Alexandria without achieving his objective was only part of Banks's problem; Porter's gunboat fleet was stuck on the far side of the rapids above Alexandria, and they would have to remain there unless the water level miraculously rose and they could get

8. James G. Hollandsworth Jr., *Pretense of Glory: The Life of General Nathaniel P. Banks* (Baton Rouge: Louisiana State University Press, 1998), pp. 172-77.

9. Maj. Gen. Henry W. Halleck to Maj. Gen. Nathaniel P. Banks, Feb. 11, 1864; Mar. 15, 1864; O.R., I, 34, 2, pp. 293-94, 610-11.

over the rapids. Fortunately for Banks, he had Lt. Col. Bailey, the engineer, on his staff. Before the war, Bailey had built dams to control log drives in Wisconsin. Now he put together a series of wooden dams that raised the water level sufficiently to float Porter's gunboats over the rapids when the floodgates were opened.

Back at his New Orleans headquarters, Gen. Banks filed reports that put his Red River campaign in the best possible light, claiming that his movements had ensured that Confederate forces would remain west of the Mississippi. However, the Red River debacle, compounded by his earlier mishandling of the Port Hudson campaign, meant that Banks's unspectacular career as a military strategist was over. After receiving news of the failed venture, Gen. Halleck vented his frustration about all "political generals" — and Banks in particular — in a letter to fellow West Point graduate William T. Sherman. "Banks's operations in the West," he wrote, "are about what should have been expected from a general so utterly destitute of military education and military capacity. It seems but little better than murder to give important commands to such men."

However, Banks was not without his allies. He had strong support from his Republican colleagues in Congress, as well as from President Lincoln. Therefore, Halleck decided on two moves. He recommended that President Lincoln settle the matter by appointing General E. R. S. Canby, a West Point graduate, to command a new Military Division of West Mississippi encompassing the Department of the Gulf and the Department of Arkansas, which would effectively supersede Banks's military authority. This move diminished Banks's military decision-making power but did not diminish his role in establishing a reconstructed Louisiana state government that abolished slavery and provided public education for all residents, black and white, between the ages of six and eighteen — work much better suited to his prewar experience.[10]

General Canby Creates Earl's Special Scouts

Born and raised in northern Kentucky, Edward Richard Sprigg Canby, known to friends and close military colleagues as "Sprigg" (or Richard), generally used his initials E. R. S. on all formal correspondence. He

10. Hollandsworth, *Pretense of Glory*, pp. 201, 206-8; Maj. Gen. H. W. Halleck to Maj. Gen. W. T. Sherman; O.R., I, 34, 3, pp. 332-33.

Major General Edward Richard Sprigg Canby
(Library of Congress)

had attended Wabash College in north central Indiana for a time before transferring to the United States Military Academy. While at West Point, Canby's classes included lectures on Indian warfare delivered by the well-known strategist Dennis Hart Mahan, who advised his students "to employ frontiersmen and friendly Indians as auxiliaries and scouts," to pay careful attention to security against hit-and-run attacks in camp and on the march, and "to gather intelligence for the purpose of exploiting intertribal tensions." Canby used these tactics in his post–West Point assignments in Florida and the Southwest, and later he used them against partisans, insurgents, smugglers, and outlaws along the lower Mississippi as well.[11]

Canby was commissioned a second lieutenant upon graduation from West Point, and his first combat experience came shortly thereaf-

11. Andrew J. Birtle, *U.S. Army Counterinsurgency and Contingency Operations and Doctrine, 1861-1941* (Washington, DC: Center of Military History, United States Army, 2009), pp. 12-13.

ter in Florida's Second Seminole War. Fighting in south central Florida's swamps and scrub brush, he encountered small bands of Seminoles who knew the terrain of their home country, and who struck fast and disappeared, causing no end of frustration to the U.S. Army. In 1846, he fought in the Mexican War, first under General Zachary Taylor's command and then with General Winfield Scott at Mexico City, honing his skills against both regular and irregular forces in battles at Contreras, Churubusco, and Belén Gates, receiving brevet promotions to major and then to lieutenant colonel. After the Mexican War, he served once again against irregulars, this time in the Utah Territory during the Utah War (1857-58) against Mormon militiamen who fought as insurrectionaries, stampeding army animals, burning supply trains, blocking roads, and generally bedeviling the troops. Finally, on the eve of the Civil War, Canby received an assignment to New Mexico to coordinate a campaign against the Navajo, a foe whose raiding parties constantly harassed the skirts of his column, and who preferred to inflict psychological rather than military damage. Through all these assignments, Canby showed himself to be an intelligent, thoughtful officer who, when the time came, brought to his assignment on the lower Mississippi a hard-won knowledge of dealing with small groups of irregulars, and a respect for the value of small, mobile, experienced counterinsurgency units.

When the Civil War broke out, Canby was still in New Mexico, commanding the Department of New Mexico. His assistant, Captain Henry H. Sibley, resigned to join the Confederate Army. The two men faced each other twice, at the Battle of Valverde, where Sibley prevailed, and then at Glorieta Pass, where Canby's troops forced Sibley to retreat toward Texas. On March 31, 1862, immediately after that latter battle, Canby's old West Point classmate Henry W. Halleck, by that time the commander of the Union Army's western theater of operations, recommended Canby for promotion to brigadier general. Five months later, he was ordered east to report to the secretary of war for "special duty" in the adjutant general's office of the War Department in Washington, D.C.

On July 17, 1863, immediately after the deadly New York draft resistance riots, E. R. S. Canby was named Commanding General of the City and Harbor of New York, a position in which he was assigned to restore order to the restive parts of the city. He held that temporary assignment for four months, after which he returned to his job as assistant to the secretary of war. Six months thereafter, in May 1864, upon being promoted to major general, he was sent south to New Orleans as commander of the newly created Military Division of West Mississippi, effectively replacing Gen. Banks.[12]

Not long after he assumed command in New Orleans, Canby decided to form a small corps of special scouts dedicated to the disruption of guerrilla and illegal trade activities along the Mississippi River. Discussion about such a unit had begun under Gen. Banks, who appears to have been receptive to the special scouts. On his arrival, Canby endorsed the proposal, and he issued orders creating a corps of those scouts that would be led by 1st Lt. Isaac Earl. (The unit became generally known as "Earl's Scouts," though it was occasionally referred to as "Canby's Scouts.") Canby's orders instructed Earl and his Scouts to gather intelligence about illegal activity, ranging from guerrilla raids to smugglers, to pursue and arrest perpetrators wherever possible, and to seize illegal goods and weapons.

Although Canby never formally explained his reasons for selecting Isaac Earl to lead the new group, the young Wisconsin lieutenant's exploits were well known, and Canby very likely learned of them soon after his arrival and concluded that Earl was an obvious choice to lead the unit. Earl was informed of his selection in a letter on June 6, 1864, from Canby's assistant adjutant, Major C. T. Christensen, which authorized Earl to "organize a corps of mounted citizen scouts," and for that purpose to select thirty "reliable men . . . specially fitted for this kind of service." Each man was to have a "written engagement" for his service, specifying a pay rate of $40 to $60 per month, with extra compensation "in cases of extra danger." The increase in pay doubtless served as an incentive for veteran soldiers who had been receiving $16 per month. The authorization letter placed recruiting responsibility on Earl, informing him that, "[i]f you know of any soldiers who are fitted for this duty they may be ordered to report to you at Natchez, Mississippi, where furloughs will be granted them." Christensen's letter also made clear that anyone who joined the scouts had to understand that they would still be members of the United States Army, and "held subject to strict military discipline and all the Rules and Articles of War." Concerned that he be kept informed about where the Scouts were and what they were doing, Gen. Canby concluded his instructions by instructing Earl to send reports of the Scouts' activities directly to his New Orleans headquarters every ten days.[13]

12. Canby's career prior to 1864 is covered in Max L. Heyman Jr., *Prudent Soldier: A Biography of Major General E. R. S. Canby, 1817-1873* (Glendale, CA: Arthur H. Clark, 1959), pp. 27-202.

13. Maj. C. T. Christensen to Lt. I. N. Earl, June 6, 1864; O.R., I, 34, 4, p. 243.

The Special Scouts Assemble

As soon as he received Christensen's letter, Isaac Earl set about assembling his "Special Scouts." Word traveled fast among 4th Wisconsin veterans, who were all well aware of Earl's exploits. They knew that he almost always achieved success, and that even though he took risks and had been captured more than once, he managed to return unscathed. Estimates of the number who volunteered vary. In his memoir Lucien Bennett put the number at an unlikely 400, while Newton Culver suggested a more probable "over 100." Either estimate meant that there were more than enough volunteers willing to accept the risks inherent in such unorthodox service to achieve the thirty seasoned veterans Canby authorized.[14]

When fully constituted, Earl's Special Scouts consisted of thirty-two Union veterans (thirty from the 4th Wisconsin, two from the 2nd Wisconsin Cavalry), sixteen Southern civilians (including a deserter from the 20th Mississippi Infantry), and ten black laborers. Most of them joined at the time the Scouts were formed; a few signed on later to fill vacancies. Three years earlier, these young Wisconsin men had left remote farming and lumbering communities in all corners of the state; now they were seasoned soldiers who were ready to apply their skills and experience in a difficult, challenging assignment.

The single largest group were ten men who came from Company G, the "Hudson Guards": Charles Fenlason, Edward Harris, George Hayes, brothers Samuel and William Jewell, William Kent, Byron Kenyon, Andrew Ryan, Warren Knowles, and Nelson Porter (who served as clerk for the group during their entire existence). Hudson, on Wisconsin's western border with Minnesota, was the area's largest city and the county seat of St. Croix County. Seven men — Charles Baker, Lucien Bennett, Miller Graham, William Hine, Archibald Rowin, James Shaw, and Henry Stafford — were members of Company I, known as the "Monroe County Volunteers." Also on the western side of the state, Monroe County was south of Hudson and immediately east of La Crosse. Isaac Earl, Lewis Hatch, Albert James, and Nathaniel White were part of Company D, the "Columbia Rifles," organized in Adams County.

The remainder of the Special Scouts came from Wisconsin's southern and eastern counties. Two, Charles Van Norman and Jacob Ripley,

---

14. Bennett, "Sketch of Military Service," p. 13; Culver, "Brevet Major Isaac N. Earl," p. 319.

Earl's Special Scouts Photo Gallery *(left to right, top to bottom):*
Lt. Isaac Earl and Pvt. Henry Stafford (State Historical Society of Wisconsin)
Pvt. Newton Culver (State Historical Society of Wisconsin)
Pvt. Nelson Porter (Hughes Family Collection)
Pvt. Lucien Bennett (State Historical Society of Wisconsin)
Pvt. Charles Fenlason (State Historical Society of Wisconsin, *Proceedings,* 1916)
Pvt. Charles Baker (State Historical Society of Wisconsin)

were members of Company F, the "Geneva Independents," from Walworth County, and Albert Woodward came from Company E, organized as the "Jefferson County Guards." John Adams, from Company B, had begun his service as a member of the "Ripon Rifles" from Fond du Lac. Sheboygan County was home to Luther Struthers and Newton Culver, who were members of Company C, the "Sheboygan County Volunteers." Lying further north was Calumet County, home of John Billings and Nicholas Wait of Company K, the "Calumet Rifles." From farthest north, on Wisconsin's border with Michigan's Upper Peninsula, came Oconto County's Spencer Bills of Company H, the "Oconto River Drivers." Two men, Louis Simpson and Frank Wallace, came from Company I of the 2nd Wisconsin Cavalry, which was stationed in the Vicksburg region. These men did not all serve at the same time; some joined and were discharged, leaving as their enlistments expired, to be replaced by others.[15]

Riding out on patrol, Earl's Scouts presented the same appearance as any group of Union soldiers did: white, young (averaging about twenty-five years old), native-born, predominantly farmers, more Protestants than Catholics, and mostly unmarried. Physically, they were also average: about five feet eight inches tall, weighing approximately 145-155 pounds.[16]

In addition to the veteran Union soldiers, there were several nonmilitary members of Earl's Scouts. Southern civilians and black freedmen, who served as informants and laborers, joined and left the organization as they were needed. In July, Earl added three civilians, identified only by surname and first initials: W. J. Laughman, W. D. Mead, and M. Bowers acted as advance scouts and spies for the group. Each received $60 per month, plus traveling expenses, and Earl listed them as "on secret duty" in his reports. Other civilians — J. W. Carlin, Sidney M. Cook, Thomas Franklin, James Mulloy, Harmon Netterfield, Samuel R. Porter, John E. Roberts, and Joel Southwick — rode with the Scouts for varying lengths of time. A few civilians had special roles with the Scouts. Phillip (Pat) Daugherty lived "out back" of Baton Rouge, and on several occasions he served as an informant and guide for scouting parties in that area. He went with the Scouts to Natchez and continued his role as informant and guide there. His mother also went to Natchez, where she supervised cooking and laundry at their headquarters. Lieutenant W. R. Smylie, a deserter from the

15. *Roster of Wisconsin Volunteers, War of the Rebellion, 1861-1865*, 2 vols. (Madison: Democrat Printing Company, 1886), vol. 1, pp. 156-201; Love, *Wisconsin in the War of the Rebellion*, p. 529; Bennett, "Sketch of Military Service." Rosters included with Trimonthly Reports submitted by Lts. Isaac N. Earl and Warren P. Knowles, Sept. 10, 1864–March 10, 1865; Culver, "Brevet Major Isaac N. Earl," pp. 308-38.

16. General information about the soldiers who served in the Civil War can be found in E. B. Long, *The Civil War Day by Day* (Garden City, NY, 1971), pp. 706-9. Biographical information about the Special Scouts can be found in their service records, veteran pension files, and the Trimonthly Reports of Lts. Earl and Knowles, supplemented by information from the *Roster of Wisconsin Volunteers in the War of the Rebellion* (Madison: Wisconsin Adjutant General's Office, 1886). A complete roster, including brief biographies of the Special Scouts, and a listing Southern civilians, spies, and associated support workers can be found in Appendix A at the conclusion of this book.

20th Mississippi Cavalry, became a Scout on October 5, 1864, and served as a guide and spy until March 10, 1865. Sixteen-year-old Johnny Hays joined the Scouts in late fall of 1864 as Lt. Earl's orderly. In addition to Jane O'Neal, Mrs. G. F. Fischer also served briefly as a paid spy.[17]

A group of black laborers worked at the Special Scouts' Natchez headquarters, and some of them accompanied the Scouts on extended expeditions. James Hardman, Josiah Haygood, Thomas Johnson, Matthew Keeney, Charles Parker, Daniel Webster, Mack Harper, and Alec Jones provided "care of horses and general labor" at a $10 monthly rate. Thornton Stewart received $15 per month as their "waggoner" (teamster), and Jerry Williams earned $40 per month as their "saddler," repairing saddles and harnesses.[18] Although Earl only occasionally refers to receiving information from blacks, it is reasonable to assume that these men were valuable not only as laborers, but also for their knowledge of the area and their acquaintances in its large black population.

Lazy Days around Natchez

In early June, Earl secured a former warehouse building in the steamboat wharf area known as Natchez-Under-The-Hill to serve as headquarters for his Special Scouts. Under-The-Hill hosted all forms of commerce — with its "wharf, boats, warehouses, stores and hotels, and haunts of vice." From the wharf, an inclined road cut into the side of the soft limestone bluff and rose 170 feet above the river to Natchez proper. Atop the bluff was a different, more genteel world of broad boulevards and large homes, with a park at its crest "commanding a view — none finer on the Mississippi — down the river for miles and up the river a short distance where it disappears behind a bend to the west twenty miles around, only to appear again across a narrow neck, about two and one-half miles to the north." From

17. Rosters included with Trimonthly Reports submitted by Lt. Earl and Lt. Knowles, Sept. 10, 1864–March 10, 1865; Abstract of Expenditures on Account of Special Services by Lt. I. N. Earl Comndg, Special Scouts, for the month of October 1864, included with Trimonthly Report (payment for September services); Culver, "Brevet Major Isaac N. Earl," pp. 337-38. An additional civilian is listed in Culver's article as McLaughlin, with no first name. Culver wrote the article fifty years later, and it is possible that the McLaughlin he recalls was really W. J. Laughman.

18. Rosters included with Trimonthly Reports submitted by Lt. Earl and Lt. Knowles, Sept. 10, 1864–Mar. 10, 1865.

The Scouts' headquarters in Natchez-Under-The-Hill, with its steamboat wharfs and warehouses, enabled them to board their steamboat and move up and down the Mississippi on short notice and without attracting undue attention. (Accessed in: https://otrwjam.wordpress .com/tag/natchez-under-the-hill/)

the bluff one could view to the west "for many miles the fertile bottom lands of Louisiana." Immediately to the east of these handsome residences was "the business part of the city."[19]

On June 15, Earl's first group of twenty-four recruits arrived from Baton Rouge aboard the riverboat *Sallie Robinson* and moved into their headquarters building. As soon as they settled in and shed their army uniforms for civilian garb, they set out to explore the city, observing friend and foe alike. It would be another six weeks before they were to begin regular patrols; in the interim they spent nearly every day walking and riding around Natchez and its environs, familiarizing themselves with their new home.[20]

Newton Culver was part of the first group to report to Earl. They had received orders to report on June 13, when they turned over their horses and equipment to the quartermaster at Baton Rouge and boarded the *Sallie*

19. Matilda Gresham, *Life of Walter Quintin Gresham, 1832-1893*, vol. 1 (Chicago: Rand-McNally, 1919), pp. 240-41.
20. Culver, Diary, June 15, 1864; Culver, "Brevet Major Isaac N. Earl," p. 320.

As late as the 1970s, Natchez-Under-The-Hill contained several unused warehouses and boarding houses, one of which may have been used by Earl's Scouts over 100 years earlier. (Gordon Olson)

Robinson for Natchez, where new horses, equipment, and weapons awaited them. Culver did not arrive in Natchez totally unarmed; he brought with him the Colt revolver that he had seized as a battle trophy from Lt. Golden. Culver liked the choice of cities for the Scouts' headquarters. To his eyes, Natchez was "by far the pretyest place I have seen in the South & in many respects surpasses any I ever saw in the North."[21] Others shared his assessment. Prior to the war, one observer called Natchez the cultural capital of the state. Before the war it had been a prosperous regional commercial center where leading citizens hired foreign gardeners, and horseflesh dominated men's conversations. A traveler in 1852 noted:

> [T]he streets are broad; some of the public buildings are handsome; and the entire scene makes an impression of comfort and opulence. Natchez is the most important city in this region for shipping [cotton], and during the proper season the streets are almost barricaded with bales. . . . The city has three churches, a handsome courthouse, four

21. Culver, Diary, June 13-14, 1864.

banks, two bookstores, three printing offices, and the usual number of mercantile stores.[22]

Although the early Civil War years had nearly destroyed nearby Vicksburg and Port Hudson, Natchez felt little of the war's destructive power. Save for a single Union gunboat bombardment, Natchez avoided virtually all of the fighting along the river. The city's only engagement came after civilians fired on a Union gunboat crew who were putting in for ice, and on September 2, 1862, the gunboat *Essex* retaliated by firing on Natchez's "under hill" area, claiming two victims. An old man died of a heart attack during the excitement, and merchant Aaron Beekman's daughter was killed as he took his family from his dry goods and grocery store and ran for safety atop the bluff. As they ran, his seven-year-old daughter, Rosalie, suddenly called out and fell to the ground. When Beekman called to his daughter to get up, she answered, "I can't. I am killed." He hurried back, picked up his daughter and carried her up the hill, but he could not stem the bleeding where she was struck by a shell fragment. She died the next day, the only direct war fatality to occur in Natchez.[23]

Natchez spent the last two years of the war as an occupied city. In mid-July 1863, shortly after the Union capture of Vicksburg and Port Hudson, Gen. Grant assigned about 5,000 Union occupation troops, which eventually included about 3,000 black soldiers, to establish a base for military operations in Natchez. Their goal was to prevent Mississippi cotton from crossing the river and moving to Texas ports for shipment to European markets; in turn, they were to keep western cattle, supplies, and troops from crossing the Mississippi River to supply Confederate forces further east.[24]

Once on the scene, Union troops took over all available space, including the city's racecourse, bluff-top park, and many of its large mansions. Immediately north of the city they built Fort McPherson, which over-

22. John K. Bettersworth, *Confederate Mississippi: The People and Policies of a Cotton State in Wartime* (Baton Rouge: Louisiana State University Press, 1943), pp. 206, 270-71; George Conclin, *New River Guide, or a Gazetteer of all the Towns on the Western Waters* (Cincinnati, 1852), p. 106, quoted in Henry L. Lewis, *The Valley of the Mississippi*, ed. Bertha L. Heilbron (St. Paul: Minnesota Historical Society, 1967), pp. 380-81.

23. Aaron D. Anderson, *Builders of a New South: Merchants, Capital, and the Remaking of Natchez, 1865-1915* (Jackson: University of Mississippi Press, 2013), pp. 12-13.

24. For a lengthy description of Natchez in 1863 from the viewpoint of a Union general's wife, see Gresham, *Life of Walter Quintin Gresham*, pp. 239-64.

looked the river. A second, smaller fortification looked back from Vidalia, Louisiana, across the Mississippi. Brigadier General M. M. Crocker, initially the commanding general of the Union troops, established his headquarters at Rosalie, "the handsomest of the [city's] residences." With so many Union soldiers present, white residents who had not fled the city were subject to a new routine. They were required to carry passes when they moved about the city and surrounding area. Determined Confederate sympathizers who refused to comply faced the prospect of jail. For those who accepted the rules and acquired passes, there was regular socializing with their occupiers, especially between young officers and many of the young ladies of Natchez. As General Walter Gresham's wife, Matilda, noted when she visited her husband for two months in 1863, "When it came to flirtation there was neither blue nor gray."[25]

More than half of the Natchez region's population was black, most of whom had been slaves prior to 1863, with a small community of freedmen and their families living in the city. Slaves, who had been offered a chance to "self-liberate" by the Union troop presence, had left their owners' plantations in large numbers and moved to "contraband" camps located in the swampy, pestilent lowlands, immediately north of Natchez-Under-The-Hill, and at a former slave market known as "Forks of the Road," at the intersection of Liberty Road and Washington Road at the city's eastern boundary, about a mile east of downtown. Washington Road tied the city to the Natchez Trace, a well-traveled route that extended nearly 450 miles, from Natchez to Nashville. Liberty Road connected Natchez to destinations east and south. Earl and his Scouts passed by "Forks of the Road" regularly, observing its squalid conditions, inadequate food, primitive shelters, polluted drinking water, and nonexistent medical care. Disease and death spiraled out of control at both of these black camps. One account claims that over three hundred camp residents had died at the Under-The-Hill camp by January 1, 1864. Despite these conditions, former slaves continued to arrive, seeking freedom and work with the Union army and civilian contractors. Many joined the army, and those who were assigned to Natchez found themselves patrolling the same streets they had previously walked as property — now challenging former masters for proof of identification. Some new arrivals brought information about nearby partisan and guerrilla movements that Earl could use to plan his surprise raids into the countryside, and he may have selected from

25. Gresham, *Life of Walter Quintin Gresham*, p. 241.

among them the teamsters and laborers he hired to care for his horses and equipment.[26]

Byron Kenyon, another of the first group of Scouts, wrote to his parents as soon as he arrived in Natchez, telling them of "the change I have made." He reported that his new group's headquarters were in Natchez, but "our field of operations is anywhere in the department from Cairo to New Orleans." He also wrote of their modus operandi: "When we are inside the lines we dress in citizens' clothes," he noted, adding that "we have to clothe ourselves," and "board in hotels keeping our business secret from everyone. We do not even speak to each other when anyone is in sight, but go to our rooms if we have anything to say. Outside the lines we dress in our uniform, and go as cavalry." Initially, Kenyon thought that being a Scout would afford him opportunity to earn extra cash; he told his parents that "if any of us feel disposed we can go into the country as spies and receive extra pay." But in a subsequent letter he reassured his parents that they "need have no fear of my volunteering as a spy for I am too much of a coward." He also told them that the Scouts would divide among themselves "one half of the goods we confiscate." That idea was short-lived: at the end of July, Kenyon ruefully informed his parents that the lesson of the Marine Brigade had not been forgotten. He wrote: "We are making rich seizures for Uncle Sam, but the old gent has decided to not give any of the captured property to the captors." He concluded with a final assurance: "One good thing about our company is drunkenness is not allowed. The first one that is found under the influence of liquor is sent back to the regiment."[27]

Earl's recruits had little to do at first. Newton Culver and Luther Struthers spent their first few days exploring Natchez's sights, strolling along its streets and nearby roads and trails, picking blackberries, and catching up on correspondence with friends and family in Wisconsin. On Sunday, Culver attended a church meeting conducted by Northern missionaries who had come to the South to teach recently freed blacks. In the city, wearing civilian clothing, the Scouts deliberately tried to confuse

26. Joyce L. Broussard, "Occupied Natchez, Elite Women, and the Feminization of the Civil War," *Journal of Mississippi History* 71 (2008): 189; Jim Barnett and H. Clark Burkett, "The Forks of the Road Slave Market at Natchez," *Mississippi History Now*: http://mshistorynow.mdah.state.ms.us/articles/47/the-forks-of-the-road (accessed May 7, 2013).

27. Byron Kenyon to Parents, 6-16-64 and 7-30-64, Kenyon Letters, Port Hudson State Historic Site.

residents. Culver and Struthers were twice mistaken for Rebels, creating a bit of difficulty if there were Union troops about. In one misguided effort at humor, Culver tricked an elderly black man into thinking he was a Rebel guerrilla; he got his proper comeuppance when the man reported him to Union authorities forthwith. The next day, two Union cavalrymen followed Culver, watching his every move as he toured the city.[28]

Soon after the recruits arrived, Earl put them to work gathering information for his first report to General Canby's headquarters. One of Canby's concerns was the security of the lines around occupied Natchez, and Earl reported that a remarkably relaxed atmosphere existed among many of the Union troops in Natchez. Based on information gathered by his scouts, including Newton Culver and Charles Baker, who dressed in "citizen's clothes [and] passed around among the people and quietly reconnoitered our own picket lines . . . [and found them] very open. For instance, a road that skirted along the river under the bluff below the city had not a picket on it. A regiment could have been marched into Natchez Under-the-Hill without being detected." Culver and Baker also found unguarded gullies running adjacent to roads coming into the city, making it very easy to enter and leave the city undetected. Culver and Baker mapped the bridges, fords, and paths over St. Catherine's Bayou, which curled around the city on the east. Tracing the St. Catherine's Bayou's route was a three-day task, but Culver understood the maps' importance. "I need not say," he later wrote, "that we needed to be very careful for we often wanted to leave the city as secretly as possible and might have found it necessary to return in some haste."

The last group of recruits for the Scouts from the 4th Wisconsin arrived at the end of June. The addition of civilian informants, stable hands, cooks, and laundresses brought the Scouts to full strength by early July. On July 4, the men received permanent passes, which permitted them to go wherever they chose within the lines and to pass beyond into the countryside. At the same time, unable to secure what he deemed "reliable" horses in Natchez, Earl sent four Scouts to Vicksburg for better horses and gear. Discovering that no usable horses were available in Vicksburg, they continued on to the Union supply depot in St. Louis to secure the needed animals and tack.[29]

Though the Scouts were not yet fully outfitted, Earl was eager for ac-

28. Culver, Diary, entries for June 18, 19, 20, 26, 1864; Trimonthly Report of Lt. Earl, Sept. 1-10, 1864.
29. Culver, "Brevet Major Isaac N. Earl," pp. 320-21.

tion. On July 5, he took Newton Culver and two others east of Natchez to a point three miles beyond the small town of Washington, viewed the countryside and "ate all the apples and peaches they wanted," and then returned to the city. During the next week, Earl and several of the Scouts continued to explore Natchez's environs. Riding to the plantation of a Colonel Bingham on one day, and south toward Kingston on another, they settled for all the watermelons and peaches they could eat at one place, and peaches and milk at the other. It was beginning to look as though the Scouts were more concerned about filling their stomachs than about enemy guerrilla activities or illegal cotton trading.

Before the Scouts could officially begin their new duties, there was the usual military paperwork to be done. Original members of the 4th Wisconsin had enlisted in June 1861, so they were completing their three-year enlistments. Those who wished to serve with Earl's Special Scouts had to secure a discharge from the regiment and then reenlist for service as a Special Scout. Their discharges arrived on July 15, and they immediately left Natchez for New Orleans to receive back pay and enlist with the Special Scouts. Some used a portion of their earnings to enjoy a few days in the Crescent City.[30]

The New Orleans of 1864 offered a variety of diversions for a soldier with money in his pocket. Union forces had occupied the city for more than two years, and a large number of establishments catering to soldiers had grown up in that time. Alcohol, gambling, and prostitutes were all available. Gallatin, Girod, and St. Thomas Streets were lined with saloons and brothels. In one six-block stretch on St. Charles Street there were forty-five such establishments. These places varied, ranging from the "barrel-houses," which offered cheap liquor and the good likelihood of being robbed if the soldier got too drunk, to the "concert-salons," where the customers were offered food, dancing, and floorshows. For the more serious, there were numerous theaters. Newton Culver, who also attended several plays in Natchez, went to the St. Charles Theater, where he saw two productions. He judged *Pizarro*, a depiction of the life of the Spanish conquistador, to be "poorly executed," but he enjoyed *Dead Shot*, a one-act farce, which he felt was better, with "recitation fair." After nearly two weeks in the Crescent City, a weary group of Scouts returned to their Natchez headquarters.[31]

30. Culver, Diary, July 5-14, 1864.
31. Culver, Diary, July 26-27, 1864.

Additional Instructions

While his recruits were in New Orleans clarifying their new status with headquarters clerks, Earl received a letter from Gen. Canby's adjutant, Maj. Christensen, with additional instructions. In this remarkable document, Canby ordered Earl to report directly to the former's headquarters, bypassing all intermediate steps; gave him the best equipment available; and authorized him to operate wherever his information took him. It reads in full:

> Hdqrs. Military Division of West Mississippi,
> New Orleans, La., July 15, 1864.

First Lieut. I. N. Earl,
Fourth Wisconsin Cavalry:

Sir: I am directed by the major-general commanding to state that in addition to the authority granted in the letter under which your scouts were organized the following instructions are given you:

First. Your operations will not be limited to any particular section of the country, but at all times you will assist the general operations of the army by deceiving the enemy, intercepting their couriers, carrying off detached parties, breaking up his mail communications, &c. You will endeavor to give all possible information of the country, the general conditions of the inhabitants, the roads, by-ways, bridle-paths, &c.: the condition in reference to trade and agriculture outside the lines, the resources of the country as regards food for men and horses, securing guides, sending spies, reconnoitering fords, passages, defiles, and positions; gain all possible information in regard to position and number of the enemy, their fortifications, caliber of their guns, position of their magazines and store-houses, strength and position of their guards and picket-lines, preparations to stop fires, &c.

Second. You are authorized to call on the quartermaster, commissary, and ordnance departments for such supplies as you will need for the use of your party. Requisitions will be made in the proper form, and when possible will be sent first to this office for approval, but in cases of emergency you are authorized to draw at once, and the requisitions will be approved afterwards.

Third. The policy of the United States Government has been distinctly stated that "no supplies whatever will be allowed to pass beyond the line of pickets of the U.S. forces to go into the country either occupied by the enemy or unoccupied by either party within the States of rebellion." If at any time, therefore, you find parties engaged in carrying out supplies, you will seize them in the name of the United States and hold them subject to the decision from these headquarters, reporting immediately the names of all parties concerned in giving the permits, selling the goods, &c.

Fourth. You are authorized to seize and turn over to the Treasury agents all property which you have good reasons for supposing belongs to the Government of the so-called Confederate states.

Fifth. You are authorized to make such disbursements of money, not exceeding $250 per month, as in your opinion are necessary for the purpose of gaining information. You will keep regular accounts of this money, forwarding monthly reports of amount on hand, amount expended, and for what purpose, and the amount probably required for the coming month. In case of any unforeseen emergency, you can call for additional sums of money during the month.

Sixth. You will make tri-monthly reports to these headquarters of the number of men employed by you, and the duties they have been engaged in during the previous ten days. This report will embrace a full account of your operations during the time specified. When special causes demanding immediate notice arise you will report them at once.

I enclose herewith a copy of a form under which you will employ your men.

> I am, sir, very respectfully, your obedient servant,
> C. T. Christensen,
> Major and Assistant Adjutant-General[32]

On occasion, Earl's impulsive behavior had annoyed some of his fellow officers, and perhaps for that reason Canby instructed him to report directly to his headquarters. Scout Lucien Bennett declared in his memoir that, in addition to the letter, Canby appointed Earl to be assistant adjutant general on his staff, enabling him to sign the general's name to any order, thereby preventing post commanders in the department from thwarting the Scouts' activities, especially those involving contraband trade. Military documents do not verify Bennett's claim, but it is plain that Canby

32. Maj. C. T. Christensen to Lt. Earl, July 15, 1864; O.R., I, 41, 2, pp. 196-97.

was prepared to give Earl great latitude in taking innovative and aggressive steps to maintain order along the lower Mississippi.[33]

Enforcing Trade Regulations

General Canby's orders made enforcement of the U.S. trade policy in oc-cupied regions a central feature of the Special Scouts' responsibilities. The Civil War split an interdependent commercial system, creating spe-cial problems for the civil and military leadership of both governments. Former commercial partners became enemies, and hostilities severed customary trade routes. The logical policy after war broke out would have been for the Union and the Confederacy to prohibit trade with each other. Any other policy meant giving some kind of aid and support to the enemy; but this was a civil war, and problems of trade were not so easily resolved. Southern agricultural products, primarily cotton, were needed in the North. Likewise, the Confederacy needed Northern manufactured goods and currency (or gold). Furthermore, European manufacturers de-sired Southern cotton for their textile mills, and neither of the belligerents in the Civil War could ignore their need. Initial arguments over *whether* trade should be permitted soon evolved into considerations of *what kind* and *how much* to allow.[34]

As President Lincoln and the United States Congress grappled with trade issues, a variety of lobbyists compounded their difficulties. Promi-nent Northern business leaders argued for open trade with the Confeder-acy, claiming it would do no more than redirect goods that were escaping

33. Bennett, "Sketch of Military Service," p. 15.

34. Contraband trade and its role in the war has been examined by several authors. E. Merton Coulter, "The Effects of Secession upon the Commerce of the Mississippi Val-ley," *Mississippi Valley Historical Review* 3 (December 1916): 275-300; and "Commercial Intercourse with the Confederacy in the Mississippi Valley," *Mississippi Valley Historical Review* 5 (March 1919): 377-95; A. Sellow Roberts, "The Federal Government and Con-federate Cotton," *American Historical Review* 32 (January 1927): 262-75; Joseph H. Parks, "A Confederate Trade Center under Federal Occupation: Memphis, 1862-1865," *Journal of Southern History* 7 (1941): 289-314; and Ludwell H. Johnson, "Contraband Trade during the Last Year of the Civil War," *Mississippi Valley Historical Review* 49 (March 1963): 635-52. Thomas H. O'Connor, "Lincoln and the Cotton Trade," *Civil War History* 7 (March 1961): 20-35, is more sympathetic to Lincoln's policy formulations. The evolution of Confederate policy is discussed in Ludwell H. Johnson, "Trading with the Union," *Virginia Magazine of History and Biography* 78 (July 1970): 308-25.

to Europe through the Union blockade. On the other side, several newspaper editors and congressional war hawks opposed trade with the South, arguing that it threatened irreparable damage to the Union cause. Military leaders held similarly conflicting opinions. Regular army officers, such as Gens. Grant, Canby, and W. T. Sherman, opposed trade in any form, while political appointees, such as Butler and Banks, offered a more sympathetic ear to those proclaiming their commercial needs. Writing in 1862, Butler intended to promote trade and announced that he would "assure safe conduct, open market, and prompt shipment of all cotton and sugar sent to New Orleans; and the owner, were he Slidell himself [John Slidell, former U.S. Senator from Louisiana serving as Confederate envoy to France], should have pay for his cotton if sent here under this assurance." Gen. Sherman set forth the opposite position: he claimed that "gold, silver, and money are as much contraband of war as powder, lead, and guns, because they are convertible items. . . . The spending of gold and money will enable our enemy to arm the horde of people that swarm the entire South. . . ." Gen. Grant emphatically agreed, declaring, "I regard a mercenary, pretended Union trader within the lines of our army as more dangerous than the shrewdest spy."[35]

Initially, federal legislation prohibited commercial intercourse with districts the President declared to be in rebellion, excepting regions occupied by Union troops. Treasury Secretary Salmon P. Chase summarized the intent of this early policy as one that "let commerce follow the flag." As the extent of occupied area along the Mississippi River grew with each Union victory, the federal licensing system became increasingly unwieldy. Smuggling, forgery, and bribery accounted for more trade than did that of licensed traders, and some Union officers were accused of leading expeditions that were little more than cotton raids. Finally, in July 1864, Congress stepped in to prohibit further licensed private trade and created a government monopoly. However, the new policy was superseded when Secretary Chase's successor, William P. Fessenden, with Lincoln's approval, promulgated guidelines declaring that cotton was to be purchased by government agents, with three-fourths of the price paid on the spot in greenbacks. The seller could then spend one-third of the money in

35. O'Connor, "Lincoln," pp. 20-35; Maj. Gen. Benjamin F. Butler to Hon. Reverdy Johnson, July 21, 1862; O.R., III, 2, p. 239; Maj. Gen. W. T. Sherman to Maj. Gen. H. W. Halleck, August 11, 1862; O.R., III, 2, p. 350; Maj. Gen. U. S. Grant to Brig. Gen. B. M. Prentiss, March 17, 1863; O.R., I, 24, 3, pp. 118-19.

government-designated stores, and could take his purchases back to the place the cotton came from. Those who could get cotton out of the South, or provisions and equipment through the lines to the beleaguered Confederacy, stood to make fortunes. For example, according to New York businessman Charles Gould, a speculator-trader could purchase a 400-pound bale of cotton for $100 in greenbacks, bring it through the lines and sell it for $375, and take one-third of that value back to the South in goods, such as pork and beef, worth nearly $3,500 in Confederate currency (or half that amount in greenbacks). Even after one discounts costs such as transportation, it is no wonder that such profit margins drew speculators aplenty and an unrestrained demand for trading permits.[36]

Gen. Canby vigorously opposed licensed trade, arguing that trade in the lower Mississippi Valley gave support to the Rebel army that was equivalent to an additional 50,000 men, while requiring at least 10,000 of his men to enforce the regulations. To his way of thinking, traders were "a class who follow in the track of the army, traffic in its blood, and betray the cause for which it is fighting with all the baseness of Judas Iscariot, and without his remorse." He shared Admiral David Dixon Porter's contention that assigning civilian treasury agents to regulate trade did not solve the problem, but was "like setting a rat to watch the cheese that the mice don't get it."[37]

Jefferson Davis faced similar problems. The Confederate Congress never outlawed trade with the United States; they passed laws restricting exports to the Union in 1861 and 1862, but they never prohibited imports. Even these regulations were increasingly ignored as the need for munitions, medical supplies, currency, and foodstuffs grew. Late in the war, Confederate Generals Leonidas Polk, P. G. T. Beauregard, and Commissary General Lucius B. Northrup argued the economic necessity of regulated trade with the Union. Beauregard believed that government cotton, properly managed and regulated, could be used to procure needed army

36. Coulter, "Commercial Intercourse," pp. 379, 388; Johnson, "Contraband Trade," pp. 637-38; J. W. Schuckers, *The Life and Public Services of Salmon Portland Chase* (New York: Appleton Co., 1874), p. 319; U.S. Congress, House of Representatives, *Executive Documents*, 38th Cong., 2nd sess., vol. 7, no. 3, (Washington, DC: Government Printing Office, 1865), pp. 335-37, 342-49; David G. Surdam, "Traders or Traitors: Northern Cotton Trading during the Civil War," *Business and Economic History* 28, no. 2 (Winter 1999): 302-3.

37. Rear Adm. David Dixon Porter to Maj. Gen. W. T. Sherman, Oct. 29, 1863; O.R., I, 31, 1, p. 780; Maj. Gen. E. R. S. Canby to Secretary of War Edwin M. Stanton, Dec. 7, 1864; O.R., I, 41, 4, pp. 785-86.

supplies from beyond enemy lines. West of the Mississippi, Gen. Edmund Kirby Smith organized a cotton bureau in August 1863 to purchase or impress cotton for resale by Confederate authorities to any and all buyers, with the proceeds to be used to purchase materials necessary to continue the war. In February 1865, as the Confederacy struggled to maintain its existence, its congress passed a law allowing government representatives to deal directly with Northern and foreign cotton buyers.[38]

Illegal trade was as big a problem as the management of regulated commerce. Smugglers used their knowledge of the land and people to move goods through the Union lines in both directions — and into the hands of eager buyers. The illicit nature of the trade makes it impossible to determine its full extent, but even if estimates are exaggerated, they leave little doubt that smuggled cotton, wool, and other goods provided the South with materials to prolong the struggle. One report claimed that an estimated $50,000 worth of supplies went through the lines around Memphis to the Confederacy every day; and the report identified another location where $100,000 in goods found their way to the enemy. In total, the report claimed that goods going directly to the Confederacy, either by smuggling or by circumventing Union trade regulations, reached an aggregate $500,000 per day in 1864. After the war, estimates for the value of the traffic in cotton alone reached $200,000,000.[39]

Canby expressed his determination to strictly interpret federal trade policy in his letter to Isaac Earl, declaring that "no supplies whatever will be allowed to pass beyond the line of pickets of the U.S. forces to go into the country either occupied by the enemy or unoccupied by either party within the states of rebellion." Anytime Earl discovered infractions of this policy he was to arrest those involved and turn them over to department headquarters, along with the names of all parties in any way connected with the operation. Whenever his Scouts came into contact with materials that Earl had "good reasons for supposing [belong] to the Government of

38. Johnson, "Trading with the Union," pp. 308-25; James M. Matthews, ed., *The Statutes at Large of the Provisional Government of the Confederate States of America* (Richmond, VA: R. M. Smith, first published in 1864; facsimile reprint, Indian Rocks Beach, FL: D. & S. Publishers, 1970), pp. 152-53, 170; *Acts and Joint Resolutions Passed at the Second Session of the Second Confederate Congress* (facsimile reprint, Holmes Beach, FL: Wm. W. Gaunt & Sons, 1970), p. 40; Robert L. Kerby, *Kirby Smith's Confederacy: The Trans-Mississippi South, 1863-1865* (New York: Columbia University Press, 1972), p. 160.

39. Roberts, "Federal Government and Confederate Cotton," pp. 267-69; Coulter, "Commercial Intercourse," pp. 386-87; Schuckers, *Chase*, p. 323.

the so-called Confederates States," his orders were to seize them immediately and turn them over to an agent of the U.S. Treasury.[40]

On the Road at Last

When the Scouts returned from their furlough in New Orleans, their new horses, equipment, and weapons awaited them. Fully outfitted, each man possessed a Sharps Carbine, a Spencer repeating carbine, two Remington revolvers, and a saber. Many Scouts, on their own, purchased and carried a small pocket pistol as well. Years later, Newton Culver boasted: "Each of them when fully armed was a small walking arsenal." The Sharps and Spencer carbines were effective weapons for horsemen: the Sharps was an accurate, long-range .52 caliber single-shot breechloader, and in the hands of an experienced soldier it was capable of firing five rounds per minute; the Spencer, loaded by tubular magazines that passed through the gun stock, held seven metallic rim-fire cartridges and fired much faster than did the Sharps — without sacrificing accuracy. The Scouts carried extra magazines, and Confederates who encountered the Spencer on the battlefield were said to have referred to it as the weapon you loaded on Sunday and shot all week.

President Lincoln, who often took a personal interest in military weapons, test-fired the Spencer and hit seven of seven shots from "a few score feet." Unsatisfied, he stepped further back and emptied two more magazines, hitting twelve of fourteen additional shots. The Spencer underwent a more rigorous controlled test at Fortress Monroe and emerged with a perfect score. An army marksman fired a Spencer repeating rifle eighty times. He buried it in sand and when he dug it up and fired again, it did not clog. He soaked it in saltwater and left it exposed for twenty-four hours with similar results. The rifle was not cleaned during the entire contest, but it worked as well at the end as it did at the beginning.[41]

The Scouts' revolvers were single-action .44 caliber percussion Remingtons. Earlier in the war the government had purchased mostly Colt revolvers, but in 1864 the less expensive Remingtons became the pre-

40. Maj. C. T. Christensen to Lt. Earl, July 15, 1864; O.R., I, 41, 2, pp. 196-97.

41. Culver, "Brevet Major Isaac N. Earl," pp. 319-21; Arcadi Gluckman, *Identifying Old U.S. Muskets, Rifles, and Carbines* (Harrisburg, PA: Stackpole, 1965), pp. 349-52, 388-90; Berkeley R. Lewis, *Small Arms and Ammunition in the United States Service, 1776-1865* (Baltimore: Lord Baltimore Press, 1956), pp. 101, 103.

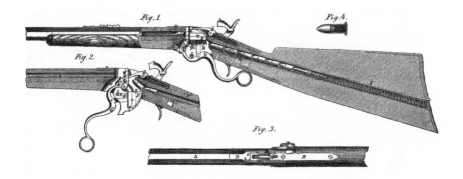

Each Scout had a Spencer seven-shot repeating carbine. Brass rim-fired cartridges (fig. 4) fed through the wooden stock to the lever action (fig. 1) which ejected the spent cartridge and moved the next into firing position. Confederate enemies said that the weapon could be "loaded on Sunday and fired all week." (*Scientific American*, 25 January 1862)

ferred sidearm. The sabers the Scouts carried were standard Model 1860 light-cavalry sabers; however, even though the weapon was narrower and lighter than sabers used at the beginning of the war, they still got in the way during raids, and the men were quite likely to leave them in Natchez. In surviving photos, none of Earl's Scouts are shown with their sabers.[42]

Earl had his newly outfitted Scouts in their saddles soon after they returned from New Orleans. On the morning of July 28, they were on the road before sunrise, heading east of Natchez on the road to Palestine and then south on the Kingston road, chasing a rumor that Gen. Wirt Adams was in the neighborhood. After riding eight miles, they discovered that Adams and his much larger force was about a mile and a half ahead of them, and judging "discretion the better part of valor," hurried back to Natchez.[43]

42. Arcadi Gluckman, *United States Martial Pistols and Revolvers* (Harrisburg, PA: Stackpole, 1960), pp. 194-96; Robert Reilly, *United States Military Small Arms, 1816-1965* (Baton Rouge: The Eagle Press, 1970), pp. 235-36; Harold L. Peterson, *The American Sword, 1775-1945* (New Hope, PA: Robert Halter — The River House, 1954), pp. 32-35.

43. Culver, Diary, July 28, 1864.

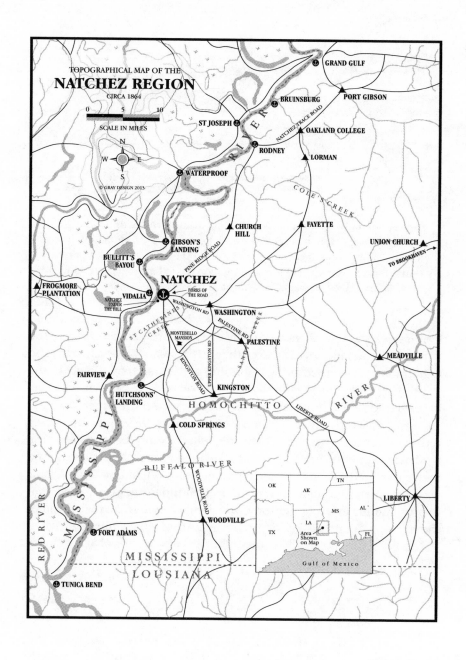

TOPOGRAPHICAL MAP OF THE
NATCHEZ REGION
CIRCA 1864

0   5   10
SCALE IN MILES

N
W   E
S

© GRAY DESIGN 2013

GRAND GULF

BRUINSBURG   PORT GIBSON

NATCHEZ TRACE ROAD

ST JOSEPH   OAKLAND COLLEGE

RODNEY   LORMAN

RIVER

WATERPROOF

COLE'S CREEK

CHURCH   FAYETTE
HILL

UNION CHURCH

GIBSON'S   TO BROOKHAVEN
LANDING

BULLITT'S   PINE RIDGE ROAD
BAYOU

NATCHEZ

FROGMORE   FORKS OF
PLANTATION   THE ROAD

VIDALIA   WASHINGTON RD   WASHINGTON
NATCHEZ
UNDER   PALESTINE RD
THE HILL   PALESTINE

ST CATHERINES CREEK

MONTEBELLO
MANSION   MEADVILLE

FAIRVIEW   KINGSTON ROAD   SANTE CREEK

UPPER KINGSTON RD

HUTCHSONS'   KINGSTON
LANDING

HOMOCHITTO   RIVER

COLD SPRINGS   LIBERTY ROAD

MISSISSIPPI

BUFFALO RIVER

WOODVILLE ROAD

LIBERTY

RED RIVER

FORT ADAMS   WOODVILLE

OK   TN
AK

MISSISSIPPI   MS   AL

LOUSIANA   LA
TX   Area
Shown
on Map   FL

TUNICA BEND   Gulf of Mexico

CHAPTER SIX

"The Country's Terror"

AFTER NARROWLY ELUDING GEN. ADAMS'S FORCES, THE SCOUTS remained in Natchez until Lt. Earl led them out on the evening of August 2. This began a busy month during which they conducted thirteen patrols into the countryside around Natchez. They almost always left Natchez at night to avoid alerting their targets.

Their first trip took them southwest on the Liberty road beyond the Union picket lines, in the direction of the home of a man identified as A. Boyd, where, Earl had been informed, smugglers were operating. Because recent rains had raised the level of St. Catherine's Bayou, they had to swim their horses across a ford in order to get to Boyd's house undetected and surprise the occupants, arresting one man who could not produce proper identification papers. With their prisoner in tow, they continued on, leaving the Liberty road and heading south toward Kingston, where they captured a quantity of Confederate mail before turning back. Along the way they stopped at the home of their guide, who, perhaps fearing the retribution he might suffer for assisting Earl's Scouts, brought his family back to Natchez with him. It was 8:00 a.m. the next morning before they returned to Natchez, exhausted. Newton Culver estimated that they had traveled a total of fifty-four miles and had been in the saddle for fourteen hours. Culver wrote in his diary that he "slept a long time in forenoon then again in afternoon." The next three days produced more ventures into the countryside, but no success.[1]

But the Scouts' trip from Natchez on August 8, though it began like the

1. Culver, Diary, August 2-3, 5-6, 1864.

others, before long became their most notable accomplishment thus far. As usual, they left at sundown, heading southeast on the Kingston road; they then left the Kingston road and crossed northeast through fields and woodlots to the Palestine road. Earl had information that a large body of Confederates was somewhere in front of them and, rather than stumble on an enemy of unknown size in the darkness, chose to make camp and wait for first light. Early the next morning they found a black man who agreed to take them off the main road and guide them to the Confederate camp through fields and little-used trails. He led them to Palestine, where they found a dozen or more Confederates hiding in an abandoned house. As the Scouts rushed the house from the front, the Rebels tumbled out the back, leaving most of their supplies behind. Newton Culver recorded that they found "horses, blankets, boots and everything but their arms." Culver grabbed a good pony that had been left behind; but before the Scouts left the house to return to Natchez, a young woman came hurrying up to claim the pony. According to Culver's diary, she "plead and used all her facinating smiles and promises to get me to give her the pony. I could not see it." Culver kept the horse. Although they took no prisoners, the Scouts reported that they had seized nine horses and three mules and turned them over to the quartermaster at Natchez. A day later, on the evening of August 10, the Scouts headed east on the Pine Ridge road in search of smugglers. Dressed in civilian clothes, they passed themselves off as Confederate irregulars and traveled about thirteen miles before heading back early the next morning without making contact with enemy soldiers or smugglers.

After allowing the Scouts to rest at their headquarters for two days, Earl once again led them out on the evening of Saturday, August 13. Using the same tactic he had used earlier, he began in one direction — southwest on the Kingston road — and then changed course, turning west to connect with the Woodville road, which was closer to the river. After about five miles, Newton Culver, Phillip Daugherty, and William Hine, who were riding ahead, came upon an elderly man driving a carriage behind several mounted riders. When one of the horsemen called out to the advancing Scouts to halt, the latter instead spurred their horses forward. The riders fired a shotgun at them, hitting Daugherty and Hine and their horses with buckshot, and then galloped away with the Scouts in pursuit. The shooters got away, but a short distance down the road, the Scouts came upon two huge wagonloads of cotton, each drawn by four pairs of oxen. With the willing help of the black wagon drivers, Earl learned that the cotton was owned by the man in the carriage, whom they knew as "Johnson." His plan

At the beginning of the twenty-first century, Palestine Road near Natchez has changed little from the Civil War era. (Gordon Olson)

was to cross it over the Mississippi to Vidalia, Louisiana, and send it on to Texas for shipment to Europe. Based on that information, and Johnson's inability to produce the proper trade permits, Earl arrested him and ordered the drivers to head back to Natchez. Leaving the slow-moving wagons, their cargo, and drivers safely hidden in a ravine at the edge of town, the Scouts delivered their prisoner to the provost marshal and returned to their headquarters at about 3:00 a.m. for a few hours of sleep. They rode out the next morning and brought in the cotton.[2]

Torpedoes at Tunica Bend

On August 10, three nights before capturing "Mr. Johnson" and his cotton, Lt. Earl had received a message from Major Christensen, of Gen. Canby's

2. Culver, Diary, August 8-10, 13-15, 1864; Newton Culver, "Brevet Major Isaac N. Earl: A Noted Scout of the Department of the Gulf," *Proceedings of the Historical Society of Wisconsin* (1917): 321.

headquarters, informing him that a squad of Confederate soldiers was "engaged in crossing torpedoes [explosive mines] across the Mississippi River at Tunica Bend," and asking him to send agents to investigate. It was the kind of assignment for which the Scouts had been created, and Earl immediately sent four undercover agents about forty-five miles south to the point where the Tunica Bayou enters the Mississippi from the east, and the big river and its tributaries twist and turn like writhing snakes. It was an ideal area for Confederates to hide from river patrols while they prepared and planted exploding mines in the river. Gunboats in the area had reported seeing "floating torpedoes," as the mines were usually called, and the gunboats *Lafayette* and *Osage* had even struck mines, though they failed to detonate. With each report about the torpedoes, commanders were becoming more and more anxious about the hazards the area held for their vessels and crews.[3]

Earl dispatched civilians W. D. Mead and M. Bowers, plus one of the Wisconsin boys, Edward Harris, to learn all they could about the Confederates and their "infernal machines." At the same time, he sent Anna Jane O'Neal, who was using the name "Jennie" (listed in Earl's pay records as "A.J."), to find the camp of "Major Ravana reported to be in charge of the Confederate submarine corps." Her task was to determine the number of men present, and, if possible, its leader's intentions.[4]

All four spies returned in about a week, having gathered valuable information, in some cases at great risk. Confederate Colonel John S. Scott was in the Woodville area with his 1st Louisiana Cavalry regiment, and he also had informants. Thomas Hart of Natchez sent Scott a coded message warning him that a spy would be operating in his area. It is quite likely that the spy Scott identified and detained was Anna Jane O'Neal. In his correspondence with Maj. Christensen, Earl always referred to the spies and agents he sent as his "men"; but in this case he identified the agent only as "the person sent by me." O'Neal was identified in Earl's records

3. Lt. Earl to Maj. C. T. Christensen, Aug. 17, 1864; O.R., I, 41, 2, pp. 741-42; Milton F. Perry, *Infernal Machines: The Story of Confederate Submarine and Mine Warfare* (Baton Rouge: Louisiana State University Press, 1965), p. 189.

4. Culver appears to be wrong about the man's name and rank. Gen. Gabriel J. Rains was chief of the Confederate Torpedo Service responsible for creating Confederate land and water mines used by the Confederacy. No reference can be found of a Confederate Maj. Ravana. Gabriel J. Rains and Peter S. Michie, *Confederate Torpedoes: Two Illustrated 19th Century Works with New Appendices and Photographs*, ed. Herbert M. Schiller (Jefferson, NC: McFarland, 2011), pp. 3-8.

"Torpedoes" (mines) were a threat to Union vessels on the Mississippi.
Anchored by weights, they were detonated either by lanyards from
shore or trip cords tied between floating logs on the river's surface.
(*Harper's Weekly*, February 7, 1863)

as paid spy, "A. J. O'Neal," but she was always known and referred to by
the scouts as "Jennie." In any case, once she was detained, she was either
exceptionally persuasive or lucky. Scott released the female spy after a
lengthy interrogation because, Earl reported, the "person" he sent was
misidentified in Hart's coded message. Jane (or A.J.) O'Neal was not Jennie,
and that apparently was enough of a difference.

Mead and Bowers learned little about the torpedo operations; but
during her detention, O'Neal learned a great deal about Col. Scott's force.
She reported that he had about 1,000 soldiers and planned to disrupt traffic on the Mississippi and its tributaries. However, her report concluded
that his men were poorly armed, and they had insufficient artillery to
significantly disturb river traffic.[5]

Of the spies Earl sent out, Edward Harris was the most successful. He
scouted the area from Fort Adams, a small river town about forty miles
south of Natchez, to the foot of Tunica Island, about ten miles further

5. Culver, "Brevet Major Isaac N. Earl," p. 322; Lt. Earl to Maj. C. T. Christensen, Aug.
27, 1864; O.R., I, 41, 2, p. 884.

Torpedoes were also constructed by means of placing explosives in wooden barrels or hollow logs, which were spiked with percussion triggers.
(*Harper's Weekly*, April 29, 1865)

downriver, gathering information from talkative residents. They told him that a detachment of "torpedo builders" from Mobile had established a base about eight miles inland from Tunica Bend and were building river torpedoes. The demolition experts, identified only as Hill, Hunter, Weldon, and Perkins, were using two different types of explosive devices. The procedure of Hill and Perkins was "to float [the torpedoes] down or make one fast between two skiffs at a distance of a hundred yards from each, then in the night the skiffs are one on each side of the boat, which brings the torpedo under the boat, when one of the men in the skiff explodes the torpedo by means of a lanyard." Hunter and Weldon used a percussion device. They anchored their torpedoes on the surface or just below the surface of the river, waiting for passing boats to strike them and trigger an explosion.

Edward Harris ended his report with an encouraging note — at least for vessels on the Mississippi. He was informed, he said, that the mine-makers had been ordered back to Mobile to operate against Union blockaders there and had left the area. Unfortunately for riverboat captains,

Hunter had left several of his torpedoes behind, and Harris could not learn where they were located. As a result, in December 1864, Gen. Canby was still receiving reports of river torpedoes in the Tunica Bend area.[6]

As soon as he received O'Neal's and Harris's reports, Earl forwarded them to Canby's headquarters. At the same time, he requisitioned a steamboat from the quartermaster, Colonel Charles G. Sawtelle, at New Orleans. The reports brought back by the spies, and the limited success of the Scouts' mounted patrols during August, convinced Earl that they needed to extend their area of operations to more distant points along the river, and for that they needed their own steamboat. In his requisition Earl said that he often heard of "opportunities for doing good service, but at too great a distance for my corps to go by land at the present." He also told Canby's office that not all of his men had received Spencer carbines and that he needed more arms and better maps of the Mississippi River to replace the older ones he was using.[7]

While waiting for Sawtelle's response, Earl continued to do what he could in the Natchez area, leading his men on one- and two-day patrols into the countryside. In the twenty-four days between August 17, when he made his request for a steamboat, and September 10, when the vessel finally arrived in Natchez, his Scouts made nine trips beyond Natchez's picket lines, capturing two prisoners, horses and mules, and weapons and ammunition. On August 17, a squad of eight Scouts patrolling on the Woodville road captured a shotgun and a rifle, a horse and a mule, and two saddles from Thomas Williams, who fled as they approached. Another group of Scouts headed downriver toward the crossing to Vidalia, Louisiana, stopping at every house along a four-mile stretch of road to search for Confederates and contraband, but finding nothing.

Despite efforts to limit their visibility, the Scouts had become well known in Natchez, and their movements were watched by Confederate sympathizers in the city. Their notoriety around Natchez made it difficult for the Scouts to slip out of town unnoticed, and that enabled smugglers and partisan groups to disappear before they arrived.[8]

6. Lt. Earl to Col. Albert J. Myer, Aug. 30, 1864; O.R., Navies, I, 26, pp. 525-26; Acting Master J. B. Devoe to Rear Adm. S. P. Lee, Dec. 1, 1864; O.R., Navies, I, 26, pp. 750-51.

7. Lt. Earl to Maj. C. T. Christensen, Aug. 17, 1864; O.R., I, 41, 2, pp. 741-42.

8. Culver, Diary, Aug. 17-18, 19-24, 1864.

Gunfight at Montebello

The Scouts encountered a particularly testy situation on August 29, when they pursued information that Gabriel Shields, a well-known planter, was harboring smugglers and contraband goods in his large home, "Montebello," just beyond Union picket lines east of the city. Earl heard from several sources that Shields regularly aided partisans, operating under cover of a permit to move in and out of Natchez, which he had managed to obtain, in part, because of his social relationships with Union leaders. One of the wealthiest plantation owners in the region before the war, Shields had once owned nearly 450 slaves. By 1864, most were gone, along with much of his other tangible fortune, and he lived at Montebello with his wife, two daughters, and two sons, using his remaining resources to entertain Confederates and Yankees alike. Among his guests was Union General Lorenzo Thomas, a prewar acquaintance described by one family member as a "renegade Virginian [i.e., a Unionist]," who was in Natchez briefly to recruit black troops.[9]

Earl first sent Phillip Daugherty and Nelson Porter to Shields's home to determine if he was concealing weapons. Their instructions, perhaps because of the family's good relations with local federal authorities, were "to treat [Shields and his family] politely and use no violence." Whether or not he was approached "politely," Shields refused Daugherty and Porter entry to his house. The two Scouts persisted for a time, but without success; then, mindful of Earl's caution to them, they left and returned to headquarters. Earl responded by sending the two men back to Montebello with four additional Scouts as reinforcements, telling them that if the people at the house continued to resist, they should arrest them and bring them to headquarters. Back they went, only to be rebuffed again. This time Daugherty remained at the site, but sent a message back to Earl asking if he should force his way into the home. Rather than authorizing that, Earl sent word that he was on his way and that his men should do nothing until he arrived.

Earl set out at once toward Shields's home, but as he approached the edge of the city he met his men coming back in the custody of Union soldiers. The latter explained that Shields had complained to the Union picket commander, Lieutenant James Willis of the 4th Illinois Cavalry, who im-

9. Joyce L. Broussard, "Occupied Natchez, Elite Women, and the Feminization of the War," *Journal of Mississippi History* 71 (2008): 179-80.

Gabriel Shields's Montebello mansion, located on the southeast edge of Natchez (Historic Natchez Foundation)

mediately placed the Scouts under guard and ordered them back to the city. Earl told Willis that the men were under his command and asked that they be turned over to him. When Willis agreed to do so, Earl turned his men around and led them back to Shields's house, where he told the Scouts to hold back while he attempted to talk to Shields. However, Shields would only speak to Earl through a closed door, and when Earl told him that he believed "they had arms and ammunition in the house intended for the Confederate army," the door remained locked.

Believing that the reports he had received were sufficient to warrant entering and searching the house, Earl ordered Luther Struthers to break down the door with an axe, while Newton Culver and Charles Baker stood at the sidelights (the small vertical windows on each side of the door) watching the men inside. As Struthers attacked the door, Baker shouted that someone inside was about to shoot through the window. Culver recoiled just as a pistol was fired, and glass and putty flew in his face. The angry Scouts then responded with several shots that shattered what remained of the already damaged door.[10]

10. Lt. Earl to Lt. Smith, Actg. Asst. Adjt. Gen., U.S. Forces, Natchez, Miss., Aug. 30, 1864; O.R., I, 39, 2, pp. 351-52.

There are two versions of what happened next. Shields's daughter Ellen, who was in an upstairs room with her mother and sister, offered one version in an account written over forty years later. She recalled that the Scouts fired first, and that a two-hour gun battle ensued before James Surget, a neighbor and Shields's brother-in-law, arrived to intervene, only to be arrested. A second neighbor finally convinced Shields to surrender and let the Scouts enter his house — unarmed. Earl, who Ellen remembered as "the country's terror," agreed to the conditions, and Shields came out of the house, accompanied by his seventeen-year-old son, Surget, and his daughters Kate and Ellen. In Ellen's version, the Scouts threatened to beat her father and nearly executed Surget, before she calmed the situation down by challenging Earl to "behave as an officer and a gentleman."[11]

Earl's official account of the episode and Newton Culver's diary agree with Ellen Shields in broad outline only. In their versions, Shields fired first, and the entire battle was over in a few minutes. Neither Earl nor Culver mentions the role of Shields's neighbors, or the threats to Shields and his son. The Scouts did not have a record of beating or killing prisoners, but they were not above threatening them to get information, which is likely what happened in this case.

After delivering their prisoners to Union authorities in Natchez, several Scouts searched Shields's home. They found a Remington revolver, two shotguns, a rifle, and about 200 rounds of ammunition, along with nine two-piece bullet molds and one minie ball mold. They also found three bottles of quinine — a valuable commodity in a region with a serious shortage of medical supplies — which, they were informed, had been brought to the house by Gen. Thomas. Shields and his family had not supported secession, but neither had they taken the loyalty oath, and they may have helped to move arms and contraband goods to partisans active in the Natchez area. However, the weapons and small amount of medicine Earl found were not sufficient grounds to punish Shields or his children.

Federal officials released Shields shortly after his arrest, but not before questioning him about his resistance. Shields explained that other federal soldiers and Union sympathizers in the area had taken silver and furniture from his house, and that when he had reported this to Gen. Thomas, whom he knew from their prewar service together in the U.S. Army, he was advised to "defend himself if similar trouble occurred again." Shields claimed that he had rid himself of nearly all his arms and ammunition

11. Broussard, "Occupied Natchez," pp. 179-80.

before Earl and the Scouts arrived, but he feared that there would be further thievery if he permitted the Scouts to enter his home. Newton Culver remained unconvinced. In his mind, Shields "belonged to that class of Confederates who secured exemption from surveillance by keeping open house for our officers."[12]

A day after their encounter with Shields, the Scouts were again on the road, this time in search of horses. They had learned that a planter who lived twelve miles out on the Woodville road had four good young horses, a mare and three geldings, and they headed out to seize them. They found the horses as reported and set to work corralling and haltering them. While his companions worked with them, Newton Culver stayed mounted outside the corral to recapture any that jumped the fence. Typical of young horses, they quickly grew skittish and one did leap the fence. Culver, riding a racehorse that he had earlier confiscated, pursued the colt, and the chase was on. Culver never caught the runaway, and his own horse was the reason. "I leaned forward to give him all the help I could," he later wrote, "when suddenly he stopped with back humped up and head down, while I pitched over his head carrying the reins and bit with me. I struck on my back and rolled over several times before I stopped. I had to be taken to Natchez in a cart." Culver rejoined the Scouts three days later, but the back injury continued to bother him and was cited many years later in his request for a veteran's partial disability pension.[13]

Their Own Steamboat

Other than the seized horses, the trip had no impact on illegal trade or guerrilla activity. Clearly, Earl needed to take his Scouts further and faster if they were going to maximize their effectiveness. They needed a steamboat and, in his next report to Maj. Christensen, Earl reminded Canby's adjutant of his earlier request. This time he got results. Christensen sent a

12. Culver, Diary, Aug. 17-24, 29, 1864; Culver, "Brevet Major Isaac N. Earl," pp. 322-23; Lt. Earl to Lt. Smith, Actg. Asst. Adjt. Gen. U.S. Forces, Natchez, Miss., Aug. 30, 1864; O.R., I, 39, 2, pp. 351-52; Maj. Gen. N. J. T. Dana to Maj. C. T. Christensen, Sept. 9, 1864; O.R., I, 39, 2, p. 350; Ellen Shields, "Genealogical Memoir of Ellen Shields," quoted in Broussard, "Occupied Natchez," pp. 201-4.

13. Culver, "Brevet Major Isaac N. Earl," pp. 323-24; Culver, Diary, Aug. 31–Sept. 4, 1864; Newton Culver Pension File No. SC383647, Washington, DC: National Archives and Records Administration.

terse message to Quartermaster Sawtelle, which said: "General C. says that he is under the impression that the small steamer asked for by Lieutenant Earl was sent up. Is he correct?" Knowing a demand for a prompt response when he saw one, Sawtelle replied that, while he had been unable to comply with the request so far, he expected to be able to make a small steamer available to Earl and his Scouts "within a day or two."[14]

Meanwhile, the Scouts arranged for people to perform various housekeeping chores at their Natchez-Under-The-Hill headquarters. They hired a black woman at 75 cents a day to keep their quarters clean, and hired a black man at 50 cents a day to polish their boots and shoes. Several men put money together and hired Scout W. J. Laughman's mother to cook for them at a rate of $1.00 a day.[15]

Finally, on Monday, September 5, word came that Sawtelle had come through with a steamer and crew. Lt. Earl departed for New Orleans to take charge of the vessel, leaving the Scouts under the command of Cpl. Albert James, with instructions to continue operating around Natchez. James led them out on the morning of Saturday, September 10, feinting toward Washington and then crossing through fields and woods north to the Pine Ridge road. Riding up to a house where a group of about ten horsemen that he described as "rebs" rested with their horses in the front yard, James ordered the Scouts forward at a gallop, firing their revolvers as they came. At the first sign of trouble, a young woman, who was sitting on the front porch talking with the horsemen, ran to a side gate and held it open so that they could escape into the thicket in back of the house. Then, despite the oncoming Scouts' gunfire, she shut and latched the gate. Only momentarily slowed, the Scouts pushed through, capturing one prisoner, a mule, and four horses. Their toll might have been higher, but Kenyon's and Baker's horses fell at the head of the squad, obstructing everyone's forward progress.[16]

Cpl. James and the scouts returned to headquarters on Saturday evening, just before Lt. Earl and the steamer *Ida May* pulled in from New Orleans. Built in Pittsburgh in 1858, she measured 157 feet long by 32 feet wide, and drew 4.8 feet of water. She had initially carried passengers and freight between Pittsburgh and Cincinnati on the Ohio River. With rooms

14. Maj. C. T. Christensen to Col. C. G. Sawtelle, Quartermaster at New Orleans, Aug. 22, 1864; O.R., I, 41, 2, pp. 741-42; Col. C. G. Sawtelle to Maj. C. T. Christensen, n.d.; O.R., I, 41, 2, pp. 742-43.

15. Culver, Diary, Aug. 12, 13, 18-31; Sept. 3, 1864.

16. Culver, Diary, Sept. 10, 1864; Culver, "Brevet Major Isaac N. Earl," p. 324.

capable of accommodating approximately sixty persons and stalls for their horses, the *Ida May* suited the Scouts' needs well. Her size enabled her to traverse both the Mississippi River and the adjoining bayous where smugglers and guerrillas hid. Brought south in 1863, she had briefly run a regular schedule between Natchez and New Orleans before being acquired by the Union Army's quartermaster.[17]

Earl and the Scouts spent Sunday and Monday, September 11 and 12, turning the *Ida May* into their floating headquarters. By sundown on Monday, men and horses were aboard and ready to depart. However, in order to arouse as little attention as possible, Earl waited until midnight before he ordered the steamer's captain to ease the vessel away from the dock, slip into the Mississippi, and turn north toward Vicksburg.[18]

North to Vicksburg

The way the Scouts went about their operations and how they were able to perform changed the moment they boarded the *Ida May*. Steaming upriver through the night, the vessel arrived at St. Joseph, Louisiana, at ten o'clock the following morning. There, hoping to surprise Confederates reported to be in the area, Earl had the captain ease the *Ida May* against the Mississippi's bank and drop the gangplank. As soon as the gangplank touched ground, the Scouts led their horses ashore and galloped west on a plank road into the bayou country. They had scarcely begun their ride when they saw about fifteen horsemen in the distance ahead of them and set out in hot pursuit. But their prey had a head start and fast horses and, after losing ground for three miles, the Scouts gave up the chase. Slowing to a trot, in another couple of miles they came upon a man in a linen duster walking beside a buggy. They hurried forward and stopped the buggy and took into custody Lieutenant Charles Wilson of Gen. Adams's 1st Mississippi Cavalry. They also detained the buggy's black driver and his passenger, "a good-looking woman about 30 years of age." In the back of the buggy they found a sizable trunk that contained, among other items, a letter describing the movement of Confederate forces west of the Mississippi, including

17. Culver, "Brevet Major Isaac N. Earl," p. 324; Frederick Way Jr., *Way's Packet Directory, 1848-1994*, rev. ed. (Athens: Ohio University Press, 1983), pp. 220-21; *Natchez Courier*, June-November 1863. The army used the *Ida May* for several purposes, including the Special Scouts, before she sank in the Red River in December 1865.

18. Culver, Diary, Sept. 12, 1864.

General Sterling Price's plan to invade Missouri from Arkansas. Newton Culver regarded the letter as especially valuable. "It was this information" he later wrote, "which gave the first hint of . . . Price's intended raid into Missouri, thus enabling our army to be in readiness to meet him."[19]

Along with the mail, the trunk also contained a flask of wine, and the lady in the carriage invited several of the Scouts to join her in a toast "that the war might soon cease and that the North and the South might ever live in peace." Earl kept the letter and arrested the man, but he released the woman and her driver. Years later, Newton Culver speculated that the woman, with whom several Scouts shared that toast, was the infamous Confederate spy Belle Boyd. (That was an erroneous speculation because records show that Boyd was in England at the time.)[20]

With their prisoner and the captured documents, Earl and the Scouts turned around and returned to the *Ida May*, where they found that their comrades who had stayed with the vessel had captured a suspected guerrilla who had ventured too close to the boat before realizing it was occupied by several Union soldiers. Earl decided to put the prisoners and intercepted mail aboard the *Ida May* and continue north.[21]

The next morning, as the sun rose over the bluffs at Vicksburg, the *Ida May* pulled into the city's wharf. The Scouts had not seen the town since 1862, when they were part of the ill-fated effort to divert the Mississippi River away from the city. What they now saw was a city struggling to recover from the siege of a year before. Vicksburg remained a trading center, but now Union soldiers, northern speculators, local merchants who had obtained licenses by signing an oath of allegiance, and former slaves and freedmen rubbed shoulders on its busy sidewalks. Trading permits were the key to success. An able man with a permit, few scruples, and a bit of luck could realize a good profit in a relatively brief time. Cotton was the prime commodity. Brought in under permit from the surrounding region, it was traded for food, clothing, medical supplies, fancy goods, and many other commodities — virtually anything except military goods.

19. Culver, "Brevet Major Isaac N. Earl," p. 325; Culver, Diary, Sept. 13, 1864.

20. Culver's speculation may have been based on a visit that Belle Boyd made to Isaac Earl's hometown, Kilbourne City (Wisconsin Dells), Wisconsin, on June 11, 1900, while touring the country presenting lectures about her life as a Civil War spy. Coincidentally, she died there while on tour, and she was buried in the city's Spring Grove Cemetery. *Civil War Trust*, "Maria (Belle) Boyd": http://www.civilwar.org/education/history/biographies/maria-belle-boyd.html (accessed May 8, 2013).

21. Culver, "Brevet Major Isaac N. Earl," p. 325.

Active wholesale and retail trade stirred the recovering city's social life. Citizens joined occupying soldiers in dancing parties, a theater had opened, and a showboat was tied at the wharf. But not everyone accepted the mingling on the streets and in private homes. Alice Shannon, a loyal Confederate, wrote to her sister: "It would surprise you to see how mean some of the Vicksburgers are. A great many of them seem to be turning blue. . . . Mrs. West has had several large dancing parties in her house and she invited all the young ladies and Yankee officers in town."

While some found opportunity in Vicksburg's recovering circumstances, many others struggled. Residents sold valuable possessions for food or clothing; homeless families lived in tents and caves and begged in the streets. Union officials and northern religious groups made efforts to assist former slaves in adjusting to lives as freed persons, but all too often those freed slaves were left to their own devices. As the city operated under martial law, the destruction of the old society and the influx of newcomers contributed to increased tensions.[22]

Isaac Earl saw in the illegal trade and insurrectionary activity around Vicksburg work for his Scouts. The *Ida May* already needed repairs, so while she was being tended to, Earl took his men on a two-day reconnaissance of the region west of the river in Louisiana. The scouts crossed the Mississippi at Young's Point, about ten miles north of Vicksburg, and rode inland to Roundaway Bayou, stopping along the way at the plantations operated by men he identified as McFarland and Paine, both friendly to the Union. They had dinner at the first plantation and rested for the night at the second. After dinner, Earl called his men together to announce additional organizational plans for the Scouts. When they were first formed, he had established three squads of ten men each, led by Henry Stafford, Phillip Daugherty, and himself. However, while they were in Natchez, the group most often acted as a single unit under his leadership, and he eventually abandoned the squad plan. On occasion he would dispatch a small group under the leadership of one of their peers; but there was no formal squad structure. When he transferred most of their operation to the *Ida May* — and with the experience of more than two months in Natchez behind him — Earl concluded that he needed a more complete noncommissioned officer structure, similar to that of an army company, to handle

22. Peter F. Walker, *Vicksburg: A People at War, 1860-1865* (Chapel Hill: University of North Carolina Press, 1960), pp. 210-22.

organizational matters for the group. Therefore, he made the following appointments:

Albert James, 1st Sergeant
Lewis Hatch, Commissary Sergeant
E. A. Harris, 2nd Sergeant
Byron Kenyon, 3rd Sergeant
Newton Culver, 1st Corporal
Charles Fenlason, 2nd Corporal
Miller Graham, 3rd Corporal

Nelson Porter continued as clerk, recording financial transactions and filing Earl's trimonthly reports and other correspondence with Gen. Canby's headquarters. Earl had begun filing the required reports every ten days when the Scouts were in Natchez, and those reports continued until the end of the war. Generally, the reports consisted of an alphabetical roster of all the Scouts and the black workers on duty or on special assignment, their pay rate, an inventory of the horses and weapons at their disposal, and a narrative of several paragraphs describing their activities for the most recent ten days. Although signed by Earl, the reports were written in Porter's hand.[23]

After a quiet night at Paine's plantation, Earl and the Scouts continued on their way, noting the totally desolate conditions all around them, evidence of the viciousness of the siege of Vicksburg. The Shreveport and Vicksburg Railroad ran west through northern Louisiana from the Mississippi. Fifteen miles inland the railroad crossed over Roundaway Bayou near the small village of Richmond. Heavy fighting to capture a Confederate supply route during the siege of Vicksburg had devastated that town, and there had been no recovery. Newton Culver reported: "There is nothing left but chimneys. The roads are all grown over with weeds, the fences are gone so that it was most impossible to follow the roads." Lt. Earl described the area as "thoroughly desolated, nearly every house being burned and scarcely any of the inhabitants remaining." Scout William Hine demonstrated the countryside's desolation another way. Spotting a half-starved raccoon beside the road, he got off his horse and picked up the animal. "Poor thing," he declared for the benefit of those within earshot.

23. Culver, Diary, Sept. 15, 1864; Culver, "Brevet Major Isaac N. Earl," p. 337.

"I will give you a lift to where there is something for you to eat. General Grant has so skinned the country that not even a coon can live in it."[24]

Southwest of Richmond, the Scouts came upon a large plantation that had been occupied by Union soldiers; their signalers had built a lookout station during the siege. By contrast to the rest of the landscape, its buildings stood in remarkably good repair. When Earl rode up to the main house and asked that the Scouts be served dinner, the woman who met them pled shortages, saying she had no food to spare. Earl pointed out that they had seen cows in the pasture and chickens around the yard as they rode up, and he urged her to reconsider. Probably hoping that the Scouts would eat and be on their way, she complied. The Scouts slaughtered several chickens and turned them over to the plantation's black cook, and before long they were seated at a table of fried chicken, cornbread, and "a good supply of rich milk and plenty of butter."

Instead of thanking their hostess and moving on, Earl and the Scouts, now curious about how the plantation had managed to remain in such good repair, decided to investigate. Earl ordered the Scouts to search the house room by room for contraband goods. Led through the house by the owner, who carried a large ring of keys, they made their way through eleven rooms and found no contraband. When they reached the door of the twelfth and final room, however, their guide denied them access. "There is nothing in this room that you need to see," she said. Newton Culver, leading the search, responded that this, then, was the room he *had to* see. She resisted until he threatened to break down the door, at which point she unlocked it. One peek explained why she had refused the Scouts entry. Inside, lining its sixteen-foot-long walls were floor-to-ceiling shelves filled with U.S. medical stores. By way of explaining their presence, the woman produced an itemized bill of sale and a permit to take them through Union lines, an order signed by the major general commanding the Vicksburg district.[25]

Earl joined the group to examine the permit and inspect the medical supplies. Surprised to find such a large amount of contraband goods beyond Union picket lines, he ordered a search of the plantation's out-

24. Culver, Diary, Sept. 16, 1864; Trimonthly Report of Lt. Earl, Sept. 10-20, 1864; Culver, "Brevet Major Isaac N. Earl," p. 326.

25. Culver, "Brevet Major Isaac N. Earl," p. 326. Culver, the source for this account, identifies the signer of the permits only as "a prominent-major general of the United States then commanding the [Vicksburg] district." From August to November, 1864, that was Maj. Gen. N. J. T. Dana.

buildings. The widened search revealed additional contraband goods hidden under the large one-story house, which was built on six-foot pilings to protect it from flooding. Tightly fitted boards, some with new nails, enclosed the entire area under the house. Since Culver's suspicions were already heightened by the discovery of the medical supplies, he checked the boards carefully and found one section that had been recently closed. Prying off several boards with an axe, he discovered that the area under the house was "filled with barrels of pork and beef standing on end two barrels deep." Asked to explain this new discovery, the woman once again produced a signed bill of sale and permit. Earl was not satisfied with her response, but he had no wagons or draft animals to haul the goods to the *Ida May*. So he decided to leave them with the woman while he reported the entire incident to Gen. Canby.

Unwilling to take more decisive action, Earl led the Scouts away from the plantation and back to the Mississippi River near the small river landing of Carthage. There they learned that two guerrillas named Winslow and Brownlow were staying in a house a few miles north, opposite Vicksburg. They rode up the west bank of the river and made a dash at the house, but the two men escaped, leaving behind horses and weapons, which Earl seized and took aboard the *Ida May*. The vessel had been repaired and, with the Scouts back on board, it headed back downstream on the evening of September 18.[26]

A Busy Morning at St. Joseph

The region around St. Joseph was home to active Rebel partisans and smugglers, among them John Powell, who regularly ferried Confederate mail across the Mississippi. The *Ida May* dropped the Scouts at a point six miles above St. Joseph at 2:00 a.m. on September 19, and embarked on the nighttime raid that I have recounted in the prologue of this book. In the course of twelve hours, they covered more than thirty miles, captured thirty-five prisoners, seized a valuable pile of mail, and captured nine riding horses, thirty-six mules, and the six-wagon train they were pulling,

26. Culver, "Brevet Major Isaac N. Earl," p. 327; Lt. Earl to Col. C. T. Christensen, Sept. 20, 1864, with accompanying Trimonthly Report for Sept. 10-20, 1864; O.R. I, 41, 3, pp. 263-64. The Mississippi has changed its course, and today the abandoned remains of Carthage lie on a backwater bayou west of the big river.

which contained about nine tons of wool. They completed their raid by burning a ferryboat and a skiff that were waiting to carry the wool train across the Mississippi. Three of their captives immediately swore an oath of allegiance and were freed; the remaining thirty-two, along with the wool, wagons, and draft animals, were turned over to the provost marshal in Natchez.[27]

The *Ida May* pushed away from the St. Joseph wharf and headed downstream shortly after noon on September 19, and six hours later it landed at Natchez. Isaac Earl and his Scouts had clearly demonstrated the advantages of river travel to their mission. With the *Ida May* they could appear anywhere on the lower Mississippi on short notice, disembark in out-of-the-way places, and ride up on their quarry before word of their presence spread. Instead of having partisans and smugglers flee before them, they could now surprise and arrest their targets, and seize the illegal goods they were handling. After a week operating between St. Joseph and Vicksburg, a period that resulted in more captures than had their previous two months around Natchez, they were eager to be out on the river again.

27. Bennett, "Sketch of Military Service," p. 13; Culver, "Brevet Major Isaac N. Earl," pp. 327-29; Culver, Diary, Sept. 18-19, 1864; Lt. Earl to Col. C. T. Christensen, Sept. 20, 1864, with accompanying Trimonthly Report for Sept. 10-20, 1864; O.R., I, 41, 3, pp. 263-64; *Daily True Delta* (New Orleans), Sept. 25, 1864 (www.Genealogybank.com; accessed Sept. 19, 2013).

CHAPTER SEVEN

"A Valuable Agent of the Government"

MOST SOLDIERS WELCOME A DAY OFF WITH COMRADES, AND
Earl's Scouts were no exception. After leaving the 4th Wisconsin's
encampment for Natchez in mid-June, they had not been back to Baton
Rouge until Lt. Earl ordered them aboard the *Ida May* on September 23 for
a quick run downriver. Besides catching up on news of the 4th Wisconsin
Cavalry, the trip had more practical purposes. Guerrillas and smugglers
continued to plague the area around Baton Rouge, and a raid by the Scouts
might exert some temporary restraint on their activities. The Scouts also
needed more arms and equipment. After the initial distribution of weapons
in Natchez, some of Earl's men were still without Sharps carbines and Remington revolvers. Earl had sent a requisition for the needed weapons, and
also for twenty saddles and bridles, to the quartermaster in Baton Rouge.

For Earl, there was also the matter of Jane O'Neal. When the Scouts
began to range farther from Natchez, O'Neal did not travel with them.
And perhaps because she had been identified as a spy while in Natchez in
September, she was removed from the Scouts' payroll and returned to the
Baton Rouge area. Thus, a visit downriver afforded Isaac and Jane a short
time together.[1]

Rather than having the Scouts stay aboard the *Ida May* all the way to
Baton Rouge, Earl told the captain to dock at Port Hudson. There, he and
the Scouts disembarked to ride their horses along the east side of the Mississippi the remainder of the way, looking for smugglers and partisans. This

1. Newton Culver, "Brevet Major Isaac N. Earl: A Noted Scout of the Department of the
Gulf," *Proceedings of the Historical Society of Wisconsin* (1917): 329; Abstract of Expenditures
on Account of Special Services by Lt. Earl, Commanding Special Scouts, for the month of
October 1864, included with Trimonthly Report (payments for September services).

tactic of landing in one place and riding quickly through backcountry to another had surprised insurgents upriver, and now it worked again. From Port Hudson the Scouts headed toward the nearby Plains Store, where they encountered "a few rebs with some cotton"; they arrested one man and confiscated his horse. They also learned that T. Winthrop Brown's Company D of Colonel Daniel C. Gober's mounted Louisiana infantry regiment was positioned between them and Baton Rouge. Rather than engage the larger unit, Earl's group rode east to the Clinton road and then into Baton Rouge, taking another prisoner and three horses along the way.

Settled back in their quarters aboard the *Ida May,* the Scouts had a day of leisure while Earl conferred with military leaders. He also likely visited Jane before rejoining his men for the trip back upriver. While in Baton Rouge, Newton Culver and several other scouts accompanied their 4th Wisconsin comrades to a funeral service for the popular regimental surgeon, Dr. Harvey Merriman, who had died of disease a few days earlier. Following the service, some 4th Wisconsin veterans visited their comrades aboard the *Ida May,* sharing news from home and hearing tales of the Scouts' adventures during the past three months. Soldier gossip and laughter rang through the vessel until it was time for their guests to return to their barracks and for the *Ida May* to return to her work on the river.

As they pulled away from the dock, the Scouts took with them twenty new Sharps carbines, twenty Remington revolvers, twenty sabers, and a like number of saddles and bridles. The new weapons and equipment meant that every Scout — soldier and civilian alike — was fully equipped with arms, horses, and gear. They had not requisitioned army horses because, as Newton Culver boasted, "we had more than supplied ourselves from those captured from the enemy." Culver also reported that the Scouts field-tested their weapons on the trip north. "We had fine practice," he wrote, "the many alligators sunning themselves along the banks of the river affording us fine targets."

The *Ida May* docked at the wharf in Natchez at 6:00 a.m. on September 27, but only for a few hours. Earl ordered everyone out for an inspection and drill to assure that they all had proper weapons and horse gear, then instructed them to retrieve their personal trunks from their Natchez-Under-The-Hill headquarters and return to the *Ida May* by evening. They were going upstream again.[2]

2. Culver, Diary, Sept. 26-27, 1864; Culver, "Brevet Major Isaac N. Earl," p. 329; Tri-monthly Report submitted by Lt. Earl, Sept. 20-30; O.R., I, 41, 3, pp. 500-501.

Ferryboats conveyed everything legal and illegal, from cattle and cotton to Confederate soldiers and mail, across the Mississippi.
(*Harper's Weekly*, August 16, 1862)

Mr. Douglas's Unwanted Guests

After darkness settled over the Mississippi River on that Tuesday evening, the *Ida May* slipped away from her moorings and, as quietly as possible, began another run toward Vicksburg. Although it was impossible for the boat's noisy engines to run in total silence, leaving in darkness and traveling through the night made it difficult for smugglers and partisans to know her identity and destination.

By the next morning Earl and his Scouts had gone nearly fifty miles, past St. Joseph, to a point across the river from Grand Gulf, Mississippi. Above this point the Mississippi began a series of twists through bayou country that more than doubled the distance a steamboat had to travel to Vicksburg. Numerous plantation landings and out-of-the-way points allowed steamboats to unload contraband cargo to be taken inland. At the tiny settlement of Hard Times Landing, located on a tiny peninsula created by the river's doubling back on itself, Earl had the *Ida May*'s captain ease the vessel to the river's west bank and unload the Scouts, who rode across the small point of land while the *Ida May* took the longer water route around the peninsula.[3]

3. Map of the country between Milliken's Bend, LA, and Jackson, MS. Compiled,

160

Guerrillas and outlaws roamed both sides of the Mississippi, harassing Union troops and seizing or destroying the property of Confederate and Union residents alike. (Harper's Weekly, December 24, 1864)

Hard Times, however, was not their destination. Instead, Earl led the Scouts on an exploration of the surrounding territory, taking them several miles west on an inland road, where they came upon a slow-moving wagon loaded with clothing, hats, knives, and other domestic goods that were being taken further inland. Seizing the goods as contraband, he led the Scouts back to the *Ida May*, which awaited them at Hard Times; they then pushed further upstream — to Point Pleasant Plantation. Earl learned from those he took prisoner with the seized wagon that they had purchased their cargo at James Douglas's landing, about four miles above Point Pleasant. Earl planned to question Douglas, who was known throughout the region for having access to a ready supply of domestic goods for sale.

surveyed, and drawn under the direction of Lt. Col. J. H. Wilson by Maj. Otto H. Matz and 1st Lt. L. Helmle, 1895, David Rumsey Historical Map Collection, Stanford University: http://www.davidrumsey.com/luna/servlet/detail/RUMSEY~8~1~26868~1100164 (accessed Aug. 18, 2012).

At Douglas's landing, they found that its owner and several armed guards had barricaded themselves inside the house, which was fortified with cotton bales. Douglas explained that, as a government lessee, he was often "molested" by thieves and guerrillas, and he had to defend himself. The day before Earl arrived, he claimed, five outlaws had tried to rob him; but he and his guards killed three, and the other two fled. Inside the house Earl found about 1,500 yards of "fine quality" cloth, along with other goods for which Douglas produced itemized bills of sale and trading permits issued at Vicksburg; he argued that the goods were for use on his plantation. However, Earl informed Douglas that he had evidence that Douglas had been engaged in an active wholesale and retail trade with Confederate government agents, and that the goods found inside the house were thus "liable for confiscation."

Earl and the Scouts remained at Douglas's home through the night, then took the smuggler and his family, together with his retail inventory, to the *Ida May* at first light. A surprise awaited them at their boat: the men guarding the vessel had seized Douglas's small steam-powered "canal boat," the *Buffalo*, which operated up the area's many bayous and ferried goods across the Mississippi. The *Buffalo* had pulled up to the landing not realizing that the *Ida May*'s guards were Union soldiers. The latter wasted no time seizing her cargo when they found documents on board that proved she was engaged in smuggling.

Late that morning the Scouts took their prisoners, the seized goods, and the *Buffalo* to Vicksburg and turned them over to the provost marshal. Douglas's illegal activities — and the official who issued him permits to purchase large quantities of goods — raised Newton Culver's ire. "No wonder," he later complained, "large industries were built up in the years that followed the war by some of our officers who thought more of gaining dollars than of gaining victories over our enemies."

The Scouts remained in Vicksburg only long enough to unload their cargo and for Earl to report their recent activities to Major General N. J. T. Dana. During their meeting, Dana invited Earl and his Scouts to join a brigade, under the leadership of Colonel Embury D. Osband, that was about to leave in pursuit of a large partisan contingent active in the area south and east of Vicksburg. Osband's brigade numbered about 1,100 men from the 2nd Wisconsin Cavalry, 5th Illinois Cavalry, 11th Illinois Cavalry, and 3rd U.S. Colored Cavalry, together with a four-gun detachment from the 26th Ohio Battery Light Artillery, and a Signal Corps squad. Because of their knowledge of the area and experience,

**Arrested guerrillas and smugglers, as well as goods seized by
Earl's Scouts, were brought to the provost marshal's office in
Baton Rouge, or the ones located in Vicksburg or Natchez.**
(Louisiana State University Libraries, G. H. Suydam Collection)

Earl's Scouts were to serve with the advance patrol, riding at the front and sides of the main force.[4]

While Earl and Gen. Dana conferred, Osband and his brigade were boarding transport vessels and traveling downriver to Bruinsburg, Mississippi, about thirty-five miles below Vicksburg, across from St. Joseph. Eager to join them, Earl returned to the Scouts after his meeting with Dana and ordered the *Ida May* south to catch up with Osband. They arrived on Friday morning, September 30, joining the expedition as it began to march inland. At the same time, the 50th U.S. Colored Infantry, commanded by Colonel Charles Gilchrist, had left Vicksburg and disembarked about eight miles further downstream at Rodney, intending to move inland and be the anvil on which Osband's cavalry hammer would pound partisan forces.[5]

4. Culver, Diary, Sept. 28-29, 1864; Culver, "Brevet Major Isaac N. Earl," p. 330; Tri-monthly Report submitted by Lt. Earl, Sept. 20-30; O.R., I, 41, 3, p. 501.

5. Maj. Gen. N. J. T. Dana to Lt. Col. C. T. Christensen, Oct. 13, 1864; O.R., I, 39, 1, pp. 568-69.

Major General N.J.T. Dana (Library of Congress)

Tense Days with Colonel Osband

In Gen. Dana's office, attaching Earl's Scouts to Osband's expedition seemed like a good idea. In the field, however, merging the two commands did not go well. Although Osband outranked Earl and commanded this expeditionary force, Earl held to Gen. Canby's assurance that he reported directly to the commanding general and no one else. Osband expected his orders to be carried out by everyone in the expedition. But Earl treated them more as suggestions: he would accept them on most occasions, but he would disregard them when he chose to follow his own counsel.

Osband had commanded the 3rd U.S. Colored Cavalry since its creation in September 1863, and had molded the regiment into a respected fighting unit that had prompted Gen. Grant to comment favorably on its "rapid progress" and "the celerity with which they acquired a knowledge of their duties as soldiers." Born in New York, Osband was the son of a

Colonel Embury Osband
(United States Military History Institute)

Methodist preacher and had become a teacher and, after marrying and moving to Chicago, a successful publisher. After joining a volunteer militia company at the outbreak of the war, he was promoted to captain of an Illinois cavalry company, and then promoted to colonel and commander of the 3rd United States Colored Cavalry.[6]

Osband's initial objective was Port Gibson, some ten miles east of

---

6. Promoted to brevet brigadier general in the fall of 1864, Osband remained in Mississippi as a cotton grower after the war. He died in 1866, and is the highest-ranking officer buried in the Vicksburg National Cemetery. Col. Embury D. Osband, "And Speaking of Which . . .": http://andspeakingofwhich.blogspot.com/2012_03_01_archive.html (accessed Aug. 21, 2012); see also Edwin M. Main, *The Story of the Marches, Battles, and Incidents of the Third United States Colored Cavalry* (New Orleans: Globe Printing Co., first published in 1908; facsimile reprint, New York: Negro Universities Press, 1970), p. 60; Dudley Taylor Cornish, *The Sable Arm: Negro Troops in the Union Army, 1861-1865* (New York: Longmans, Green and Co., 1956); William Dobak, *Freedom by the Sword: The U.S. Colored Troops, 1862-1867* (Washington, DC: Center for Military History, United States Army, 2011), pp. 193-94, 196-99, 201-2, 220-27.

Bruinsburg, where he hoped to surprise a partisan group known as the Black River Scouts, led by Captain J. T. Cobb. It is difficult to imagine more than a thousand horsemen sneaking up on anyone, but Osband somehow managed to nearly catch Cobb and his men at Port Gibson. Two of Cobb's scouts and one of Osband's soldiers were killed as Cobb fled south. Earl's Scouts rode with Osband to Port Gibson, where they paused for the day. Resting in the yard of a prominent resident, they relaxed and fed their horses and talked with two young women who lived there. One of the girls asked if the men in her yard knew "General Earl" and his men. Newton Culver, whose diaries suggest that he needed little encouragement to engage young Southern women in conversation, replied that he had frequently met Earl and his men, and sometimes rode with them. The girls asked if there might be a way for them to meet "General Earl," and since the latter was only a few steps away, Culver called his lieutenant over and made the introductions. One of the girls claimed to be the daughter of General Earl Van Dorn, and the other the sister of General Joseph Wheeler's adjutant; they both acted impressed with Earl. This may well have been a case where all parties to the conversation showed interest in each other — all the while hoping to gather useful information for their leaders.[7]

After their conversation with the young women, the Scouts overnighted near the Port Gibson home of an unnamed attorney and Unionist. The next morning, they headed south with Osband's force on the Fayette road toward the small community of Lorman, then turned west to the little settlement of Rodney, about ten miles away. There the *Ida May* and Col. Gilchrist and his 50th U.S. Colored Infantry awaited them.[8]

Osband's next destination was Fayette, about eighteen miles southeast, and it was here that the tension between his military discipline and Earl's spontaneity burst into the open. Before sunrise on Sunday, October

7. Arthur W. Bergeron Jr., *Guide to Louisiana Confederate Military Units, 1861-1865* (Baton Rouge: Louisiana State University Press, 1989), pp. 52-55; Culver, "Brevet Major Isaac N. Earl," pp. 330-33; Culver, Diary, Sept. 30, 1864; Maj. Gen. N. J. T. Dana to Lt. Col. C. T. Christensen, Oct. 13, 1864; O.R. I, 39, 1, p. 569.

8. Lorman was home to Presbyterian Church–sponsored Oakland College, whose Unionist president had been murdered by an ardent secessionist in the 1850s. The school closed because of the war and failed to reopen. The property was sold to the state of Mississippi, which established it as a black college in 1871. It was renamed to honor James L. Alcorn, then the state's governor, as Alcorn State University: http://www.alcorn.edu/default.aspx (accessed Aug. 24, 2012); Maj. Gen. N. J. T. Dana to Lt. Col. C. T. Christensen, October 13, 1864; O.R. I, 39, 1, p. 569.

2, Osband had his force on the road to Fayette, arriving outside the small community at noon. Earl's Scouts were not in advance when the expedition set out, but they moved ahead after the advance guard was fired on by a picket as they approached a bridge at the edge of town. The Scouts galloped into town, drawing fire as they went. Ahead, at the far edge of town they found a large number of saddled horses tied in a small grove next to a church. Services were underway, but, alerted to the Scouts' presence, soldiers and civilians rushed out of the church. Advance scouts Charles Fenlason and Newton Culver rode on past, while Earl and the remaining Scouts stopped and began making arrests. They detained several worshipers, but others got to their horses and escaped; still others ran down side streets and alleys and disappeared into homes — behind locked doors and drawn curtains.

As Culver and Fenlason passed the church, a new party became the focus of their chase. A two-horse carriage entered Fayette's main street from the east, and upon seeing the two Scouts coming toward him, the driver turned south and "ran as if for dear life." Culver and Fenlason spurred their horses in pursuit. The carriage's destination now was safe haven with a group of mounted partisans camped south of Fayette. The Scouts urged their horses on, intent on capturing the buggy before it made the camp. They were closing fast, and suspecting that whoever was in the carriage was a person of importance, they brushed past the camp's outlying picket, who fired once and ran. They captured the man in the buggy short of his goal and turned around as quickly as they had come, taking their captive back to Fayette, where they found an Osband-Earl tempest brewing.

As they reentered Fayette, the Scouts slowed to get a better look at their prisoner and especially the two valises in the back of his carriage. To their amazement, in addition to some clothing and personal items, they found that rolls of Federal currency filled both bags. The man they had captured turned out to be a Confederate army lieutenant and cotton agent who was planning to purchase more than 600 bales of cotton hidden among the scrub oaks on the east bank of the Mississippi, near Fort Adams, about forty miles south of Natchez. Earl, thanks to his civilian spies, who had continued their underground activity while he and the Scouts traveled the river on the *Ida May,* already knew about that huge cache of cotton, and he understood the cotton agent's mission. Since that amount of cotton was much too large for the Scouts to carry away, a federal force seized the cotton and delivered it to Natchez. Newton Culver thought that the seized cotton's value was over $300,000 — a fair estimate. Culver and Fenlason

167

turned over their prisoner and his cash to Earl, who passed them on Col. Osband and his provost marshal.[9]

While Culver and Fenlason were chasing the cotton buyer, other Scouts were venting their anger at a storeowner from whose building they had been fired on as they entered Fayette. In response, they broke through the door of the store and began seizing large amounts of clothing and other goods. Their action incensed Osband's provost marshal, a Captain Woods, who ordered them to desist at once. Earl and Cpt. Woods "had some words in reference to this matter," in the course of which, Osband later claimed, Earl "grossly insulted and abused" Woods.

There are widely divergent accounts of what happened next. In broad outline, Earl rode up the street to Osband, and the two men became embroiled in a disagreement over the handling of papers that Culver and Fenlason had captured from the cotton agent, as well as the matter of the Scouts' taking goods from the Fayette store. Earl told Osband that he and his men reported only to Gen. Canby, and that they would not obey Osband's order to turn over the mail and cease taking goods from the store. Osband complained that Earl addressed him in "the most ungentlemanly and unofficer-like manner" during that confrontation.

Osband fumed that he "did not receive from him one particle of information during the entire trip; I know of nothing that he did, except to plunder, take horses, and by keeping in advance of the column, enable the people to drive away their stock before the column came up." Osband "requested" that Earl take a "road upon my flank, so that I might not have any further altercation." Earl initially complied, but then returned the Scouts to the main unit, whereupon Osband ordered him to a position in the "center of the column." Earl responded by leaving the expedition with his men and heading for Natchez. In the conclusion to his report of the incident, Osband angrily declared that he planned to make "formal charges and summon every commissioned officer in my command as witnesses."[10]

9. There are numerous accounts of the incident at Fayette. In general, they agree on its initial events, but have much different versions of the Osband-Earl encounter. Maj. Gen. N. J. T. Dana to Lt. Col. C. T. Christensen, Oct. 13, 1864; O.R., I, 39, 1, p. 569; Trimonthly Report of Lt. Earl, Sept. 20-30, 1864; O.R., I, 41, 3, p. 501; Report of Col. Embury D. Osband, 3rd U.S. Colored Cavalry, Oct. 4, 1864; O.R. I, 39, 1, pp. 575-76; Bennett, "Sketch of Military Service," p. 16; Culver, Diary, Oct. 2, 1864; Culver, "Brevet Major Isaac N. Earl," p. 332.

10. Trimonthly Report of Lt. Earl, Sept. 20-30, 1864; O.R., I, 41, 3, pp. 500-501; Maj. Gen. N. J. T. Dana to Lt. Col. C. T. Christensen, Oct. 13, 1864; O.R. I, 39, 1, pp. 568-71;

Scout Lucien Bennett saw the store incident from a different perspective. In his memory, the confrontation's script was far more melodramatic. Osband said to Earl: "Lt. Earl I order you under arrest, you have allowed your men to plunder that store." Earl answered: "Yes, sir, I ordered it done. I told the men to help themselves. As we passed through town the rebels fired on us from that building. I therefore told my men to take what they wanted. As for your order of arrest, I don't care a fig. I am not subject to your orders." Bennett recalled that Osband then began to draw his pistol, but thought better of it when he saw the Scouts around him with Spencer carbines leveled in his direction.[11]

Newton Culver also saw the confrontation differently. "Not being satisfied with the conduct of Colonel Osband, who had partaken too freely of rum," he stated simply: "Earl left him at Fayette and returned to Natchez." Culver did not comment on his commanding officer's behavior, and Lucien Bennett's recollection was probably embellished by the filter of time that passed between the incident and when he wrote his memoir. In any case, Earl had made a decision, and the two men separated: Osband rejoined his column, while Earl took his Scouts and headed for Natchez, no longer part of Osband's expedition.[12]

Both Earl and Osband filed reports of the incident with Gen. Dana, each blaming the other for the altercation — leaving Dana to resolve the matter. Significantly, neither report suggested that Osband had been drinking or that he reached for his pistol, nor did anyone else mention that the Scouts raised their weapons in defense of Earl. Basing his decision on the formal reports, Dana searched for a way to avoid limiting the activities of Lt. Earl and his Scouts, and at the same time to support Col. Osband's Woodville expedition. He resolved the situation by doing nothing to restrict Osband's mission and by permitting the Scouts to carry on as they had before, but forbidding them to go near Osband's command.[13]

Report of Col. Embury D. Osband, 3rd U.S. Colored Cavalry, Oct. 4, 1864; O.R. I, 39, 1, pp. 575-76; Bennett, "Sketch of Military Service," p. 16; Culver, Diary, Oct. 2, 1864; Culver, "Brevet Major Isaac N. Earl," p. 332.

11. Bennett, "Sketch of Military Service," p. 16.

12. Culver, "Brevet Major Isaac N. Earl," p. 332.

13. Reports of Maj. Gen. N. J. T. Dana to Lt. Col. C. T. Christensen, Oct. 3, 1864; O.R., I, 39, 1, pp. 573-74. Earl and Osband were more effective when operating independently. Earl soon captured a large amount of contraband cotton, and Osband completed his successful expedition on October 11, having captured 86 prisoners and 3 cannon, and seizing 1,000 cattle, 300 sheep, 300-400 horses and mules, and 12 wagons. He also destroyed 350

The Scouts left their prisoner with Osband's provost marshal, but they kept the Confederate's valises and papers, and they returned to Natchez with them on the evening of October 2. Before leaving on a new foray, Earl prepared his report for the last ten days of September, noting with justifiable pride the large quantity of goods the Scouts had seized at Douglas's plantation, and the forty prisoners they had arrested, at a loss of only two horses that had broken down from hard riding. The mail taken at Fayette at the beginning of the month would be forwarded, he said in conclusion, as soon as it was "thoroughly examined." Earl's report does not mention the cotton agent's rolls of greenbacks. Col. Osband arrived in Natchez the following afternoon, but he had no further contact with Earl or his Scouts.[14]

Osband and Colonel Charles A. Gilchrist, of the 50th U.S. Colored Infantry, continued their mission without Earl and the Scouts, though they did use information from the report filed a month earlier by Jane O'Neal. She had reported that Colonel John Scott's Cavalry Brigade (including 500 of Scott's own men), together with Colonel Frank Powers's Cavalry (300 men), Captain John C. McKowen's Cavalry (250 men), and Bradford's Mississippi Battery of seven captured guns, were operating out of Woodville east and north. "They do not stay in Woodville," she reported, "but have their general headquarters there." A month later, Osband and Gilchrist pursued the partisans, based in part on O'Neal's intelligence.[15]

Back to Natchez

The acquisition of the paddle steamer *Ida May* had turned Earl's Scouts into the highly mobile unit Gen. Canby had envisioned when he issued their letter of authorization. By the end of September they were known from Baton Rouge to Vicksburg. Earl's leadership inspired not only his men but also the former slaves and Southern Unionists on whom he depended for information. As the Scouts continued their raids against partisans and smugglers who plagued the Union occupation forces, Gen. Canby began mentioning their activities in his reports to the Union Army's chief of staff, Gen. Henry Halleck.[16]

stands of small arms, $100,000 worth of subsistence stores, and the telegraph station and printing office at Woodville, MS; Main, *Third United States Colored Cavalry*, pp. 192-93.

14. Trimonthly Report of Lt. Earl, Sept. 20-30, 1864; O.R., I, 41, 3, pp. 500-501.

15. Lt. Earl to Maj. Christensen, Aug. 27, 1864; O.R., I, 41, 2, p. 884.

16. Maj. Gen. Canby to Maj. Gen. Henry W. Halleck, Oct. 10, 1864; O.R., I, 39, 1,

October began quietly. Gen. Dana's decision to restrict the Scouts' activities kept the *Ida May* tied up at the Natchez wharf for several days, limiting them to a series of mounted missions around Natchez in which they managed to capture a few prisoners and seize several horses. Their expedition to Kingston, Mississippi, is an example. Crawling with partisans and smugglers, Kingston required a cautious approach. Newton Culver, Earl's advance scout, thought that his leader behaved too carelessly during the two-day trip. The Scouts left for Kingston on the morning of October 5, "made a dash" through the village, and then proceeded to the home of a suspected smuggler named Farrar. They searched Farrar's house and found nothing; but as they were about to leave, three men rode up to the house. When these newcomers saw that Farrar's visitors were Union soldiers, they made an abrupt about-face, abandoned their horses, and ran for the woods behind the house. They got away, but they left their horses and a double-barreled shotgun behind. Newton Culver thought that the men were some of Colonel Frank Powers's partisans, who were regularly seen on the roads around Kingston.

Giving up on the chase for Powers's men, the Scouts continued down the road to the home of a known partisan sympathizer and smuggler by the name of Bowers. There they found a quantity of leather and cloth, which Earl ordered burned. As they were destroying these goods, a squad of Confederate cavalry rode near them and then quickly disappeared. Despite the presence of Confederate partisans, Earl seemed unconcerned — even reckless. Finally, the loyal Newton Culver could stand it no longer and aired his concern. Earl, he remembered, "only laughed at me."

After spending the day on the roads around Kingston, and having only three horses, a shotgun, and the destruction of a small amount of contraband goods to show for their effort, Earl turned the Scouts toward Natchez, stopping at a house outside the city for a meal. Before they could eat, their picket reported the approach of more of Powers's partisans. Not wanting to confront Powers's superior numbers, the Scouts hurried to their horses, mounted up, and rode off toward Natchez. Near the outskirts of Natchez, Earl ordered a halt at the home of another friendly family, and he arranged a meal for the Scouts, who had not eaten since early morning. Now beyond the reach of Confederates, he proceeded to explain the behavior that had so concerned Culver. "Boys," he said, "I am disappointed

pp. 828-29; Brig. Gen. Mason Brayman to Lt. Col. C. T. Christensen, Dec. 9, 1864; O.R., I, 41, 4, p. 810.

in you. None of you knew the situation today any better than Culver, yet no one but he showed any concern. Had the situation been as it seemed, we were in a most critical condition." He then explained: "Other forces of ours were out and we were to draw the enemy on or attract their attention while our forces should get in their rear." The seeming carelessness that had so bothered Culver was a ruse intended to draw out Powers's men. But, Earl said, "They did not bite at the bait."

Setting decoys and attempting to draw out the enemy was one of several tactics used by both sides. What is unusual in this case is that Earl did not inform the Scouts of his intention. On numerous earlier occasions, they had been informed participants in his subterfuges. He had ridden one way and then changed directions to confuse his prey, used Southern civilians as spies, and occasionally had the Scouts don civilian garb to present the impression that they were Confederate partisans.[17]

Confederate Officers, Battle Flags, Mail, and Money

On October 6, the Scouts brought their horses and equipment on board the *Ida May* for another trip upriver, intending to travel north to Waterproof, Louisiana, which was between Natchez and Vicksburg, about fifteen miles south of St. Joseph. Waterproof, so named because it sat on a higher piece of ground generally not susceptible to floods, was known to be a haven for smugglers and illegal traders. Earl and the Scouts had made important communication and contraband seizures in the area just two weeks earlier.

Landing at Waterproof in late morning, they headed inland in search of a partisan camp they had been informed was in the area. But their prey was warned of their arrival and was nowhere to be found, leaving Earl little choice but to return to the *Ida May* and try to figure out who had alerted the Rebels. His best guess was a plantation owner, Gustavus Bass, who lived a short distance upriver and was known to watch river traffic for Union vessels from the cupola of his house. Because the *Ida May* had become known as Earl's transport, its passing prompted alerts from Bass and others along the river, negating much of the initial advantage the Scouts had enjoyed on their earlier trips upriver. Bass also posted signals in his cupola (perhaps a flag during daylight hours or a lantern at night) to tell

---

17. Culver, Diary, Oct. 5-6, 1864; Culver, "Brevet Major Isaac N. Earl," p. 333.

any Confederates approaching the river from the west when it was safe to be ferried across.[18]

Someone, perhaps one of Bass's slaves, informed Earl that when Bass learned that the Scouts were headed his way, he sent several blacks to hide his horses in a nearby woods. Learning of Bass's move, Earl resorted to a deception of his own. He instructed his men to light a chicken coop afire to draw out the blacks to extinguish the flames. This they did, bringing with them Bass's horses, which Earl promptly seized. Now in control of the plantation, Earl and his Scouts decided to stay for a time — in hopes that he could intercept partisans or guerrillas. He placed pickets on the levee road for a distance of six miles up and down the river; but no one came up the road, and after a time he and his men returned to the *Ida May.*[19]

Earl learned from another source that there was to be an attempt to cross the Mississippi with a valuable Confederate mail shipment on the morning of October 8. Gen. Edmund Kirby Smith, commander of the Confederate Trans-Mississippi Department, intended to send a large shipment of important materials to his eastern counterparts. With Union troops in control of the Mississippi, it was increasingly difficult for Confederates to keep communication lines open between the western Confederacy and Richmond. Mail went back and forth irregularly and often by circuitous routes. It was not unusual for letters to reach Kirby Smith weeks and even months after they had been issued.[20] Knowing how important such communications were for Smith, who was isolated from the rest of the Confederacy, Earl set out to intercept the shipment.

With nothing to show for the Scouts' expedition thus far, Lt. Earl ordered everyone aboard and turned the vessel back downstream. But they had traveled only a few miles before they pulled up to the river bank and waited quietly. After midnight, with all lights doused, he ordered the *Ida May* back upriver, running past Waterproof and St. Joseph to a landing opposite Bruinsburg. There they quietly disembarked in the dark and made their way back down the levee road. With Scouts Fenlason and Culver in advance, they rode through St. Joseph and out the plank road they had traveled on earlier occasions. Fenlason and Culver had come to think and act as a team, so much so that Culver said of his partner, "He was cautious

18. Culver, "Brevet Major Isaac N. Earl," p. 333.

19. Culver, "Brevet Major Isaac N. Earl," pp. 333-34; Culver, Diary, Oct. 7, 1864.

20. Robert L. Kerby, *Kirby Smith's Confederacy: The Trans-Mississippi South, 1863-1865* (New York: Columbia University Press, 1972), pp. 86, 147, 253, 280.

and brave, quick to see, and ready to act." A few miles out on the plank road, Fenlason's prompt action led to the Scouts' biggest capture up to that time.

As they rode along, "a very tall man on a short-legged, black pony" emerged into a field and, seeing the lead Scouts, "seemed to awake suddenly and started off to our left as fast as his pony could carry him." Culver took off in pursuit, while Fenlason, seeing "the top of an ambulance coming over a rise of ground in the road ahead," spurred his horse toward it with the rest of the Scouts behind him.[21] The tall man Culver was chasing got to a fence and, realizing that his pony could not leap it, jumped off and was on his way over when a shot from Culver's revolver stopped him in his tracks. Landing on the far side of the fence, he threw up his hands and, convinced he had been seriously wounded, shouted, "For God's sake don't shoot again!" From his vantage point a short distance away, Culver realized that his bullet had hit the fence. Only chips of wood had struck the man, so Culver said: "You are not hurt, only a sliver has hit you." The man looked at the rail, then checked his body, and said, "I thank God. I was sure I had got my last." He then looked quizzically at Culver and asked, "Where did you come from? You went *down* the river last night." Culver then asked him who he thought he was talking to, and the man gave unsolicited testimony to the Scouts' growing reputation: "Don't you suppose I know who you are? You are Earl's Scouts."[22]

Securing his frightened prisoner, Culver took him and his "short-legged pony" to rejoin the main group of Scouts, who, he found, had struck pay dirt. After a short pursuit, they had surrounded the mule-drawn ambulance. Its passengers turned out to be no ordinary group of guards: captured with the ambulance were Major H. F. Springer, identified as "quartermaster and chief of the secret service of the rebel war department" west of the Mississippi, and Major Eugene B. Pendleton, the nephew of General John B. Magruder, on the staff of Gen. Edmund Kirby Smith at Shreveport, together with two men identified as Cpts. McIntyre and Baker, "in charge of ferries across the Mississippi," and two enlisted men who assisted them. Smith had assigned Pendleton to accompany the contents of the ambulance, which included six bushels of mail and an estimated $1,250,000 in Confederate money, together with fourteen battle flags that had been

21. Ambulances could be any number of forms of light, covered wagons and carriages used by both sides to transport wounded and, as in this case, personnel and light cargo.
22. Culver, "Brevet Major Isaac N. Earl," pp. 334-35; Culver, Diary, Oct. 8, 1864.

lost by Gen. Banks's forces in his ill-fated offensive up the Red River and in other engagements west of the Mississippi in the two years after Union troops took New Orleans.[23]

The value of the cash lay in the fact that the Confederacy was suffering from runaway inflation by 1864, and the Confederate Congress had attempted to assert some control with its Currency Act, which replaced the old inflated currency at a rate of two new bills for three old ones. The Department of the Trans-Mississippi's financial instability was exacerbated by the difficult task of getting old bills across the Mississippi, where they could be exchanged for new currency. Many of the old notes were intercepted before they could be exchanged, and by December 1864, Gen. Smith's department's debt totaled $60 million, with only $8 million in new notes on hand. Prices climbed in the ensuing financial panic, as merchants demanded payment in specie or simply closed their doors, and soldiers went months without pay. Getting the more than $1 million exchanged for new currency would have been an immediate help.[24]

Economics aside, members of the Scouts did not require an explanation about the value of the captured battle flags. Their value was known to all soldiers. They had rallied to the 4th Wisconsin's flag during battle, and men fell holding their flag high for their comrades. It was embarrassing for a regiment to lose its flag, and an honor to return it. Earl and the Scouts enjoyed the prospect of returning so many flags — and accepting the congratulations of their commanding general.

Earl would have to wait to learn more about the mail he had captured. Soon after seizing the ambulance, his advance scouts galloped back to report that a mounted Confederate escort force of approximately two hundred men was coming up on them fast. Earl ordered his men to wheel around and return to the *Ida May* as rapidly as their seizures would permit. Barely ahead of their pursuers when they reached the boat, the Scouts scrambled up the gangplank, and the captain pulled away from the landing and set off downriver.[25]

---

23. Culver, "Brevet Major Isaac N. Earl," pp. 334-35; Culver, Diary, Oct. 8, 1864; *Confederate Military History: A Library of Confederate States History*, vol. 10 (Atlanta: Confederate Publishing Company, 1899), p. 540; Report of Maj. Gen. Edward R. S. Canby, Oct. 10, 1864; O.R., I, 39, 1, p. 829.

24. Kerby, *Kirby Smith*, pp. 264-65, 386-91.

25. Report of Maj. Gen. Edward R. S. Canby, Oct. 10, 1864; O.R., I, 39, 1, p. 829; Culver, "Brevet Major Isaac N. Earl," pp. 334-35; Culver, Diary, Oct. 8, 1864.

Off to New Orleans

Earl knew he had achieved a coup by capturing the battle flags and the accompanying officers. Rather than deliver them to the provost marshal in Natchez or Baton Rouge, as he had done in the past, he decided to stop at his Natchez headquarters only long enough to drop off most of the Scouts and their horses, and then he continued directly to Gen. Canby's headquarters in New Orleans. Nightfall on October 8 found him aboard the *Ida May* bound for New Orleans with Newton Culver, Edward Harris, and three other Scouts, who were guarding the flags and the prisoners.

It seems to have become Earl's practice to stop for a day in Baton Rouge any time he passed by, and this trip to New Orleans with the flags and prisoners was no exception. The *Ida May* docked at Baton Rouge early Sunday morning, October 9, and spent the day. Culver and two Scouts remained on board to mind the boat and their prisoners, while Earl and the others went into town, "where our regiment was encamped, in order to visit our comrades." The only record of what happened during the day comes from Newton Culver, and he does not mention Earl's destination. But since Earl had stated no business in Baton Rouge, he probably used the time for a social call on Jane O'Neal.[26]

While Earl was in town, Newton Culver had his hands full at the boat. Baton Rouge was bustling, and Union troops regularly needed vessels to cross the river. Earl had not been gone long when Major General Francis Herron's superintendent of transportation requested the use of the idle *Ida May* to ferry a regiment across the river from West Baton Rouge. Cpl. Culver, though heavily outranked, invoked Lt. Earl's unique relationship with Gen. Canby and refused to permit anyone else to take charge of the Scouts' vessel. Herron's representative replied that his general was "bigger [higher ranking] than Earl," but Culver held his ground, declaring that if Herron's superintendent of transportation wished, he could have Culver arrested — which ended the standoff. The general's man thought it better to wait for Earl to return and deal with him directly. It was a good decision. Upon returning and assessing the situation, Earl permitted the boat's main deck to be used to transport the regiment, provided his prisoners were confined on the top deck, and all others, "including officers, [would be] on the lower deck." Once the guards were in place, the regiment crossed the river, and everyone parted "in the best of humor."

26. Culver, "Brevet Major Isaac N. Earl," p. 335; Culver, Diary, Oct. 8, 1864.

Gen. Canby's headquarters in New Orleans were in the St. Charles Hotel, where Lt. Earl reported personally with the captured Union regimental battle flags recovered near St. Joseph. (National Archives)

Their ferry service work and socializing complete, Earl and the five Scouts with him took their prisoners to New Orleans, where the officers were confined at the city's federalized Carondelet Street prison. (They were later moved north to New York City, where they were held until the end of the conflict.) Having delivered their prisoners, Earl and the Scouts moved on to their proudest moment: a visit to Gen. Canby's office, where they planned to formally present the recovered battle flags and captured mail to their commander. Before entering the office, Lt. Earl gave Culver the Brashear City Garrison flag and said, "It is your due to hand this flag to General Canby."[27]

Isaac Earl was no shrinking violet. From the 4th Wisconsin's early days in Maryland to the battle for Port Hudson to Gen. Canby's office, he confidently addressed those of higher rank, freely stated what was on his mind, and accepted — perhaps some might say actively sought — their praise and gratitude for his performance in the field. He could have sent

27. *Confederate Military History,* vol. 10, p. 540; Culver, Diary, Oct. 10, 1864; Culver, "Brevet Major Isaac N. Earl," pp. 335-36.

the battle flags, mail, and prisoners to Gen. Canby through regular channels; but he knew that their impact on his career as a soldier and the reputation of his Scouts would be much greater if he delivered them personally. By the same token, Earl's success also reflected favorably on Canby, and it is perhaps no surprise that, after receiving Earl's in-person report, the general included an account of the capture of the flags and mail and the subsequent escape of Earl and the Scouts from the large confederate force in his next report to Gen. Halleck. Canby testified to his high regard for Earl and his Scouts, calling their seizure "the most important mail ever captured in his [Canby's] department, containing dispatches from Kirby Smith to the Confederate War Department," which gave the Union information about a possible Confederate attempt to cross troops to the east side of the Mississippi.[28]

L. C. Bartlett, a member of the 4th Wisconsin from Sheboygan Falls who sent a monthly column to his hometown's *Evergreen City Times*, had nothing but praise for Earl and the Scouts in his November letter to the newspaper's editor: "On arriving in camp we heard of the daring and successful exploit of the notorious Earl. . . . This was characteristic of the man. He courts danger for the sport of the thing, and he is eminently successful, that is the beauty of the thing. . . ." Gen. Canby forwarded the battle flags to Gen. Halleck to be returned to their proper regiments, who were doubtless pleased to have them back.[29]

One of the unlikeliest acknowledgments of the Scouts' success came from Embury Osband, who had earlier described them as willful plunderers whose presence was more a hindrance than a help. Upon learning of Earl's capture of the Confederate officers, the mail, and the battle flags, the man who once threatened to press charges against Earl sent a conciliatory letter to Gen. Dana retracting his threat. "While I do not desire to again

28. Report of Gen. Canby, Oct. 10, 1864; O.R., I, 39, 1, p. 829; Trimonthly Report of Lt. Earl, Oct. 20-31, 1864. Some of the returned flags are identified in the correspondence. They were from the 160th and 176th New York, 23rd Connecticut, 3rd Massachusetts, 43rd Indiana; several others were not identified. Lt. Col. C. T. Christensen to Adjutant General of the Army, Letters, May 1864–June 1865, Records of U.S. Army Continental Commands, Military Division of West Mississippi, p. 385; William DeLoss Love, *Wisconsin in the War of the Rebellion: A History of Regiments and Batteries the State Has Sent to the Field* (Chicago: Church and Goodman, 1866), p. 908.

29. L. C. Bartlett to the *Evergreen City Times* (Sheboygan, WI), Nov. 12, 1864, p. 2; Lt. Col. C. T. Christensen to the Adj. Gen. of the Army, Washington, DC, Nov. 11, 1864; O.R., I, 41, 4, pp. 515-16.

have him under my command, his gallant action in [re]capturing the flags of our armies and sealed dispatches at Saint Joseph leads me to believe that he is a valuable agent of the government and I would most respectfully decline to prosecute him for what I thought unofficer-like conduct." It was not a full retraction — and Osband still disliked Earl — but it nonetheless acknowledged that the man he earlier said performed no useful service was, with his special scouting unit, valuable to the Union cause.[30]

Earl's plan was to deliver his prisoners and captured goods, accept General Canby's appreciation, and return to the *Ida May* to continue the Scouts' activities. Unfortunately, the vessel did not cooperate. Twice before she had balked and had been laid up for repairs; in New Orleans it happened a third time. The hard-used vessel managed to limp to the city's docks, but her captain doubted whether she could make her way upriver again without a serious overhaul. Now Earl needed to find a replacement, and, unfortunately, competition for serviceable river vessels was stiff. Just days after the Scouts' greatest success, they were stranded.

For two weeks, Earl and those with him remained in New Orleans in their quarters aboard the *Ida May* — waiting for a new boat. They used the time for a bit of recreation, attending theatrical performances, and exploring the city's dance halls. Earl also took time to return to Canby for a special favor. Newton Culver, who had signed on for only a four-month extension of his original three-year commitment, had reached the end of his service and intended to return to Wisconsin. Earl appreciated Culver's work riding in advance of the Scouts, and he asked Canby to draft a letter of recommendation for Culver. The general complied, which was an extraordinary act of support for an enlisted man and a clear indication of both Earl's influence and Canby's appreciation of the work of the Scouts.[31]

Wedding Bells

On October 24, news finally came that a new vessel, the *Starlight*, was ready for Earl and his Scouts. They took immediate possession of the 166-foot side-wheeler, deemed her a "fine boat and runs well," took on coal

---

30. Col. Embury D. Osband to Cpt. F. W. Fox, Assistant Adjutant General, Vicksburg, Mississippi, Oct. 12, 1864; O.R., I, 39, 1, p. 833.

31. Culver, Diary, Oct. 13, 1864. Culver's history of the Scouts praises both men and is clearly his effort to assure that the accomplishments of Earl and the Scouts would not be forgotten.

that night, and on October 25 departed for Natchez. Their period of involuntary inactivity was over.

The *Starlight* made a brief two-hour stop at Baton Rouge for a visit with comrades in the 4th Wisconsin and other friends in the city. For Newton Culver, who had begun riding as an advance scout for Earl in 1863, when he organized squads from the 4th Wisconsin for forays into the backcountry around Baton Rouge, it was a chance to say goodbye to friends.[32]

For Earl, the stop was even more personal. Although his later report does not specifically mention Jane O'Neal, she joined the Scouts for the trip back to Natchez. Her initial confrontation with, and then spying for, Earl had turned into a love affair, and at some point in the fall of 1864, perhaps just before his momentous visit to New Orleans, the couple had decided to marry. When they wrote about the Scouts' activities long after the war, Scouts Newton Culver and Lucien Bennett mentioned the marriage of Isaac Earl and Jane O'Neal. However, the only contemporaneous information that describes the couple's marriage comes from an affidavit O'Neal filed with the Pension Bureau in early 1865. In that document she provided details of her marriage to Earl and an affidavit from Rev. Gideon B. Perry, the rector of Trinity Episcopal Church in Natchez, stating that he married the couple on October 26, 1864, the day after Jane, Earl, and the Scouts had returned from New Orleans.[33]

Isaac Earl and Jane O'Neal had little time to enjoy their new status as husband and wife. One day after their marriage, Earl led the Scouts on a mounted sortie south of Natchez. Because Newton Culver had completed his service, Earl assumed the position of advance scout. Earlier, as they were steaming toward Natchez on October 25, Earl had made one last effort to persuade Culver to remain with the Scouts; he said that if Culver left, then he (Earl) would have to personally take the advance position.

There is no doubt that Culver took pride in his service as a Scout, and he admired Earl; but he was determined to rejoin his family. On October 27, the day after Earl and the Scouts returned to Natchez, Newton Culver was on his way home.[34] With back pay totaling $265 in his pocket, and his soldier's transportation fare of $4.50, Culver set about finding a vessel that was headed north. After three days, he added an additional $4.50 to

32. Culver, Diary, Oct. 25, 1864.

33. Pension File of Jeannie Earl, WC72262, filed 11-29-1865, National Archives and Record Service.

34. Culver, "Brevet Major Isaac N. Earl," pp. 335-36; Culver, Diary, October 25, 1864.

Isaac Earl and Jane O'Neal were married in Natchez's Trinity Episcopal Church on October 26, 1864. (Gordon Olson)

his soldier's fare and took a state room on the *Luminary* with a cattle buyer from Ohio. By November 5 he was in Cairo, Illinois, where he departed the *Luminary* for a passenger train to Chicago; from Chicago he transferred to another train that was headed to Wisconsin. He checked into Kenosha's City Hotel at midnight, Sunday, November 7, and spent Monday visiting friends in the area. On Tuesday he tried to vote; but he was told that, as a discharged soldier, he could only vote in his hometown, Sheboygan Falls. He caught a late train north to Milwaukee and went on north to Fond du Lac, where he made one last transfer to an open horse-drawn coach, and rode through a cold rain to his hometown, arriving the next afternoon. As he stepped from the coach and stood looking down the town's main street, he saw his father riding up to the post office. Any disappointment he may have felt at missing his opportunity to cast a ballot for his commander-in-chief was promptly pushed aside. Newton Culver's days as a member of the Union Army were complete, capped by a happy reunion with his family and friends.[35]

35. Culver, Diary, Sept. 27–Oct. 9, 1864.

Meanwhile, back on the Mississippi River, work for the Scouts continued as usual. Isaac Earl's marriage did little to interrupt his tasks as leader of the Scouts. As soon as the *Starlight* arrived in Natchez, he began reviewing information gathered by his spies in the area. On October 27, he led the Scouts from Natchez about ten miles south toward Ellis Cliffs, where his agents had informed him that a signal corps contingent of General Simon Bolivar Buckner, commander of the Confederate District of West Louisiana, was encamped. The information was good, and the Scouts announced their return to action in the area by capturing five of Buckner's men. (Buckner had come west earlier in the year to join Gen. Kirby Smith's staff with the assignment of facilitating the movement of cotton through Union lines; he was in the area to carry out that assignment.)[36]

Returning to Natchez, Earl had planned to spend only enough time to drop off his prisoners with the provost marshal and then head north to Vicksburg, using his new boat to conduct surprise raids on those engaged in illegal ventures along the river "and to gain all possible information in regard to the movements of the enemy." Unfortunately, while the *Starlight* had looked good when Earl took possession in New Orleans, he discovered on the Ellis Cliffs trip "some disarrangement of the boat's machinery," which required them to take her to Vicksburg for repairs. The Scouts departed at about 4:00 p.m. for Vicksburg to get the *Starlight* repaired — or get her replaced with a new vessel. When the repairs turned out to be more extensive than anticipated, the Scouts found themselves stuck in Vicksburg without a boat. They left the *Starlight* with the Vicksburg quartermaster for repairs, receiving in return only a requisition for a replacement when one would become available.

While they waited, Earl decided to lead the Scouts on a mounted exploration of the desolate bayou country opposite Vicksburg. Riding as advance scout in the place of Newton Culver, he led the Scouts out of Vicksburg on the morning of October 31, taking them on an exhausting thirty-six-hour, eighty-mile ride that captured two Rebel soldiers and, at the request of Gen. Dana, arrested a civilian identified as P. James. Earl does not state why that arrest was made, but it was most likely tied to illegal trade.

Despite the long delay in New Orleans — and the *Starlight*'s mechanical problems — October had been remarkably productive. In his report filed at the end of the month, Earl noted the capture of the battle flags,

36. Culver, Diary, Oct. 27, 1864.

the correspondence, the currency, and ten prisoners. In addition, the Scouts had seized nineteen horses, ten mules, and an ambulance wagon; and they had destroyed the boats intended to move everything across the river. For November to be as successful, the Scouts needed to have a new vessel without delay.[37]

37. Trimonthly Report of Lt. Earl, Oct. 20-31, 1864.

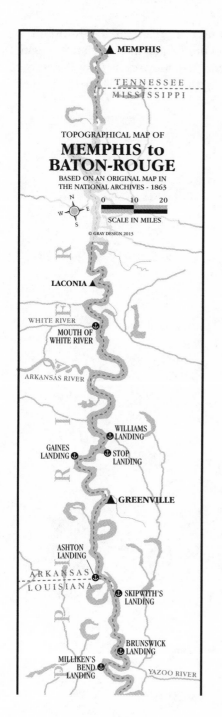

MEMPHIS ▲

TENNESSEE
MISSISSIPPI

TOPOGRAPHICAL MAP OF
MEMPHIS to
BATON-ROUGE

BASED ON AN ORIGINAL MAP IN
THE NATIONAL ARCHIVES - 1863

0   10   20

SCALE IN MILES

© GRAY DESIGN 2013

LACONIA ▲

WHITE RIVER

MOUTH OF
WHITE RIVER ⚓

ARKANSAS RIVER

WILLIAMS
⚓ LANDING

GAINES
LANDING ⚓   ⚓ STOP
                  LANDING

▲ GREENVILLE

ASHTON
LANDING ⚓

ARKANSAS
LOUISIANA

⚓ SKIPWITH'S
   LANDING

BRUNSWICK
⚓ LANDING

MILLIKEN'S
BEND ⚓
LANDING   YAZOO RIVER

BRUNSWICK
⚓ LANDING

MILLIKEN'S
BEND ⚓
LANDING   YAZOO RIVER

▲ **VICKSBURG**
▲ **WARRENTON**

BIG BLACK RIVER

POINT PLEASANT
LANDING ⚓
SHIP BAYOU LANDING ⚓
HARD TIMES LANDING ⚓   ▲ **GRAND GULF**
SAINT JOSEPH ▲   ⚓ BRUINSBURG
                          LANDING
                        ▲ **RODNEY**

WATERPROOF ▲

VIDALIA ▲   ▲ **NATCHEZ**

RED   RIVER

MOUTH OF
RED RIVER ⚓   MISS.

LOUISIANA

UPPER
TUNICA
LANDING ⚓

**BAYOU
SARA** ▲

**BATON
ROUGE** ▲

OK | AK | TN
TX | LA | MS | AL
            | FL
Area Shown on Map

Gulf of Mexico

CHAPTER EIGHT

"Invaluable Services"

A NEW STEAMER, THE SIDEWHEELER *COLONEL COWLES*, AWAITED the Scouts when they returned from their two-day trip into the Louisiana bayous across from Vicksburg. With a vessel once again at his disposal, Lt. Earl wasted no time getting the Scouts and their trunks onboard. On the evening of Wednesday, November 2, 1864, the *Colonel Cowles* pulled away from its dock in Vicksburg and started churning north up the Mississippi. Prior to this trip, the Scouts had always kept their activities south of Vicksburg; but now they were joining an inspection tour, organized by Gen. Canby, that was seeking firsthand information about guerrilla and illegal activities as far north as central Arkansas. Confederate troop movement and the possibility of a Confederate attempt to move a sizable contingent of western troops to the east side of the river also concerned Union leaders, and Gen. Canby assigned Earl's Scouts to learn everything they could about the location, current activities, and intentions of enemy troops in Arkansas. They were to keep themselves especially alert to any plan or likelihood of a Confederate attempt to move a substantial contingent of western troops to aid General John Bell Hood's Tennessee campaign.[1]

1. *Names of Steamboats*, compiled by Cpt. F. L. (Fielding) Wooldridge, Pott Library Special Collections, St. Louis Mercantile Library, University of Missouri, St. Louis. The vessel was named for Col. Daniel S. Cowles, commander of the 128th New York Infantry, who died in Gen. Banks's last assault at Port Hudson. He was known for the inspiring last words he allegedly spoke before dying: "Tell my mother I died with my face to the enemy." *The Philadelphia Inquirer*, June 9, 1863, reprinted in Web site of Donald G. Butcher Library at Morrisville State College: http://localhistory.morrisville.edu/sites/unitinfo/

Earl always did what he could to travel without attracting notice. Pulling away from the Vicksburg wharf, he and his Scouts worked their way north cautiously, stopping often to size up new terrain — physical, civilian, and military. Violence and contempt for normal civilian law raged through most of Arkansas and Missouri during the war, escalating as each new brutality was heaped on the last. One historian described an "ethical dam" bursting in the region after Quantrill's Raiders' barbarous raid on the border town of Lawrence, Kansas, in August 1863. An Arkansas guerrilla referred to 1863-64 as "dark Days," when enforcement of law "was in abeyance." With large numbers of Rebel deserters, partisans, and guerrillas roaming the state, resistance and insurrection devolved into outlawry that respected neither friend nor foe. It was a dangerous environment for anyone, but particularly for Earl and his Scouts. Captured Union soldiers could expect little mercy, and those posing as Confederates — as Earl and his Scouts were known to do — might well be hanged on the spot as spies.[2]

Undercover in Arkansas

The Scouts did not encounter Rebel activity until November 5, three days into their trip, when they arrived at Ashton's Landing, Arkansas, about eighty miles north of Vicksburg. There they found a "small-fry" sternwheeled steamer, the *Sylph*, loaded heavily with cotton, mules, oxen, and wagons. Slightly under a hundred feet long, sixteen and a half feet wide at her widest point, with a depth of only three feet, the *Sylph*'s size enabled her to move and maneuver up the Mississippi's tributaries and surrounding bayous as well as on the big river. Used by Northern war profiteers, she had come down from Cincinnati in 1863 and operated in the region since that time. On board the *Sylph*, Earl counted "32 bales of cotton, 4 mules, 4 oxen, and two wagons," and, concluding she was engaged in illegal trade, placed her under guard and sent her downriver to the provost marshal at Vicksburg. As soon as the *Sylph* was on her way, Earl ordered his remaining men to mount up for an investigation of the area west of the landing. They rode inland as far as Bayou Mason, where they discovered a lightly

cowles-david.html (accessed Sept. 6, 2012); Trimonthly Reports of Lt. Earl, Oct. 20-31, Nov. 1-10, 1864.

    2. Daniel E. Sutherland, *A Savage Conflict: The Decisive Role of Guerrillas in the American Civil War* (Chapel Hill: University of North Carolina Press, 2009), p. 210; Trimonthly Report of Lt. Earl, Nov. 1-10, 1864.

Steamboats traveling the Mississippi were vulnerable to guerrilla sharp-shooters and raiders when they stopped at remote landings to discharge or take on passengers or freight. (*Leslie's Illustrated Newspaper*, June 25, 1864)

guarded cache of "4 horses, 1 mule, and 40 bales of cotton," waiting for sale to Northern profiteers. He seized the horses and mule, but with no wagons to transport the cotton, he ordered it burned rather than permit it to remain and be transferred to dealers with questionable credentials.[3]

The Scouts spent the next five days working their way up the Missis-sippi. On November 7 they arrived at Gaines Landing, about 150 miles north of Vicksburg. Sharp bends in the river around the landing made

3. Frederick Way Jr., *Way's Packet Directory, 1848-1994*, rev. ed. (Athens: Ohio University Press, 1983), p. 440; Trimonthly Report of Lt. Earl, Nov. 1-10, 1864.

The Scouts regularly found caches of cotton bales and other goods hidden near the Mississippi, waiting to be smuggled across the river.
(*Harper's Weekly*, August 16, 1862)

it an ideal place for Confederate guerrillas to harass Union steamboats. They could attack boats as they entered a bend, cut across the neck of land while the vessel went around, and hit it again as it came out the far side — which was an especially effective tactic against boats that were heading slowly upstream. Union leaders responded by sending gunboats, infantry, and cavalry squads to drive away Rebels; but the latter usually returned as quickly as the federals withdrew.

Gaines Landing had a well-earned reputation as an active shipping depot for Confederate cotton. A convenient road led westward, enabling merchants and traders to move goods to and from the landing. Colonel Osband was also in the area, and he reported to Gen. Dana that "the Confederates boast that they constantly keep up an illicit trade through Gaines Landing and also that they sold quantities of Confederate cotton [there] last year." Gaines Landing was quiet when Earl and the Scouts arrived. They made a short trip inland, encountered enemy pickets after traveling about seven miles, "made no captures of consequence," and then returned to the *Colonel Cowles* and continued upriver.[4]

4. "Skirmish at Gaines Landing": http://www.encyclopediaofarkansas.net/encyclopedia/entry-detail.aspx?search=1&entryID=6938 (accessed Sept. 9, 2012); Col. Os-

At the same time that Canby sent Earl and his Scouts into Arkansas, he decided to travel up the river and investigate conditions for himself. Aboard the gunboat *Cricket*, he was about five days ahead of Earl. The morning of November 6 found Canby nearly forty miles up the White River. At about 8 a.m., as he stood on the vessel's top deck enjoying the morning breeze, a single shot fired by a guerrilla sniper who was hiding onshore struck him in his upper thigh, missing bone and large blood vessels, but knocking him to the deck. As his staff sprang to his aid, the *Cricket*'s captain reversed course and headed back to the Mississippi. Once on the big river, the *Cricket* made haste for New Orleans, where Canby, after receiving additional medical care, was confined to his quarters for a month. Even then, he was able to spend only a part of each day tending to the business of his command, leaving routine matters to his adjutant, Lt. Col. Christensen.[5]

Posing as Confederates

Unaware that Gen. Canby had been wounded, Earl and the Scouts continued north, arriving at the mouth of the White River on November 8, two days after the shooting. The complex at the juncture of the White and Mississippi Rivers offered docks, wood yards, and storage for goods waiting to be shipped and for recent deliveries being stored until picked up and taken inland. Also present was a ready complement of laborers who were keeping goods — legal and illegal — moving. The Scouts remained at the mouth of the White River on November 8 and 9, during which time they "drew rations and got some . . . horses shod," in preparation for heading up the White River to learn what they could about local guerrillas and who might have shot Canby.

Fast and rugged near its source, the White was a far different river nearer its mouth. Augmented by the smaller Arkansas River, it was wide, sluggish, and navigable by steamboats. On November 10, Earl and the Scouts switched to the *Kate Hart*, a 153-foot-long, 29-foot-wide stern-wheeler that provided local transport service and whose captain was an experienced White River pilot. They started up the White River, leaving

---

band to Maj. Gen. Dana, Nov. 20, 1864; O.R., I, 41, 4, p. 629; Trimonthly Report of Lt. Earl, Nov. 1-10, 1864.

5. Max L. Heyman Jr., *Prudent Soldier: A Biography of Major General E. R. S. Canby* (Glendale, CA: Arthur H. Clark, 1959), pp. 219-23.

the *Colonel Cowles*'s captain to tend to his vessel's maintenance, fuel, and supplies.

Unusually low water in the fall of 1864 made upriver travel difficult, and the Scouts got only as far as Prairie Landing, about fifteen miles north and west of the Mississippi, before Earl decided to disembark and search the region on horseback. They left the *Kate Hart* and rode overland about thirty-five miles to the village of DeWitt, founded a decade earlier to be the county seat of Arkansas County. DeWitt had a population of about 200, and its courthouse, the only brick building in town, was just two years old. In such a small community the presence of strangers was quickly noticed. However, Earl, wearing civilian clothes, "passed [himself] for a Confederate soldier" and moved among the local citizenry seeking information about the cotton trade, Confederate troops, and guerrillas. As Earl talked with DeWitt's residents, he found the people "very disloyal to the United States Government, [but] could hear of no force of Confederates between the White and Arkansas Rivers."[6]

On the morning of November 11, Earl led his Scouts out of DeWitt about fifteen miles north and east back to St. Charles on the White River. Perhaps because it served as an outpost for a small contingent of Union soldiers, he found no Rebel activity in the area, and when the *Kate Hart* arrived a day later, they steamed back to the mouth of the White River. Before returning down the Mississippi, Earl made one more exploratory trip upriver in search of enemy activity. He and the Scouts took the *Colonel Cowles* twenty miles north to Laconia Landing, but they found no guerrillas and so turned about and headed downstream.[7]

Wherever he went, Earl heard the same story: there were few Confederate soldiers in the area, but plenty of unhappy residents, armed partisans, and cotton traders with questionable permits from the U.S. Treasury. He concluded that the area would continue to be a hotbed of intrigue, illegal activity, and violence, but that there was very little likelihood of an attempt to cross large numbers of Confederate troops to the eastern side of the Mississippi. From intelligence gathered from area residents — and especially one unsuspecting Confederate officer who talked too freely — Earl concluded that Gen. Kirby Smith had given up the idea of

6. Trimonthly Report of Lt. Earl, Nov. 1-10, 1864; DeWitt (Arkansas County), *Encyclopedia of Arkansas History and Culture:* http://www.encyclopediaofarkansas.net/encyclopedia/entry-detail.aspx?entryID=819# (accessed Sept. 8, 2012).

7. Trimonthly Report of Lt. Earl, Nov. 10-20, 1864; O.R., I, 41, 4, pp. 629-30.

crossing troops to the east bank of the Mississippi and was moving instead to defend against an assault in either Louisiana or Texas. Earl reported to Canby that Smith had stationed about 7,000 men under General Buckner at Alexandria, Louisiana, and had another 4,000 to 6,000 men under his own command at Shreveport. Further north, General John B. Magruder was said to be fortifying Camden, Arkansas, with about 5,000 men.[8]

Lt. Earl's information again proved accurate and useful. His biggest error came in estimating the number of Kirby Smith's troops. As early as midsummer 1864, desertion had become a serious problem for Smith, and by the end of the year it had reached epidemic proportions. Gen. Smith still had somewhat more than 35,000 effectives spread throughout Louisiana, Texas, and Arkansas, but he had lost more than 10,000 to desertion. Thoroughly disheartened, he wrote to his mother on Christmas Day, 1864: "My stay here is uncertain. . . . My administration may cease at any moment."[9]

Back to Natchez

On November 15, after nearly two weeks in northern Louisiana and southern Arkansas, Earl and the Scouts left the mouth of the White River to return to Natchez. They made two stops on their way downriver. At Williams Landing, twenty-five miles below the White River, Earl learned that several wagons had crossed from east to west, accompanied by a large guard. Too late to interrupt that crossing and learn the content of the wagons, he moved on to Stock Landing, fifteen miles further down. There he captured a Confederate lieutenant and two privates, and he learned of a wagon train of tobacco and an accompanying group of guards located several miles inland, possibly the same one that had crossed near Williams Landing earlier. Thinking that he might add to his already valuable captures and intelligence, Earl ordered the Scouts off the *Colonel Cowles* in pursuit of the Rebels. About seven miles into the Mississippi bayou country, they came upon seven wagons loaded with a total of forty boxes of tobacco that weighed an estimated 5,000 pounds total, and two wagons outfitted with large pontoons, which were to be used to cross the Mississippi. Rushing

8. Joseph Howard Parks, *General Edmund Kirby Smith, C.S.A.* (Baton Rouge: Louisiana State University Press, 1954; 1982), pp. 420-31; Trimonthly Report of Lt. Earl, Nov. 10-20, 1864; O.R., I, 41, 4, pp. 629-30.

9. Robert L. Kerby, *Kirby Smith's Confederacy: The Trans-Mississippi South, 1863-1865* (New York: Columbia University Press, 1972), pp. 398, 405-7.

forward, the Scouts captured Confederate commissary agent Ed Montgomery, along with a captain, a lieutenant, and two privates. Earl was surprised at the weakness of the resistance he encountered. Although the wagon train "had an escort of about 100 men, and, notwithstanding his pickets saw me land, they did not try to fight. There were not more than 50 shots fired altogether." The wagon train's main force of guards fled so quickly that they left behind ten muskets, nine horses, and thirty-seven mules — in addition to the tobacco.[10]

Ed Montgomery's capture was as significant as the seizure of contraband goods. He was a key Mississippi River figure. As one newspaper put it, "There is hardly a pilot on the Mississippi and Ohio who is not well acquainted with Ed Montgomery." Even before the war, he had a well-known reputation as a pilot and commander of river steamers between Louisville and New Orleans. Mark Twain once piloted a boat captained by Montgomery and later described him as a "good man" and "worthy to be an admiral of the blue."[11] When war broke out, Montgomery lingered in St. Louis long enough to learn what he could about the construction of Union gunboats, and then headed south. For a time he served the Confederate cause as a guerrilla fighter beside his cousin Will Montgomery, who was active from Natchez to Vicksburg, but he served the Confederacy best as a builder and commander of gunboats, helping modify the ram *Tennessee*. Montgomery's immediate mission at the time of his capture was to either build a gunboat or acquire a foreign vessel, most likely the latter, considering the fact that he was carrying $250,000 in foreign currency and bank drafts. After Montgomery's arrest, Earl decided to make no more stops and turned the *Colonel Cowles* straight for Natchez. She pulled into her home port on November 21, bulging with captured goods and prisoners.[12]

From the standpoint of arrests and captured goods, the Scouts' trip up the Mississippi had been an undeniable success. They achieved much

10. Trimonthly Report of Lt. Earl, Nov. 10-20, 1864. In this context, Earl used the term "commissary" to indicate someone, not a military officer, delegated by the government for special duty.

11. Mississippi Steamboat Men in Mark Twain's Writings: http://www.twainquotes .com/Steamboats/Montgomery.html (accessed Sept. 10, 2012); *Virginia City Territorial Enterprise*, Jan. 1866.

12. Maj. Gen. Canby to Maj. Gen. Halleck, Nov. 25, 1864, *Letters Sent, May 1864–June 1865*, records of U.S. Army Continental Commands, Military Division of West Mississippi, Record Group 393, National Archives, vol. 60, p. 406. The information about Montgomery is found in a *St. Louis Democrat* article reprinted in the *Vicksburg Herald*, Dec. 10, 1864, p. 3.

**As restrictions were loosened in the last two years of the war,
U.S. Treasury Department offices that issued passes and trade permits
became increasingly busy.** (*Harper's Weekly*, January 18, 1862)

of what they had set out to do, and they incurred no losses of their own. Spending almost three weeks along the Mississippi in northern Louisiana and Mississippi, and in southern Arkansas, often passing themselves off as Confederates, they infiltrated enemy camps and won the confidence of several informants. That effort produced valuable information about troop numbers and placement, information Gen. Canby used as he deployed his troops along the Mississippi. They also seized the steamboat *Sylph*, seventy-two bales of cotton, 5,000 pounds of tobacco, forty-one mules, fifteen horses, and eleven wagons, and brought twelve prisoners to the Union provost marshal at Natchez.[13]

Instructed to survey illegal trade north of Vicksburg, Lt. Earl sent Canby's headquarters a letter summarizing his investigation. In it he confirmed Gen. Canby's greatest concerns, writing that he found that the cotton trade "is carried much further than you are aware of. . . . I find that

13. *The American Annual Cyclopedia and Register of Important Events of the Year 1864*, vol. 4 (New York: D. Appleton and Co., 1864), p. 193; Trimonthly Report of Lt. Earl, Nov. 10-20, 1864; O.R., I, 41, 4, p. 630.

persons claiming to be agents of the United States Government, most of whom have papers from the local agent at Memphis, Tenn., are scattered all along the river for the purpose of buying cotton for which they are to pay one-third in produce." These "agents" operated under two separate standards. "They say when they talk to U.S. soldiers that the produce is to be such as will be of no material aid to the Confederate Government." When talking to Confederates, however, they promised Southerners "gray cloth, provisions, boots and shoes, and some ammunition, and some quinine for family use." Furthermore, Confederate agents had unfettered access to Union camps and transports. "Our agents," said Earl, "are permitted to go through their camps and their agents to go on board our transports, and in some cases [so do] their soldiers."[14]

Earl used specific incidents to corroborate his conclusions. Along Bayou Macon, he had talked with members of Major General Mosby Parsons's 6th Division of the Missouri State Guard detailed to guard cotton. These men told him that they could get anything they wanted at Gaines Landing. Parsons's brigade's reputation was that of a hard-fighting mounted unit that had participated in close to fifty skirmishes and small battles, and had served for three years as pickets and scouts in the Little Rock and Shreveport regions. To Earl, "the fact that two regiments of Parson's [sic] brigade are employed guarding [cotton] at a time that they need their troops as much as at present is good evidence that the cotton trade is a profitable one for them." To further prove his point, Earl reported capturing a Rebel lieutenant and private who had just made a trade with a cotton agent from Memphis who was staying at the same house where the Confederates had their headquarters. "This agent wants me to treat the lieutenant very kindly, for he was a nice man and had been riding with and aiding him [the agent] ever since he had been there."[15]

All the events Earl reported occurred during a time when official Union policy permitted the cotton trade to be carried on only under rigid regulation and standards. Trade was not permitted with the Confederate government or its agents. The cotton agent whom Lt. Earl found in the same house with Confederate soldiers was aware of these restrictions; yet when Earl asked him if his papers permitted him to buy cotton from the

---

14. Lt. Earl to Lt. Col. C. T. Christensen, Nov. 24, 1864; O.R., I, 41, 4, p. 663.

15. Earl to Christensen, O.R., I, 41, 4, p. 663. Anne J. Bailey, "Parsons's Brigade," *Handbook of Texas Online*: http://www.tshaonline.org/handbook/online/articles/qkp01 (accessed Sept. 12, 2012) (published by the Texas State Historical Association).

Confederate Government, "he said they did, and added that the agent at Memphis told them to buy of Jefferson Davis if they could." Earl concluded his report with a pointed opinion about the wisdom of the trade policy:

> I have conversed with many leading men in that country [the area around Stock Landing] who are in favor of the Confederacy, and they all expressed the same opinions in regard to the benefit to be derived by the Confederacy from this cotton trade, I being at the time in Confederate uniform and supposed by them to be a good Confederate. And from what I have seen and heard in regard to it, and the way it is and is likely to be carried on, I consider it one of the worst measures that could well be adopted.[16]

Earl did not name the cotton agent with whom he had the discussion. Quite possibly, however, based on the description he received — and information from other letters that may have since been lost — Gen. Canby knew the man. Two days after Lt. Earl filed his letter, a notice from Canby's headquarters revoked the permit granted to a trader named Nicholls and further stated that such permits would no longer be granted except by orders from the general's headquarters.[17]

Gen. Canby had formed his opinion of the cotton trade and traders well before he received Earl's letter. He had, after all, authorized the Scouts' formation for the express purpose of monitoring and controlling speculators and illegal traders along the Mississippi River. Earl's letter served to reinforce Canby's view of the federal licensing policy. Like other hard-liners, he believed that the existing practice of licensed trade created problems that far outweighed its benefits. In his eyes, the issue would not be solved until the U.S. government adopted a program that combined tight control with consistent enforcement.

More Success around Natchez

The *Colonel Cowles* pulled into Natchez on November 19 and remained there for five days, giving the Scouts time to rest, clean and repair weapons

16. Lt. Earl to Lt. Col. Christensen, Nov. 24, 1864; O.R., I, 41, 4, p. 663.

17. Lt. Col. C. T. Christensen to Brig. Gen. N. B. Buford, Helena, Arkansas, Nov. 26, 1864; O.R., I, 41, 4, p. 691.

With their shallow-draft steamboats, Earl's Scouts eased quietly up to the Mississippi's sandy banks, like this location about five miles above St. Joseph, and surprised nearby guerrillas. (Gordon Olson)

and equipment, and catch up on correspondence from home. In addition to spending time with Jane, Isaac Earl used the days to review intelligence reports that had come in during his absence and to plan his Scouts' next action. By November 24, he was prepared to return to the river. Based on a report of an illegal cotton shipment at the plantation of Robert Scott, forty miles upstream, near Rodney, Mississippi, he ordered the Scouts back on board the *Colonel Cowles*. They proceeded to the plantation, seized sixty-seven bales and seventeen bags of cotton, and then engaged in a bit of deception by misdirection: they traveled farther north, to a point five miles above St. Joseph, Louisiana, where they landed and made an about-face. Disembarking in the dark of night, the Scouts turned back to St. Joseph, surprising the townspeople, who had relaxed after the *Colonel Cowles* passed. Earl and the Scouts arrived in St. Joseph on the morning of November 26, with three prisoners they had captured on their way.[18]

Leaving the prisoners under guard to await the arrival of the *Colonel Cowles*, Earl led the Scouts westward over the same road they had used on

18. Trimonthly Report of Lt. Earl, Nov. 20-30, 1864.

earlier occasions, going about twelve miles to a place where they had been told there was a load of tobacco previously brought over the Mississippi and now awaiting transport further west. They located and seized twenty-five boxes of tobacco and took them back to the *Colonel Cowles* "during the night of the 26th and also captured 2 other prisoners, making 5 on this trip and 17 during the month."

Captures and arrests like those the Scouts made in November spread Earl's reputation far beyond Natchez, and they deepened the animosity of the Confederate locals toward him. At the same time, the Scouts' known willingness to fight caused those they encountered to think twice before engaging them. On his way back to the *Colonel Cowles* after seizing the tobacco boxes, Earl noted the respect his Scouts had earned. "Just before dark on the evening of the 26th," he reported, "while I was in the country with my command, a party of Confederates attacked and drove to their boat eighty Union marines from one of the gun-boats, with a loss of 1 killed and 1 missing." He proudly ended his report by pointing out that "the skirmish took place only a few hundred yards from where my boat was lying. A portion of my command passed over the only road which led to the interior twice during the night, escorting teams, but were not molested." The distance between the Confederates and the Scouts may have been greater than Earl noted, and there may have been fewer Rebels. But in broad outline the facts of the case attest to the amount of activity along the river in the St. Joseph region, and Earl's Scouts' ability to function in that environment.[19]

Ambushed!

While they were resting in Natchez, Earl learned that Gen. Dana had authorized an offensive in the area of Brookhaven, Mississippi, about sixty-five miles due east of Natchez. Dana wanted the Scouts to participate, and Earl complied. On the morning of November 29, he ordered his men back aboard the *Colonel Cowles*, where they were joined by fifteen soldiers from the black 3rd Mississippi Cavalry, for a run of about fifteen miles upstream, where they would land and ride east to Brookhaven. A twenty-five-mile ride brought them to Fayette after sunset, but they had no intention of stopping. Their destination was still forty miles distant, and knowing from

19. Trimonthly Report of Lt. Earl, Nov. 20-30, 1864; Byron Kenyon to Parents, 11-27-64, Kenyon Letters, Port Hudson State Historic Site.

their past visit that this was hostile territory, "they were passing through as silently as possible with the intent . . . of not halting at all."

With Newton Culver gone, Earl was riding as an advance scout when they passed through the center of Fayette. Businesses were closed, and dim lights shone from the windows of a few homes. Initially there was a flurry of action in front of the hotel in the center of town; two men hurried inside at the first noise of the Scouts' arrival. But then no one was on the street, and everything was quiet until the Scouts reached the hotel. At that moment, "when [we were] just opposite the hotel, two or three shots were fired," their sound amplified by the quiet of the night. Isaac Earl, alone in front of the hotel, was struck and tumbled from his horse onto the street. Then the shooting stopped as suddenly as it started. The shots that brought Earl down were fired from a double-barreled shotgun loaded with a combination of a single large ball in one barrel and smaller balls in the other. Several of the lead projectiles "took effect . . . wounding Earl in the left breast a little above the nipple, and in the right cheek (not severely) and in the right wrist."[20]

In the quiet darkness, some Scouts scanned the street for the shooter, while others rushed to their fallen leader. Although he was gravely wounded, Earl remained conscious, giving them hope that he could be saved if they could get him back to Natchez. Charles Baker, the only Scout to write a contemporaneous account of the event, described what happened next in a letter to Newton Culver two days later: "The boys took him to the home of [Charles] Duncan and left him as he was so badly injured as to be unable to ride in a carriage, and then they started for this place [Natchez] which they reached at daylight yesterday morning [November 30]." Baker said that Duncan's seventy-eight-year-old father, John, was a physician and the first to tend to Earl's wounds. Earl's orderly, Johnny Hays, a young Southern boy whose age is variously listed as between twelve and sixteen, remained with his leader while the others retraced their route to Natchez in search of help.[21]

20. Charles Baker to Newton Culver, Dec. 1, 1864, Newton Culver Papers. A later account suggested that one of his wounds was in his leg. No matter their precise location, the facial wound and the wound to his limb do not appear to have been life-threatening. The chest wound was another matter. He was struck solidly, and there was danger of serious injury to vital organs.

21. Charles Baker to Newton Culver, Dec. 1, 1864, Newton Culver Papers; Surgeon P. A. Willis and Ass't Surgeon A. E. Carothers to Brig. Gen. M. Brayman, Dec. 2, 1864; O.R., I, 41, 4, pp. 756-57.

Back in Natchez the next morning, the sleepless scouts reported to Brigadier General Mason Brayman's headquarters as soon as they arrived, hoping that he would send a cavalry force to bring Earl back. Brayman responded by ordering two surgeons, P. A. Willis from the 48th Ohio Veteran Infantry and the post surgeon in Natchez, and A. E. Carothers, of the U.S. Volunteers, who was in charge of the general hospital in Natchez, to gather medical instruments and supplies and accompany six Scouts and Jane Earl to Fayette. He told them to aid Earl if permitted and to bring him back if possible. Having sent the relief party on its way, Brayman sent a letter to Canby's headquarters informing him of the shooting, and expressing his concern that the wounds might be fatal because Earl had been "bleeding profusely," and the physician at Fayette had very few medical supplies. Pointing out that his cavalry was away with Gen. Dana and not available to respond in force, Brayman wrote that his only option was to send, along with the surgeons, Jane Earl to attend to her husband, hoping that she and the surgeons could bring him back with them. Concluding his report with what appeared to be an attempt to limit his own responsibility in the matter, Brayman stated that he was not aware of Earl's trip to Brookhaven until the Scouts returned with news of his wounds, reminding Canby's office that Earl was not "under my direction."[22]

The Scouts, surgeons, and Jane Earl departed Natchez in a carriage at about 2:00 p.m., with credentials signed by Gen. Brayman. They traveled until early evening before stopping at the home of a Unionist named Hoggett. In addition to getting a meal and resting, they wanted to avoid encountering Rebel partisans who might be patrolling the dark road — or having a carriage accident. Rising early and getting back on the road at daybreak, the relief party arrived at Fayette by midday, December 1, and were met at the edge of town by Lieutenant B. B. Paddock, commander of a small company of Confederates. The surgeons gave Brayman's letter to Paddock and requested to see Lt. Earl so that they could treat him. After reading the letter, Paddock told them that it would be impossible for any of them to see Earl because he had been taken thirty miles further inland to Confederate-held territory, where the group could not be permitted to go.

The surgeons, however, "insisted upon going on without our escort

---

22. Brig. Gen. Mason Brayman to "Commanding Officer Confederate Forces," Nov. 30, 1864; O.R., I, 41, 4, pp. 755-56; Gen. Mason Brayman to Lt. Col. C. T. Christensen, Nov. 30, 1864; O.R., I, 41, 4, pp. 722-23.

under charge of a guard of his men, offering him any pledges of secrecy that he might wish, but to no avail." In a letter that he gave the surgeons to return to Gen. Brayman, Paddock explained that he could not assent to the request, "it being contrary to usual custom to allow [them] to enter the lines." The surgeons made their attempt to reach Earl even though they had received information that Johnny Hays, the boy who had been left to attend Earl, had already been made a Confederate prisoner. To volunteer to go thirty miles past Confederate pickets was to invite a similar fate. While resisting their efforts to reach Earl, Lt. Paddock persistently maintained that he was alive, with wounds that were serious but not fatal. In the letter to Gen. Brayman, he said that Earl "shall have every attention in my power to bestow. . . ." The only immediate satisfaction he gave Jane Earl and the physicians was to take the delicacies, liquors, and clothing that were intended for Earl and assure them they would be given to the wounded Scout.[23]

Before leaving Fayette, the frustrated surgeons talked with "Dr. [B. G.] Greenfield, the physician who first attended Lieutenant Earl after being wounded." Charles Baker's letter to Culver identified Earl's first physician as Dr. John Duncan, a much older man living with his planter son, Charles. John Duncan probably referred Earl's care to other physicians. Later information mentioned — in addition to Dr. Greenfield — treatment by a Dr. Patrick Wade, also of Fayette. The fact that several doctors were involved may indicate that none of them had the necessary resources with which to treat a serious wound. In any case, the Union surgeons sent to care for Earl came away frustrated and unimpressed. "Either through ignorance or from a worse motive, [the physician] gave us such conflicting accounts of his wounds that we are unable to state with any degree of certainty whether they are mortal or not." From the information provided to the doctors, their best conclusion was that Earl had a buckshot wound in the face which was painful but not serious, and "another buckshot or ball on the left side of the chest near the clavicle, but whether it opened the cavity of the left thorax [the heart and lungs] we are unable to determine."

The question of whether the bullet had entered the thorax was critical to understanding Earl's chances for surviving. If it had, there was good reason to believe that a lung had been punctured. If this were true, there was very little hope that he would survive without immediate and com-

23. Surgeons P. A. Willis and A. E. Carothers to Brig. Gen. Mason Brayman, Dec. 2, 1864; O.R., I, 41, 4, pp. 756-57; Lt. B. B. Paddock, Commanding Confederate Scouts, to Brig. Gen. Brayman, Dec. 1, 1864; O.R., I, 41, 4, p. 756.

petent care. If, on the other hand, the bullet had entered higher in the shoulder, he was not in nearly as much danger. From the report of the Fayette physician, the doctors could only express a cautious optimism for Earl's survival.[24]

Nearly fifty years later, information about the wounds and the weapon that made them was confirmed by one of the Rebels present at the shooting. In 1911, Newton Culver, then living in Montana but still determined to promote Isaac Earl's memory, placed an announcement in a Natchez newspaper seeking information about Earl's shooting and his treatment while in Confederate hands. In response, he received a letter from Thomas G. Dicks, a native of Natchez and former member of Lt. Paddock's Scouts. Dicks stated that he was sitting in front of Fayette's hotel with Sergeant James Smith, also a member of Paddock's Scouts, when Earl and his men approached. Smith ordered the lights extinguished, and when Earl came within about forty yards he fired two shots from his double-barreled shotgun.[25]

In his report to Gen. Canby's office about the shooting of Lt. Earl, Gen. Brayman had concluded that Earl was not wounded in a fight, but "a murderous fire from houses" — an ambush. Thomas Dicks's acknowledgment that the Rebels had doused lights, waited in darkness, and fired only twice from short range before fleeing into the night confirmed that version of events. Killing Earl may not have been a planned assassination, but it certainly was a response to a moment of opportunity.[26]

24. Surgeons P. A. Willis and A. E. Carothers to Brig. Gen. Mason Brayman, Dec. 2, 1864; O.R., I, 41, 4, pp. 756-57. Dr. B. G. Greenfield is listed in the 1860 census as a thirty-two-year-old physician originally from Tennessee. The Dr. Duncan mentioned by Charles Baker is Dr. John Duncan, seventy-eight years old and a longtime Fayette resident from Virginia. Dr. Pat Wade was a thirty-five-year-old physician originally from South Carolina. 1860 U.S. census, population schedule, *Fayette, Jefferson County, Mississippi,* NARA microfilm publication M653, Roll 584, pp. 587, 629, 657, Washington, DC: National Archives and Records Administration.

25. Newton Culver, "Brevet Major Isaac N. Earl: A Noted Scout of the Department of the Gulf," *Proceedings of the Historical Society of Wisconsin* (1917): 337. Thomas G. Dicks to Newton Culver, Sept. 6, 1911, Newton Culver Papers. Thomas Dicks was a well-informed source. A carpenter and lifelong Natchez resident, he maintained contact with many of the area's former Confederate soldiers. He spent his last years as a resident at Beauvoir, Jefferson Davis's former plantation, converted to a Confederate Soldier's Home. *Beauvoir Confederate Soldiers Home:* http://www.beauvoir.org/vetshome.html (accessed Sept. 16, 2012); *Mississippi Confederate Grave Registry:* http://mscgr.homestead.com/MSCGRdi .htm (accessed Sept. 16, 2012).

26. Gen. Mason Brayman to Lt. Col. C. T. Christensen, Nov. 30, 1864; O.R., I, 41, 4, pp. 722-23.

Exhausted, angry, and frustrated, the Scouts who returned from Fayette with the surgeons remained convinced that their leader was alive, and they began making urgent preparations to rescue him. Earl had trained them well, and performing as though he were still in charge, they sent out several undercover agents to determine his whereabouts, the number of Rebels guarding him, and his condition. The rest of the Scouts remained in Natchez, trying to learn anything they could from rumors making their way around town, ready to ride on short notice if word of his location was heard. Unfortunately, when a message finally arrived, it brought not the news the Scouts had been hoping for, but a report of the worst possible kind. They were told that Lt. Earl was dead and that he had died shortly after being shot.[27]

The spies also brought back a rumor that Earl had been poisoned, an idea that persisted among some members of the Scouts as long as they lived. The spies were told that, just before he died, Earl went into convulsions and that after his death a fluid as clear and transparent as water flowed from his wounds in large quantities. To give credence to this story, the spies recounted tales that it was the "medicine" given to him that caused his death. The Scouts were incensed at the idea that they might have lost their leader in such a way, and they went to several physicians in Natchez to determine whether poison might have been the cause of the unusual circumstances of Earl's death. Some of them later claimed that these physicians stated that such a fluid was not the result of the wounds — and could only be produced by poison. In his letter to Culver, Thomas Dicks denied that Earl had been mistreated in any way. "I can assure you," he wrote Newton Culver, "that all was done for him that could possibly be done with the limited amount of drugs at our command." He assured Culver: "There never was any symptoms of poisoning or foul play, for I am sure Lieutenant Paddock would never have allowed any such practice especially upon an enemy as brave as Lieutenant Earl had proved himself and one whom he knew personally."

When Lt. Earl's young orderly, Johnny Hays, escaped three months later and returned to the Scouts, he, too, discounted the poisoning rumors and confirmed the formal reports the Scouts had received about their lead-

27. Jane Earl was exhausted when she returned from Fayette. Unable to rouse herself from her carriage, she was carried to her lodging by the Scouts and left to be cared for by her landlady. Charles Baker to Newton Culver, Dec. 1, 1864, Newton Culver Papers; "A Friend" to Newton Culver, reprinted in the *Evergreen City Times* (Sheboygan, WI), Mar. 11, 1865, p. 2.

er's death. With similar stories coming from different sources, perhaps the best that can be concluded is that, while Earl was not poisoned, he may have been hastened to his grave by the lack of medical treatment he received.[28]

Another rumor about Earl's death also gained credence among many of his supporters and friends. In this version of the shooting, Lt. Earl was killed as an act of vengeance by a man he had bested in an affair of the heart. According to that story, Lieutenant Buckley Burton Paddock, the man credited with taking Earl prisoner after the shooting (and the officer who denied the Union surgeons access to him), had lived in Wisconsin before the outbreak of war. Supposedly, Paddock's animus toward the Scouts' leader stemmed from an incident in which he had lost the favors of a young lady to Earl. While it is true that Paddock, who was born in Ohio, lived in Wisconsin for a time, he was only fifteen years old when he moved to the South with his family in 1859, arguably too young to have formed a lasting bitterness over an equally youthful woman. When the war broke out, Paddock joined Company K of Col. Wirt Adams's First Mississippi Cavalry, where he was named commander of a group of scouts and later earned a promotion to captain. Earl and Paddock were active opponents in Mississippi and in Louisiana's Florida Parishes for much of the war. They knew each other, at least by reputation. Despite the questionable veracity of the story that they had met in Wisconsin, it indicates the aura of romance and legend that was growing around the heroic Earl. Those he commanded — and others who knew of his exploits — embroidered his death, seeking to add heroic proportions to his life.[29]

News of Earl's wounds and capture spread rapidly. Gen. Brayman sent a report to Lt. Col. Christensen of Gen. Canby's headquarters, telling him

28. "A Friend" to Newton Culver, reprinted in the *Evergreen City Times* (Sheboygan, WI), Mar. 11, 1865, p. 2; Thomas G. Dicks to Newton Culver, Sept. 6, 1911, Newton Culver Papers. The Dicks letter is quoted at length in Michael J. Martin, *A History of the 4th Wisconsin Infantry and Cavalry in the Civil War* (El Dorado Hills, CA: Savas Beatie, 2006), pp. 384-85. In 1973, a member of the professional staff at the Veterans Administration Center in Cheyenne, WY, examined the accounts of Lt. Earl's death and concluded that his wounds were very likely fatal. He felt there was insufficient evidence to make any conclusions regarding the story that Earl was poisoned (Dr. John W. Horton to Gordon Olson, Jan. 16, 1973).

29. Bennett, "Sketch of Military Service," p. 16; Patricia L. Duncan, "Paddock, Buckley Burton," *Handbook of Texas Online:* http://www.tshaonline.org/handbook/online/articles/fpa03 (accessed Apr. 28, 2013) (published by the Texas State Historical Association).

of Earl's death and offering such details as he had gathered in the days after the shooting. He reported that two privates, Thomas Rodgers and James Mitchell, members of Col. Frank Powers's partisan Mississippi and Louisiana Cavalry Regiment, had deserted and made their way to Natchez. They had seen Earl buried at Union Church, a small settlement about twenty miles east of Fayette. "I have no reason to doubt this statement," Brayman assured Christensen. Another witness, a young woman not further identified, told Brayman:

> [W]hen Earl dashed into Fayette with less than 30 men, four companies of rebels ran away, supposing him to have a larger force; that they returned the next day and carried him off. . . . She says the inhabitants, especially the women remonstrated against his removal and offered to take care of him, and that Doctor Duncan, at whose house he was and who kindly attended him, protested that to remove him would cause his death, and that his murder would rest upon them, but that they swore they would carry him to Jackson "dead or alive."

Continuing his report, Brayman eulogized Earl as "a brave and chivalrous officer. He was a terror to the enemy and had by his successes awakened deep hostility. I have heard of their threats to destroy him. I did not suppose they would wish or dare to kill him by violence, but was too well satisfied that they would treat him so as to make him die. He will be sorely missed in the peculiar service in which he was fast becoming distinguished."[30]

Gen. Canby considered Earl's shooting of enough significance to mention it in his report to Washington, assuring Gen. Halleck that if Earl survived, he would make every exertion to have him exchanged at an early date. Canby was as good as his word, immediately sending a message to the exchange agent, Colonel Charles Dwight, asking him to make a special exchange for Lt. Earl. On December 7, Dwight sent a message to his Confederate counterpart, Major J. R. Curell at Mobile, stating: "I shall be glad to make . . . a special exchange for Lieut. I. N. Earl, Fourth Wisconsin Cavalry, who was wounded and taken prisoner by your forces . . . on the 29th." Dwight offered "in exchange for Lieutenant Earl any officer of like rank from among the prisoners now held by us in this department captured from the forces of your department," offering one of "several officers

---

30. Gen. Brayman to Lt. Col. C. T. Christensen, Dec. 9, 1864; O.R., I, 41, 4, p. 810.

Major General Henry W. Halleck (Library of Congress)

of the staff of General [George B.] Hodge lately captured at or near Liberty [Mississippi] by the forces of Brig. Gen. A. L. Lee."[31]

Unfortunately, by that time the offer was too late. Shortly after he sent his report to Gen. Halleck, Gen. Canby received the news that Lt. Earl was dead; the general immediately sat down to compose a letter of condolence to his widow. It was a difficult moment. Canby had placed a great deal of responsibility on the shoulders of the young soldier from Wisconsin, and his confidence had been justified. He told Jane Earl of his personal sorrow "that our country has lost one of her brave sons, whose abilities were of that peculiar character that it is next to impossible to find any one worthy and capable of fully replacing him." Canby went on to say that Earl's "many excellent qualities had endeared him to me personally, and I mourn the loss

31. Col. Chas. C. Dwight to Maj. J. R. Curell, Dec. 7, 1864; O.R., II, 7, p. 1202.

Following his death, Isaac Earl was buried at the cemetery near this
Presbyterian church in the small community of Union Church, Mississippi.
(Gordon Olson)

of him, as that of a valued friend."[32] Compounding Gen. Canby's sense of
loss, a letter from Gen. Halleck announcing Lt. Earl's brevet promotion to
Major arrived shortly after his death — an honor Earl would never know.

A New Leader

Isaac Earl's death left a difficult void for Gen. Canby to fill. In October
and November 1864, success had attended the Scouts wherever they went.

32. Gen. Canby to Gen. Halleck, Chief of Staff, U.S. Army, Dec. 9, 1864; O.R., I, 41, 4,
pp. 807-8; Gen. Brayman to Lt. Col. C. T. Christensen, Dec. 9, 1864; O.R., I, 41, 4, p. 810;
Gen. Canby to Mrs. I. N. Earl, Dec. 27, 1864 (copy in pension claim of Jane Earl). Brayman's
report states that he was carried first to Jackson, Mississippi, and then to Union Church
(thirty-five miles east of Natchez), where he was buried. According to Newton Culver,
Jane Earl later claimed his body for reburial in a cemetery in Minneapolis, where she was
living at the time; but attempts to locate Earl's grave in Minneapolis have thus far been
unsuccessful. Culver, "Brevet Major Isaac N. Earl," p. 337.

The steamboats at their disposable had enabled them to operate as an amphibious unit, moving quickly from one place along the river to another. Responding to reports of suspected illegal trade and smuggling, they made arrests and seizures on the spot, carrying away or destroying large quantities of goods that Earl deemed contraband. His death left Canby searching for a replacement he could trust to handle the responsibility — one who was also acceptable to the Scouts. This would not be an easy task: Isaac Earl had been a special soldier.

As soon as Canby learned Earl was severely wounded and in enemy hands, he moved to assure the Scouts that their organization would continue unchanged, and that he had "every confidence in the bravery and integrity of the men." His first step was to name a temporary — if necessary, permanent — replacement, a process in which the Scouts would play an important role. In an unusual move, he asked the Scouts to recommend an officer to serve as their new leader, reserving for himself final approval of the man they recommended. He also informed them that "should Lt. Earle's [sic] disability prove permanent, such officer as he and his men recommend will be assigned to the command of the Party." Even in an army in which volunteer companies often elected officers, Canby's decision to give the Scouts such a large role in selecting their leader was remarkable. Their performance of duties since their organization in June certainly played a role in his decision, as did their cohesiveness as a unit. The only personnel changes that had been made occurred at the end of October, when Earl ordered Frank Wallace and Lewis Simpson returned to the 2nd Wisconsin Cavalry for "misconduct," and when Newton Culver, John Billings, Luther Struthers, and Albert James departed at the completion of their term of enlistment.[33]

Even before they received Canby's message seeking their recommendation for a leader, the Scouts had begun discussing how to fill their leadership void until Earl returned. Most of them wanted to have someone from the Scouts ranks, or the 4th Wisconsin, named to take Earl's place. One possibility was to pass leadership to Henry Stafford, whom Earl had earlier designated a squad chief. However, Stafford was a private, and the leader of the Scouts had to be an officer. Newton Culver, who had ridden

---

33. Trimonthly Reports of Lt. Earl, Oct. 20-31, Nov. 20-30, Dec. 1-10, 10-20, 1864; Lt. Col. C. T. Christensen to Nelson W. Porter, Dec. 2, 1864, *Letters Sent, May 1864–June 1865,* Records of the U.S. Army Continental Commands, Military Division of West Mississippi, Record Group 383, National Archives Building (vol. 60, p. 421).

in their advance during most of the Scouts' existence, was highly regarded by those who had fought beside him, but two factors prohibited his selection as the new leader: he had been discharged by the army and was back in Sheboygan Falls, and even if he were still in the army, he was also an enlisted man, not an officer. The Scouts had to find Earl's replacement from among the officers they knew.[34]

After talking among themselves, they settled on Lieutenant Warren P. Knowles, the commander of Company "G" of the 4th Wisconsin Cavalry as the best man they knew to succeed Earl. Like Earl, Knowles had worked his way up through the enlisted ranks to become an officer. Both men were twenty when they volunteered; the two men were also similar in height (five feet eight) and weight (about 150); even their facial features, from their fair complexions and dark hair to their mustaches, were similar. Like Earl, Knowles had taken part in the 4th Wisconsin's training at Camp Utley, and he had gotten his first taste of dealing with the enemy in Maryland and then Louisiana. For a time in 1863, during the Port Hudson campaign, Knowles had served as orderly to General Thomas W. Sherman and, like Earl, had been promoted to lieutenant "for gallantry in action" during the Port Hudson campaign.[35] Although most of the Scouts felt that Lt. Knowles would adequately replace Earl, Newton Culver's close friend Charles Fenlason, who rode beside him as an advance scout, had reservations. "I voted for him," he wrote Culver, "not that I thought him capable of filling Earl's place for I knew that he was not near as good a Scout as Earl. In the first place I did not consider him daring enough to lead such a corps of men as composed the Special Scouts and in the second place he was not energetic enough and in the third place he drank too much whiskey."

Nelson Porter, clerk of the Scouts, was selected to convey the Scouts' preference to Gen. Canby's headquarters. On December 2, just three days after the ambush that killed Earl, Porter left for New Orleans, where he went directly to Gen. Canby's headquarters. There, with a minimum of discussion, he presented the Scouts' request that Lt. Warren P. Knowles be named to replace Isaac Earl, and he received the general's approval.[36]

---

34. Charles W. Fenlason to Newton Culver, Feb. 25, 1865, Newton Culver Papers.

35. Service Record of Lt. Warren P. Knowles, Records of the Adjutant General's Office, Record Group 94, National Archives and Records Service.

36. Charles Baker to Newton Culver, Dec. 1, 1864; Charles W. Fenlason to Newton Culver, Feb. 25, 1865, Newton Culver Papers.

CHAPTER NINE

"I Shall Do All I Can . . ."

O N DECEMBER 5, 1864, WARREN KNOWLES TOOK COMMAND OF THE Special Scouts. He had just returned to Baton Rouge from his first visit to his home in western Wisconsin in three years when General Canby informed him of his new assignment. He gathered his gear and left promptly for Natchez, arriving there at 9:00 the following evening. Along with Gen. Canby's orders, Knowles received copies of Lt. Earl's original orders of June 6 and July 15, 1864, the orders that had created the Scouts and laid out their responsibilities. In an accompanying letter, Canby's adjutant, Lt. Col. Christensen, told Knowles that the same instructions applied to him, and reminded him of "the necessity of preserving the same good discipline amongst your men" as was exercised by Lt. Earl: "While bravery and dash are necessary qualifications in the execution of your important duties you must also exercise the necessary amount of carefulness and moderation, and keep in view the special duties for which the party was organized." Christensen closed his letter with the hope that Knowles would justify the confidence expressed in him by Gen. Canby and instructed him to make no changes in his command without consulting headquarters. Knowles inherited an experienced and effective organization, but Isaac Earl's accomplishments and dynamic personality loomed over him. His performance would be closely watched.[1]

As soon as his steamboat docked at Natchez, Knowles began acquainting himself with his new command and placing the Scouts' affairs in "the

---

1. Lt. Col. C. T. Christensen to Lt. Warren P. Knowles, Dec. 5, 1864; O.R., I, 41, 4, pp. 766-67.

Lieutenant Warren Perley Knowles
(State Historical Society of Wisconsin)

best possible situation." The job turned out to be bigger than he had anticipated. Isaac Earl had been much more interested in his operations than in
keeping track of his people and equipment, of seizures and arrests. Nelson
Porter's written reports, signed by Earl, had been sufficient for Gen. Canby's office. But Knowles, who became a teacher, attorney, and businessman after the war, placed a higher value on record-keeping and adminis-
trative order. He began his first full day at the head of the Scouts "taking
inventory of property and preparing such as is not necessary to arm the
command, for inspection to enable me to turn it over to the Ordnance Department in accordance with the order from your [Canby's] headquarters."
These tasks consumed his time for several days. In his first report, filed
December 10, he told Canby's office that he had been "so occupied with
these affairs that I have done nothing outside the lines," though he hoped
to "soon be able to attempt active operations." There were undoubtedly

Scouts, angry about Earl's killing and eager to exact retribution, who were pushing him to get back to active duty; but these few days of focusing on equipment and reports were important, giving Knowles time to familiarize himself with his new command before taking the field.

Knowles's inventory revealed more weapons than he felt the Scouts needed. Each man had a Sharps carbine, two Spencer carbines, and two sabers. Knowles' count also revealed 56 revolvers, 80 saddles, 62 horses, and 4 mules. His review of the Scouts' roster revealed additional discrepancies that required resolution. He removed from the Scouts' roster two Southern civilians who had served as Earl's spies: W. D. Mead, for failing to report regularly, and M. Bowers, because his services were no longer available. In his report to General Canby, Lt. Knowles said that he dropped the men "by reason of representations made by members of the command that such was the wish and order of Lt. Earl."[2]

With his paperwork in order, Lt. Knowles confronted yet another problem. At the request of the Natchez quartermaster, Captain L. W. Pierce, he had "turned over the services of the steamer *Colonel Cowles . . .* until such time as I am able to commence operations where its service will be necessary." Unfortunately, when he went to reclaim the vessel on the evening of December 13, the boat's captain informed him that it needed to go to New Orleans for repairs. While he and his men remained in Natchez for the following week, Knowles ordered the *Colonel Cowles* to New Orleans. The Scouts made a few short forays into the countryside while they waited, but heavy rains rendered the roads almost impassable, making it very difficult to accomplish anything. Despite the limitations, the Scouts gathered important information and forwarded it to Gen. Canby's office. On December 14, in a message requesting "the use of a boat immediately . . . as it will most likely be too late before the steamer Colonel Cowles can receive the necessary repairs," Knowles reported that "the enemy in this vicinity are concentrating the most of their available force on or near the river, below this place [Natchez]." Knowles went on to explain that this was a diversion and that similar moves in the past meant that they were in reality "preparing to cross men or valuable material across the river above." To buttress his point, he informed Canby: "I have positive information that there are some 500 or 600 in the vicinity of Palestine and Cold Springs [about thirty-five miles southeast of Vicksburg]. They

2. Trimonthly Report of Lt. Knowles, Dec. 1-10, 1864; Trimonthly Report of Lt. Earl, Nov. 20-30, 1864.

have just arrived from above and are moving toward the river." He did not, however, know their destination or intent: "I know of nothing for them to make a demonstration upon in that direction, and consider that it must be to cover some other move."[3]

When the *Colonel Cowles*'s replacement, the *Mustang*, finally arrived on December 20, Knowles felt that it was far less than an ideal vessel for the Scouts' purposes. It was a 172-ton wood-hulled side-wheeler that was built in Pittsburgh in 1860 and purchased by the U.S. Army quartermaster department in May 1864. The *Mustang* "came lacking some things absolutely necessary, among which is stage planks [for loading and unloading horses and wagons], which will be furnished here as soon as possible." Furthermore, she lacked "sufficient accommodation for our horses. Also the howitzer and ammunition, and many other things necessary, which are expected to be placed upon any boat which was assigned to this service. . . ." Knowles completed his review of the *Mustang* with the observation that the missing items "are all upon the steamer Col. Cowles," but pledged to Canby that, "notwithstanding these deficiencies I shall do all I can with the boat as it is until the Cowles can be repaired, or it is your pleasure to make other arrangements."[4]

Knowles followed through on his promise two days after the *Mustang* arrived, when he set out with the Scouts for St. Joseph. Along with seeking more information about Confederate troop activity in the area, Knowles was acting on a report supplied by unnamed undercover agents about illegal activities around the plantation of a suspected smuggler named Briscoe. Following Earl's pattern, Knowles led his command up the Mississippi River to a point about four miles below St. Joseph, where they quietly disembarked and proceeded northwest six miles to Briscoe's plantation. Arriving undetected, they captured two prisoners and seized a quantity of Confederate mail. They also learned of "a large quantity" of tobacco on the east side of the river, about five miles further north, near Bruinsburg, awaiting transport across the Mississippi.[5]

Upon learning of the pending tobacco crossing, Knowles hurried his prisoners and captured mail back to the boat and ordered the captain to

3. Lt. Knowles to Lt. Col. Christensen, Dec. 14, 1864; O.R., I, 41, 4, p. 852; Trimonthly Report of Lt. Knowles, Dec. 10-20, 1864.

4. Frederick Way Jr., *Way's Packet Directory, 1848-1994*, rev. ed. (Athens: Ohio University Press, 1983), p. 334; Trimonthly Report of Lt. Knowles, Dec. 10-20, 1864.

5. Trimonthly Report of Lt. Knowles, Dec. 20-31, 1864; *Evergreen City Times*, Mar. 11, 1865, p. 2.

ferry the Scouts across the river, and then meet them further north at Bruinsburg. With the *Mustang* churning north, Knowles and the Scouts set out on horseback to intercept the tobacco shipment. The mounted Scouts arrived at Bruinsburg while the *Mustang* was still a mile away. Realizing that the tobacco remained hidden inland, Knowles decided to seize it before it could be moved.

Up to this point, Knowles's first trip on the river as the Scouts' leader had proceeded much as those led by Earl. Then, about a half mile inland, similarities ceased. As they rode along a levee, the Scouts saw a man who turned and ran when he was noticed. Knowles ordered four Scouts to catch him, determine his identity, and the reason he had run. The four men had no sooner galloped off than about 200 members of the 3rd Louisiana Cavalry appeared to the Scouts' rear, separating them from the river and the *Mustang*, which was just pulling up. Unfortunately, the unarmed vessel could offer no covering fire.

Knowles's first impulse was to attempt to run through the enemy to the boat, and he started in that direction; but almost immediately he had to change his plans, because he saw the *Mustang* pull away from the bank and begin moving downstream! With no hope of rescue at the river, the Scouts made a run for a woodlot a short distance from the road — with the Confederate cavalrymen close behind. Barely a hundred yards ahead of their pursuers when they reached the woods, Knowles halted the Scouts and turned them to face the approaching enemy. When the Rebels came within twenty yards, the Scouts opened fire with their Spencer carbines and temporarily turned them back. But the Confederates regrouped, fanned out, and prepared to attack from both sides as well as the front, slowly surrounding the less numerous Scouts. Realizing what the enemy was up to, Knowles ordered his men to fall back gradually, turn, and fight their way slowly to the river, where the *Mustang* had returned and was cruising up and down looking for any of the group who escaped.[6]

Close-quarter combat followed for the next four hours. The Scouts fought their foe individually and in small groups, first through the woods and then through an "apparently impassable swamp" between them and the river. Lt. Knowles's conduct during this fight won him the respect of those who had earlier doubted his courage and ability to lead. One of the doubters, Charles Fenlason, reported that "no officer could have done bet-

6. Maj. F. W. Marston to Lt. Col. C. T. Christensen, Dec. 31, 1864; O.R., I, 41, 4, p. 968; *Evergreen City Times*, Mar. 11, 1865, p. 2.

The U.S.S. *Rattler* was a welcome sight to the Scouts when it appeared on the Mississippi to rescue them after they were outnumbered by Confederate troops near Bruinsburg. (U.S. Naval Historical Center)

ter than he did. . . . He handled his men skillfully and fought as bravely as ever a man fought, he killed the rebel, Colonel Stafford, with his own hand shot him four times before he killed him." Under these battle conditions, Knowles and fifteen Scouts reached the river shortly before noon, where they were taken aboard the "tinclad" stern-wheeler *Rattler*, which was also patrolling in the area. Once on board, they learned that the *Rattler* had earlier picked up three more of their comrades. At 3:00 p.m., the *Mustang* hove into view, enabling Knowles and the Scouts to get back on their own vessel and continue the search for their comrades. The *Rattler* found three additional Scouts at 7:15 that evening, before darkness caused the vessels' crews to anchor for the night.[7]

The *Mustang* and the *Rattler* renewed their search early the next morning. Knowles sent out a search party, which located a wounded

7. Fenlason's report of Knowles's killing of Confederate Col. Stafford in battle cannot be documented. No reference other than Fenlason's account exists, and Col. Stafford has not been identified. The colonel of the 3rd Louisiana Cavalry was Isaac F. Harrison, who survived the war. Arthur W. Bergeron Jr., *Guide to Louisiana Confederate Military Units, 1861-1865* (Baton Rouge: Louisiana State University Press, 1989), pp. 43-44.

Charles Fenlason, who was hiding in the cabin of a former slave couple; they had cared for his wounds and then reported his hiding place to his comrades. When the search party returned with Fenlason, Union officers concluded that further searching was futile. As a final gesture, the *Rattler* "commenced shelling the woods to dislodge the rebels, who were secreted there." Following the shelling, the unarmed *Mustang* retired downriver while the *Rattler* continued its patrol duties.[8]

"Lost by Capture"

The Scouts withdrew without Charles Baker, Lucien Bennett, John W. Carlin, Nathaniel White, Albert Woodward, and John Roberts, all of whom were in Confederate hands. When Knowles filed his Trimonthly Report for December 21-30, for the first time it designated several men in the hands of the enemy and included a column for "Property Lost by Capture," enumerating nine horses, nine Spencer carbines, fourteen revolvers, ten sabers, and nine saddles. After he ended the search for any Scouts still in the area, Knowles tried to secure the release of those who had been captured. Lucien Bennett later recalled: "[O]ur friends sent out a flag of truce and tried to induce our captors to exchange us, offering to release six officers below the rank of Col. who were in their hands, in exchange for us. Our captors refused and started us on the march for prison."[9]

The Confederates took the six captured Scouts across the Mississippi to Briscoe's plantation the night after the firefight. There, Charles Baker recalled, "our boots, coats, gloves, caps, and other good garments, and our blankets, were taken from us. And we were supplied in return, with the tattered garments and ragged boots, of the chivalric gentlemen who robbed us." The Confederates also informed the Scouts that, "if we survived long enough to get to Shreveport, we would be hanged as guerrillas, and consequently blankets would be unnecessary burdens." Their forced march to Shreveport was a difficult one. Approaching the Boeuf

8. *Evergreen City Times*, Mar. 11, 1865, p. 2; Charles Fenlason to Newton Culver, Feb. 25, 1866, Newton Culver Papers, State Historical Society of Wisconsin; Abstract log of the U.S.S. *Rattler*, Lt. James Laning, commanding, June 3 to Dec. 31, 1864; O.R. Navies, I, 26, p. 801. The report of Fenlason's escape is found in the Trimonthly Report of Lt. Knowles, Dec. 20-31, 1864.

9. *Evergreen City Times*, Mar. 11, 1865, p. 2; Trimonthly Report of Lt. Knowles, Dec. 20-31, 1864; Bennett, "Sketch of Military Service."

**Like this group of Confederate prisoners, the six Scouts captured near
St. Joseph were marched across Louisiana to Texas.**
(*Leslie's Illustrated Newspaper*, February 20, 1864)

River near Monroe, they encountered a freezing half-mile-wide overflow
area where icy water reached to their waists. Forced to wade through
the overflow, they waited for a raft to take them across the river. Although they built a fire to dry and warm themselves, Charles Baker and
Lucien Bennett were still wet and cold when they boarded the raft with
two guards and a horse. Halfway across the swollen stream, the agitated
horse tipped the raft, dumping the Scouts and one of the guards into
the freezing water. By the time they reboarded and gained the river's far
shore, Baker reported that "our clothes were frozen on us, and we were
compelled that night to sleep in an old open negro kitchen." The next
day, Bennett and Baker were sick, but they were still forced to march
about fifteen miles to a small military camp. The Scouts and their guards
remained at that camp for four days, confined in a ten-foot-square log
pen in freezing weather without blankets — and with only raw, unginned
cotton to lie on. Despite the brutal conditions, all the Scouts made it to

Shreveport, "always sleeping with no covering but the open sky, the ground for a bed."[10]

Their situation improved little when they got to Shreveport in mid-January. They were penned "in a stockade with about 160 other prisoners and 60 or 70 citizens who refused to do duty in their army." Imprisoned with them were "6 or 8 negro soldiers who were compelled to do all sorts of drudgery by the Rebs." Bennett and Baker and the four other Scouts remained at Shreveport about a month. To ward off the damp and cold, they built a hut "of sods and poles" covered by a roof "thatched with pine boughs." Initially haunted by the threat of being hanged, the Scouts learned that, because Gen. Canby's letter to Gen. Kirby Smith informed the latter that these Scouts were "regularly mustered into the service of the United States as scouts, guides and couriers," they would not be tried and executed as guerrillas.[11]

No longer threatened with execution, the captured Scouts were treated similarly to the two hundred other men held at Shreveport: poorly clothed, underfed, and ill-sheltered. Then they were marched about a hundred miles further west, to Camp Ford prison camp, near Tyler, Texas. Baker's health had improved somewhat by the time they left Shreveport, but Bennett continued to be "troubled with his throat and lungs; coughing & hoarse & with difficulty breathing up to the time [he was] discharged."[12]

Initially a training camp for Texas recruits and draftees, Camp Ford was the chief prison camp of the Confederate Trans-Mississippi Department. The original six-acre, stockade-enclosed camp — with a spring-fed creek for fresh water — was greatly expanded in 1864, when a series of battles increased its prisoner population to nearly 5,000. Using the labor of slaves to split stockade logs, camp administrators enclosed sixteen acres. Expected to create their own shelter, prisoners built primitive huts, which they called *shebangs*, along "streets" arranged around a parade ground and marketplace, giving the camp a remarkably orderly appearance. Although the camp had begun clean and dry, with a steady supply of food and good drinking water, crowding and the Confederacy's declining economy had

10. Affidavit of Charles Baker, sworn in Iowa City, IA, Jan. 1881 (copy in Lucien Bennett pension file No. WC634317).

11. Gen. Canby to Confederate Gen. Edmund Kirby Smith, Apr. 1, 1865 (copy in Newton Culver Papers).

12. Affidavit of Charles Baker, sworn in Iowa City, IA, Jan. 1881 (copy in pension file of Lucien Bennett, No. WC634317).

The captured Scouts were held at Camp Ford Prison Camp near Tyler, Texas, from January 1865 until the end of the war. (*Harper's Weekly*, March 4, 1865)

reduced prisoners' rations and diminished conditions in other ways by the time the six captured Scouts arrived.[13]

More Trouble: The Navy and Cotton

Knowles and the remaining Scouts were undeterred by the reversal at St. Joseph. They were back in the same area, opposite Grand Gulf, Missis-

13. Camp Ford returned to agriculture after the war, and only structural rubble and faintly visible earth features remained of it at the turn of the twentieth century. Preservation began during the 1936 Texas Centennial with the establishment of a nine-acre roadside park at the site. In 1994 the Smith County Historical Society received a Federal Intermodal Surface Transportation Efficiency Act grant for acquisition and development of the site. Subsequent archaeological work by the Center for Environmental Archaeology at Texas A&M University in 1997 and 1998 uncovered the west, south, and east walls, the trench for the original north and east walls, and over sixteen structures. For a full report, see Alston V. Thoms, ed., *Uncovering Camp Ford* (College Station, TX: Center for Ecological Archaeology, Texas A&M University, 2000); Bennett, "Sketch of Military Service" p. 18; Leon Mitchell Jr., "Camp Ford Confederate Military Prison," *The Southwest Historical Quarterly* 66 (July 1962): 1-16.

sippi, five days later, completing their reconnaissance to assess reports of growing Confederate strength. They learned that there were about 200 Confederates inland from Grand Gulf, and another 450 further upriver. They had also received a report of an additional 200 men stationed near Oakland College, inland near Rodney, who were guarding 2,500 Enfield rifles and 8,000 other weapons. Knowles surmised that these rifles were for new recruits gathered by General Sterling Price for his Missouri campaign.[14] Knowles also reported that Frank Powers's regiment remained near Kingston, and another regiment was near the Black River, west of the Mississippi. Knowles concluded his report with the judgment that, considering the large number of enemy troops in the area, he did not deem it advisable to take his unit inland any distance from the Mississippi.[15]

The Scouts returned to Natchez shortly after the first of January, where they remained about a week. Then, most likely acting on instructions from Gen. Canby's headquarters, they returned to the river and headed north to the region above Vicksburg where they had been successful in November. Gen. Canby had been investigating the area himself when the guerrilla sniper had wounded him a month earlier, and he remained concerned about its volatility.

Knowles led the Scouts to Vicksburg and then seventy miles further, to Skipwith's Landing, Mississippi, where they arrived during the forenoon of January 9. Soon after pulling into Skipwith's Landing, they became embroiled in a controversy that, in Knowles's words, was "the point toward which the command had been tending since I took command." The issue he referred to centered on the question of licensed trade along the Mississippi. Gen. Canby authorized the Special Scouts to monitor this trade — and to interrupt any illegal activities. The Scouts, who often invoked their special authority granted by Gen. Canby, were particularly resented by speculators, agents for Northern investors, and those members of the military who were motivated by a quest for profit. For these trade advocates, Earl's Scouts represented a sore that refused to heal. On at least one occasion, Earl's group had been investigated by the adjutant general's of-

14. Knowles's surmise was faulty. When Gen. Price returned from Missouri, he may have needed additional weapons, but not because of new recruits. Instead of adding men, he had lost a portion of his army. Robert L. Kerby, *Kirby Smith's Confederacy: The Trans-Mississippi South, 1863-1865* (New York: Columbia University Press, 1972), pp. 356-61.

15. Bergeron, *Guide to Louisiana Confederate Military Units, 1861-1865*, pp. 46-48, 54-55, 64.

fice after they seized six hundred bales of alleged C.S.A. cotton near Fort Adams, Louisiana. Although its owners argued that the cotton had been purchased with foreign currency, Canby believed his Scouts' assertions and ordered the cotton transferred to New Orleans. Despite efforts to have the cotton released, the confiscation was sustained. It was Warren Knowles's unfortunate fate to confront the anger of those who wished to promote trade, and he defended his position staunchly, eventually winning vindication for the Scouts' activities.[16]

The complex drama began unfolding shortly after the Scouts docked at Skipwith's Landing. Knowles was informed by Lieutenant Commander Thomas Bacon, of the gunboat *Louisville*, that the small stern-wheeled packet *Venango* had been attacked and burned by Confederates of the Louisiana 6th Cavalry, led by Lieutenant Colonel William Denson. Bacon asked Knowles to take the Scouts upstream seven miles to Pilcher's Point, Louisiana, where the attack had occurred, and to investigate the matter. Knowles agreed and set out at once.[17]

Just before the Scouts reached their destination, the *Mustang* picked up four blacks, two men and two women, who had been part of the *Venango*'s crew. At Pilcher's Point, the Scouts found the burned hulk of the *Venango* and more people milling around, unsure of what to do next. These crew members and laborers gave Knowles additional information about the raid and the guerrillas, telling him that they had only recently left with a warning that they would return. Knowles decided to order the Scouts to disembark and set out in pursuit, telling the *Venango*'s party to board the *Mustang* and make themselves as comfortable as they could until the Scouts returned.

Also at the landing were twenty-five bales of cotton, property of a

16. Bennett, "Sketch of Military Service," p. 15; Lt. Knowles to Gen. Canby's Headquarters, Jan. 23, 1865; Trimonthly Report of Lt. Knowles, Jan. 20-31, 1865; Lt. Col. C. T. Christensen to District Attorney, New Orleans, July 7, 1864; Lt. Col. Christensen to Gen. Mason Brayman, July 30, 1864, *Letters Sent, May 1864–June 1865*; papers of the Military Division of West Mississippi, National Archives, vol. 60, pp. 144, 155; Gen. Dana to Gen. Canby, Aug. 23, 1864; Lt. Col. John M. Wilson to Gen. Canby, July 21, Sept. 30, 1864; *List of Letters Received*, Department of the Gulf, Military Division of West Mississippi, National Archives, vol. 62, p. 232, vol. 63, pp. 296, 563.

17. The *Venango* had an interesting past. Built in Pennsylvania in 1858, she originally carried steam engines and boilers to that state's oil fields, returning with barrels of oil. Working the Ohio in 1862, she sank near the Cumberland River, but was raised and sold to Cpt. Victor Wilson of Vicksburg in 1864. He was her owner when she burned and sank at Pilcher's Point on December 31, 1864. Way, *Way's Packet Directory, 1848-1994*, pp. 466-67.

trader named Owens; the cotton was originally on board the *Venango*, but it was ordered unloaded by Lt. Col. Denson before the vessel was burned. Knowles was in a quandary about what to do with the cotton: he could return it to Owens, or he could seize it as property of the Confederate government and turn it over to the provost marshal's office. In any case, he did not want to leave it unguarded at the landing; he finally decided to place it onboard the *Mustang* and take it downriver.

As soon as he had loaded the cotton and arranged for the welfare of the *Venango*'s crew and workers, Knowles set out in pursuit of the Confederates. The Scouts rode about four miles inland when they "got information that all the property had been taken across Bayou Macon." Knowles was about to turn his men around and return when his advance patrol was fired on from a house owned by Benjamin Gaza. Knowles ordered the Scouts to charge "at once . . . but was too late as the Rebels had succeeded in making their escape not without some loss for one was wounded and left in our hands, and another was shot through the arm," but escaped.[18]

In his report of the incident, Knowles said that former slaves living nearby told him that other guerrillas remained hidden in the house. He dismounted and with four of his men went inside for a more careful search. After they "examined every room and fail[ed] to find anyone," they returned to the *Mustang*. The wounded Confederates were "in too bad a condition to be removed and [were] consequently left [behind]." Later, when questioned about the raid, Knowles maintained that the only item of value that he found in the house was a saddlebag containing important papers, which he took back to the boat.[19]

Back onboard the *Mustang*, Knowles decided that there was nothing more to be done at Pilcher's Point, so the Scouts returned downstream to Skipwith's Landing, where they unloaded the crew and passengers of the *Venango* and the cotton. As soon as the *Mustang* was clear of her cargo, Knowles ordered her to head back north up the Mississippi. The trip was quiet until they reached Gaines Landing, about eighty miles above Skipwith's Landing, on January 11. Nearing the landing, they noticed a Union gunboat, the *Romeo*, and two cotton traders' vessels, which were being guarded by three mounted riders on the shore, "with guns lying across

18. Lt. Knowles to Lt. Col. James Wilson, Jan. 23, 1865 (copy included in Trimonthly Reports of Lt. Knowles).

19. Affidavit taken from Samuel R. Porter, Jan. 20, 1865 (copy included in Trimonthly Reports of Lt. Knowles).

their saddles." When suspicious situations of this nature occurred, Lt. Knowles shared Isaac Earl's belief in acting quickly and making inquiries later. He "at once ran [the *Mustang*] in to land hoping to capture one or more of them, but taking fright they fled." Knowles landed his men and horses, secured the two vessels, and set out in pursuit of the fleeing guards. After two or three miles of pursuit with no success, Knowles ordered his men back to the river.

Back at the river, matters were in an uproar. An angry Thomas Baldwin, acting master of the gunboat, sent word for Knowles to come aboard at once. Knowles complied with the request and was "met very cooly and in a very rough manner." Baldwin demanded an explanation for the Scouts' "landing without his permission and seizing horses and mules belonging to citizens." Knowles gave the Scouts' standard response that his authority came directly from Gen. Canby, and Baldwin "modified his tone somewhat" — but did not change his attitude. Knowles went on to explain that "it had always been my practice whenever I landed to seize and hold all men, mules and horses near the landing to prevent couriers being sent by bypaths to give information [and] that when I returned all were set at liberty." After further conversation, Knowles returned to the *Mustang*, thinking the situation had been resolved.

More controversy awaited Knowles back at the *Mustang*, where he was greeted by a group of irate citizens claiming that the Scouts had robbed them of substantial sums of money. Upon hearing the severity of the charges, Knowles at once took the citizens on board and told them to identify the persons who had robbed them, promising to return their money as soon as they identified the robbers. Face to face with the Scouts, their accusers could not pick out a single man as a thief. Knowles then asked the civilians to return ashore so that he might talk to the members of his command. Once he was alone with his men, Knowles made his position very clear. "I demanded everything that had been taken for they well knew such work was contrary to my orders and that I would not command them longer if they had become robbers." One man, James Mulloy, "gave me a roll of money which he said he took to show me the way business was done." The money, which was still in the same envelope in which it had left New Orleans, was immediately returned to the man who claimed it.

The Scouts denied having taken anything else, or knowing of any other thefts. But if Knowles thought he had calmed the aroused citizens, he was wrong. He had no sooner given the order for "the boat to move out from land with the intention of anchoring for the night" than Baldwin again ordered him to come aboard the *Romeo*. Knowles went because, he said, he wished "to show proper courtesy to the Navy though I did not like the manner in which the order was delivered."[20]

The second conversation between the two men was more strained than the first. Baldwin, who "was very rough in his language," complained "that he had been two months restoring the confidence earlier destroyed by Lt. Earl and, just as he got confidence restored and a little trade established, I came in and destroyed the work of months." Knowles concluded his description of the incident with the comment that "seeing that he [Baldwin] was very much excited I made no answer." Knowles was then ordered back to the *Mustang* under arrest, to which he "submitted merely for the purpose of settling a question of authority." Knowles was ordered to anchor for the night, and the next morning, January 12, the *Mustang* was escorted to Skipwith's Landing, where Baldwin permitted nobody to go ashore.[21]

From Skipwith's Landing, the *Romeo* convoyed the *Mustang* to Vicksburg and remained anchored at its side while Baldwin went ashore to meet with General Cadwallader C. Washburn, who was the commander of Union troops in the area. A short time later, "two boats filled with soldiers," under Lieutenant Colonel John H. Howe of the 124th Illinois, tied up to the *Mustang* and came onboard. Howe ordered everyone on the boat, including the black crew, to form ranks on the upper deck; then he took them ashore and confined them in the Vicksburg courthouse, where they were searched, and all their money and valuables were taken from them. The searchers found only personal possessions. Miller Graham, the oldest Scout, had the most money, and he could account for every cent. He had saved the $230 discharge pay he received when he left the 4th Wisconsin, along with nearly every dollar he was paid after he joined the Scouts. Altogether he had accumulated $521.[22]

While Howe's men searched the Scouts, Gen. Washburn sent another detail to the *Mustang* to go through their possessions, again searching for stolen money, watches, and jewelry. The only money they found belonged to Lt. Knowles. His trunk contained $850, placed at his disposal for oper-

20. Lt. Knowles to Lt. Col. James Wilson, Jan. 23, 1865 (copy included in Trimonthly Reports of Lt. Knowles).

21. Lt. Knowles to Lt. Col. James Wilson, Jan. 23, 1865; Lt. Knowles to Lt. Col. Christensen, Jan. 14, 1865; Acting Master Thomas Baldwin to Cpt. G. C. Dunwell, U.S. Steamer *Mustang*, Jan. 12, 1864 (copies included in Trimonthly Reports of Lt. Knowles).

22. Affidavit taken from Miller Graham, Jan. 20, 1865; Lt. Knowles to Lt. Col. James Wilson, Jan. 23, 1865.

Major General Cadwallader C. Washburn
(Library of Congress)

ating expenses. Like Lt. Earl, he kept an account of this money and filed a report at the end of each month. In addition to taking the money, Lt. Col. Howe seized Knowles's trunk and its contents, including "an old gold watch, three pairs stockings, three white silk handkerchiefs, two fine linen handkerchiefs, two linen shirts, one pair new gauntlet gloves, one pair field glasses, and two photographs, one of my sister and one of a little child." These he brought in when he later reported his version of the entire incident to Lt. Col. James Wilson, the assistant inspector general in New Orleans. Knowles pointedly noted that he had been "unable to retain my trunk," and made it clear in his report that he expected it returned.[23]

Following the search, Gen. Washburn ordered the Scouts confined in Vicksburg's Union Prison No. 1, granted Knowles a "parole of honor," and confined him to the city limits, while the general continued to review

23. Lt. Knowles to Lt. Col. Christensen, Jan. 14, 1865 (copy included in Trimonthly Reports of Lt. Knowles).

While Gen. Washburn interrogated Lt. Knowles, the Scouts were held in the former Warren County Jail, which served as a Union prison during the war.
(http://oldcourthouse.org/photos/civil-war-tour/)

reports of the incident. On January 13, at 9:00 a.m., Knowles was ushered into the general's office. Washburn, an ardent supporter of trade along the Mississippi and a prewar politician and businessman, presented complaining affidavits against the Scouts, and he informed Knowles that his men were concealing a large amount of stolen money and other valuables. Unless these items were returned, Washburn threatened, he would send the entire command to the headquarters of the Department of the Mississippi in Memphis for prosecution. If, on the other hand, they agreed to return the stolen items, Washburn promised Knowles that they would be sent to New Orleans for the final disposition of their case. Although Knowles knew that he and his men would receive a much more sympathetic hearing from Gen. Canby in New Orleans than from Gen. Dana in Memphis, he refused Washburn's proposition. It would mean admitting to charges that he asserted were baseless. When he returned to his men and told them of the situation, "everyone said if they were to go to Memphis go they must for they did not know where anything was concealed."[24]

24. After the war, Washburn served one term as the governor of Wisconsin, but later he really made his mark in flour milling, building two large mills in Minneapolis and ulti-

Sometime between January 14 and January 16, Gen. Washburn had a change of heart. Although the Scouts had told him nothing, he concluded that they should be sent to New Orleans. It is likely that a letter Knowles sent to Gen. Canby's headquarters had something to do with that decision. In the letter Knowles complained that he had been "placed under arrest while in performance of his duties at Gaines Landing, Arkansas"; he also recounted how his men had been searched and all their money and valuables had been seized. Knowles ended the letter with a request that "myself and command be ordered to report to you as soon as possible and that all money or valuables of any kind taken from us be sent to your Headquarters, also that *all* papers whether original or copies be forwarded at the same time." No record of such an order emanating from Gen. Canby's headquarters can be found, but it would seem that Knowles's letter contributed to Washburn's decision.[25]

The Scouts were sent to New Orleans under guard on January 16, accompanied by Gen. Washburn's letter, which indicated his belief in their guilt. "They are proven to have robbed different parties of four or five thousand dollars in one day with jewelry, watches, and other property to a large amount," he wrote. "As they are acting under Gen. Canby's orders, I send them down for his action, and will not chastise them as I think their conduct merits. I had them all searched on coming here, but as they had ample time, they had concealed most of their plunder." Washburn went on to offer additional thoughts regarding the value of the Scouts to the Union cause. As he saw it, they were "the terror of both friend and foe, and plunder without discrimination or remorse whoever has the misfortune to fall into their way." The differing views regarding trade along the river

---

mately participating in the founding of the giant General Mills company. Lt. Knowles to Lt. Col. James Wilson, Jan. 23, 1865 (copy included in Trimonthly Reports of Lt. Knowles). Knowles's fears regarding Gen. Dana and his staff were not unfounded. In 1865 a special commission reported that, while he was the commander at Vicksburg, Dana's staff was involved in bribery and extortion. The commission reported that orders were issued to close stores; they were then reopened "for a consideration paid to persons connected with public offices; and the testimony leaves little doubt that all the officers in charge of the Department were cognizant of, or connected with these nefarious transactions." The commission also found that seized cotton had been released after a large bribe. William Nichols testified that he had paid $1,400 to release thirty bales held at Milliken's Bend. Maj. Gen. William J. Smith and Jason T. Brady, *Report of Special Commission, 1865* (records of the Adjutant General's Office, Record Group 94, National Archives Building, pp. 173-74).

25. Lt. Knowles to Lt. Col. Christensen, Jan. 15, 1865 (copy included in Trimonthly Reports of Lt. Knowles).

revealed themselves in Washburn's letter. To his mind, there were many Union friends among the traders; as Canby saw it, and as he had instructed the Scouts, all trade was detrimental to the war effort.

Arriving in New Orleans at 10:00 a.m. on January 18, the Scouts were taken to Parish Prison for confinement, while Lt. Knowles remained on the *Mustang* "with the privilege of going into the city for meals on 'Parole of Honor' until about 5 p.m. same day when I was allowed the city limits." He was, however, expected to report to the provost marshal every morning.[26]

While Knowles and the Scouts waited, Gen. Canby's headquarters staff began reviewing affidavits from the claimants and gathering statements from the Scouts. Though the claimants' affidavits were in close accord over the basic incidents at Skipwith's Landing and Pilcher's Point, they varied in two significant respects. The first was quite simple: the claimants accused the Scouts of stealing money totaling almost $5,000; the second concerned the question of the authority of the Scouts to disrupt trade and to treat anyone engaging in trade along the river as an enemy of the U.S. government.[27]

Affidavits from two persons made financial claims against the Scouts for their actions, not only at Gaines Landing but also earlier at Pilcher's Point and at the plantation of Benjamin Gaza. William G. Munson, a Wisconsin citizen who was a passenger onboard the steamer *Venango,* filed one of the affidavits. He did not state his occupation or purpose for being in the South, although the sizable amount of money he was carrying seems to indicate that he planned to engage in the cotton trade. He recounted the attack on the *Venango* and his imprisonment, along with others at the house of Benjamin Gaza, by the guerrillas. For reasons he did not explain, the guerrillas did not take the $3,400 he carried with him, of which he gave $2,750 to Gaza to hold for him, only to have it stolen by Lt. Knowles and the Scouts when they raided the plantation. He admitted that he was not at Gaza's home when Knowles arrived, but had gone on about a mile further to the home of Mr. Owens, the man who owned the cotton that Knowles confiscated.

Munson said that he was at Owens's home when he received notice

26. Lt. Knowles to Lt. Col. Christensen, Jan. 14, 1865 (copy included in Trimonthly Reports of Lt. Knowles).

27. Lt. Knowles to Lt. Col. James Wilson, Jan. 23, 1865 (copy included in Trimonthly Reports of Lt. Knowles). Affidavits taken from members of the Scouts, Jan. 20, 1865, and from William G. Munson and Jacob C. Forbes, Jan. 13, 1865 (copies included in Trimonthly Reports of Lt. Knowles).

that the Scouts had raided Gaza's house without provocation and had plundered it. Claiming that a large amount of Gaza's personal possessions and the carpetbag of a female passenger were taken, along with his money, Munson swore that all the statements he made were true and that any statements made by Benjamin Gaza must also be true, for he knew the man and was convinced of his integrity and veracity.[28]

Tennessean Jacob Forbes, clerk of the steamer *Mattie Cook*, claimed that he saw the Scouts seize five or six mules and horses, and rob a Mr. Stanley "of a sum of money in gold . . . and also some paper money . . . and a larger sum of gold in twenty dollar pieces." He could not state the exact amount, though "Mr. Stanley told me there was sixteen hundred dollars in gold." Forbes also claimed to have seen Stanley report the robbery to Knowles, who "took no measures to refund the money . . . or any other articles except Stanley's horse." Forbes went on to say that he "also saw this party rob and plunder another citizen, Mr. Shorter of money, some in gold and some paper money. Also of his saddle bags and his mule." The robbery of Shorter was likewise "reported to Lt. Knowles in command of the party, but he paid no attention to the complaint made to him." As to Knowles's statement that he had seen Confederate soldiers on the river bank, Forbes stated that he had been at Gaines Landing for a week and had seen no soldiers during that time.[29]

When news of the Scouts' arrest reached the editor of the *Vicksburg Herald*, he published a brief report confirming Washburn's belief that they were guilty of "sundry depredations not at all in accordance with the duties of United States soldiers," and would be sent to jail in New Orleans. The Scouts' account of events differed sharply from that of the *Herald*'s editor and the affidavits of Munson and Forbes. All twenty-three men questioned swore that they had taken no money or property, and knew of no one who had. The complaints stated in William Munson's affidavit focused on two of the Scouts in particular: James Mulloy was accused of taking the money from Gaza, and Samuel R. Porter admitted that he had taken a carpetbag from Gaza's house. He took the bag, he said, because he believed it belonged to the captain of the *Venango*. He denied that it was the possession of one of the women passengers, stating that he had found it wrapped in a

28. Affidavit made by William G. Munson at Skipwith Landing, Jan. 11, 1865 (copy included in Trimonthly Reports of Lt. Knowles).

29. Affidavit by Jacob Forbes, Vicksburg, Mississippi, Jan. 13, 1865 (copy included in Trimonthly Reports of Lt. Knowles).

bed quilt; he said that he had taken it to Lt. Knowles because it contained a large quantity of papers that he thought might be of some importance.[30]

The complaint regarding the stolen money was not as easily explained as the carpetbag affair. But James Mulloy presented a forceful defense. He readily admitted that he was the one who arrested Benjamin Gaza, and he spoke openly of his distrust for the man. He remembered Gaza from a previous encounter. Lt. Earl had arrested him as a Rebel recruiting agent, though he had later been released by higher-ranking officers. Mulloy was equally vehement in his denial that he was a thief, proclaiming that he "never took 10 cents from Gaza or any other citizen." He said that when he arrested Gaza, he inquired whether or not he had taken the oath of allegiance. He said that Gaza replied, "No and [don't] intend to." In Mulloy's eyes, Gaza deserved to be arrested and sent to jail. But he insisted that, despite his feelings, he had not robbed him or anyone else. Any member of the Scouts who did such a thing would be foolish, he said, for Lt. Knowles "gave orders half a dozen times against pillaging, threatening discharge with loss of pay, to anyone who should be guilty of it."[31]

The Munson and Forbes affidavits were the primary evidence against the Scouts. The only other evidence sent to New Orleans was a letter from Commander George Bacon of the gunboat *Louisville*, who seemed more concerned with branding Knowles and the Scouts the worst kind of scoundrels than with providing concrete evidence of their guilt. He accused them of "robbing citizens who had brought their cotton down to the bank for the purpose of shipment [probably referring to Mr. Owens] and who were loyal men having taken the oath of allegiance." Knowles's men were "no better than a gang of scoundrels & robbers who have made use of the Federal uniform to perpetrate the most flagrant outrages upon defenseless and loyal citizens." Bacon's letter again raised the question of whether or not trade should be permitted, and on what basis. He believed it was important and should be permitted, at least with "loyal men" who had taken the oath of allegiance. Both this and the question of whether or not robberies had been committed would be resolved by Gen. Canby.[32]

30. "Overhauled," *Vicksburg Herald*, reprinted in *New Orleans Times*, Jan. 22, 1865: www.Genealogybank.com (accessed Sept. 19, 2013); affidavit by Samuel R. Porter, Jan. 20, 1865 (copy included in Trimonthly Reports of Lt. Knowles).

31. Affidavit by James Mulloy, Jan. 20, 1865 (copy included in Trimonthly Reports of Lt. Knowles).

32. Lt. Com. George Bacon to Maj. Gen. C. C. Washburn, Jan. 12, 1865 (copy included in Trimonthly Reports of Lt. Knowles).

The Scouts were never brought to trial. The final decision regarding their future was made in Gen. Canby's headquarters. The record of their imprisonment is found in the list of prisoners received by the provost marshal general for the Military Division of the West Mississippi. That list indicates that the Scouts were officially placed under arrest on January 12, 1865, and confined in the military prison at 54 Barronne Street in New Orleans on January 18. The provost marshal general's list further states that they were officially charged with "robbing loyal citizens." The next category on the prisoner list, titled "Remarks," is especially instructive. With one exception, it reads simply: "Released by order of Major General Canby Jan. 25th, '65."[33]

The only Scout not released was James Mulloy. William Munson had specifically accused Mulloy of robbing loyal citizens, and Mulloy had admitted taking money, though he argued it was to be turned over to Lt. Knowles. Gen. Canby felt that the evidence was too strong to dismiss the case, and Mulloy was held for trial. But a general court martial in New Orleans acquitted him on April 19, 1865. Although he was exonerated, Mulloy did not rejoin his old companions in the Scouts. Instead, he was sent to serve under General Andrew Jackson Smith, commander of the XVI Corps, for the remainder of his enlistment.[34]

The list of prisoners provides other interesting information. Not only does it indicate that Gen. Canby intervened on the Scouts' behalf; it also indicates his full support of their activities and Lt. Knowles's judgment. On the same page, several lines lower, an entry indicates the arrest of Benjamin F. Gaza, one of the Scouts' most persistent accusers and the owner of the home where many of their troubles began, on January 25, 1865. The real surprise comes in the column under the heading "By Whom Arrested": Gen. Canby himself is listed as the arresting officer, charging Gaza with "rebel services," including "engaged in recruiting" and "for the act as a witness against Mulloy." In other words, Canby arrested Gaza for both aiding the enemy and perjury. However, Canby's intervention did not result in a trial and conviction of Gaza. According to the ledger's "remarks" column, Gaza was released on bond on February 22, and released

33. *List of Prisoners Received, 1864-65*, Records of U.S. Army Continental Commands, Department of the Gulf, Record Group 393, National Archives Building. vol. 410, pp. 6-7.

34. Information about Mulloy is found in the Trimonthly Report of Lt. Knowles, Apr. 10-20, 1865, and the provost marshal general's office to Lt. Knowles, Mar. 20, 1865 (*Letters Sent, July 1864–June 1865*, Records of the U.S. Army Continental Commands, Record Group 393, National Archives Building, p. 334).

from bond and custody on March 25. Yet, despite Gaza's release, Canby had accomplished his purpose. He affirmed his support for the Scouts and his opposition to illegal cotton dealers to everyone concerned. He stood squarely behind the group he had organized to destroy the "leeches" that he felt were "draining the lifeblood" from his army. Although the Scouts' actions may have disturbed many along the Mississippi, Canby overrode the objections of subordinates and freed the Scouts. They were too valuable to him to be languishing in a military prison.[35]

Back in Action: Mobile, 1865

The Scouts returned to Natchez shortly after Gen. Canby released them. But no sooner had they put their headquarters back in order than they received orders to return to New Orleans without delay. Knowles immediately turned over all surplus property in his possession and prepared his men to move out. They left Natchez in the gathering darkness of February 12, bound for New Orleans. Stalled by a sudden storm the next day, they made up for the delay by traveling all night. Exhausted and unsettled, the Scouts arrived at their destination early on the morning of February 14. While Lt. Knowles reported to Gen. Canby, the rest of the Scouts moved into temporary quarters in a cotton press building on Calliope Street. Soon Knowles was back with news that a major offensive was planned against Mobile, and Canby wanted the Scouts to serve as guides and couriers.[36]

By early 1865, Mobile was one of the few large Southern cities that was still in Confederate hands. Situated near the head of Mobile Bay, it stood as a forlorn symbol of the South's continued resistance. Unable to reach the blockaded waters of the Gulf of Mexico a few short miles away, Mobile had to rely solely on overland routes to maintain contact with the rest of the Confederacy. The city was defended on the east by Spanish Fort, which commanded the mouth of the Appalachee River, and by Fort Blakely, at the head of the bay. Ten thousand men, with 300 heavy guns, defended the western perimeter of the city.

General Canby planned to attack Mobile from its weak side, the east,

35. *List of Prisoners Received, 1864-65*, Records of U.S. Army Continental Commands, Department of the Gulf, Record Group 393, National Archives Building, vol. 410, pp. 6-7.
36. Trimonthly Report of Lt. Knowles, Feb. 10-20, 1865.

with two columns. He proposed to lead one column himself up from Dauphine Island at the mouth of the bay, and to send another from Pensacola under Major General Frederick Steele. He had a combined force of 45,000 men to accomplish his purpose. Gen. Grant had pushed Canby to capture the Rebel city, and he could not afford a setback. Gen. Nathaniel Banks had lost his command by blundering offensive operations; Canby would not make the same mistake.[37]

While Canby was completing his preparations, the Scouts waited in their Calliope Street quarters through the month of February and into March. Finally, on March 2, Lt. Knowles received orders to report to General Robert S. Granger at Fort Gaines on Dauphine Island. They were to begin their new duties on March 6: they were assigned to the 1st Brigade of the 2nd Division of the 13th Army Corps, commanded by Colonel Henry Bertram at Navy Cove, above Fort Morgan, at the head of Mobile Bay.[38]

When Gen. Canby opened his offensive against Mobile on March 17, the Scouts were with Col. Bertram, mainly "examining the roads in advance of his Brigade and reporting to him their condition." At times, Knowles divided up his command, sending smaller groups of Scouts on different details. Their biggest problem, aside from general fatigue, was feeding their animals. The loose sandy soil of the area around Navy Cove made even short marches an endurance test for horses. The land was so unproductive that Lt. Knowles found that, whenever he went any distance from camp, it was necessary to carry forage for the horses. He did not have the means to carry the necessary feed along with them, and Col. Bertram's supply train was too far in the rear to provide a consistent supply. "Consequently," Knowles reported, "my horses have been much of the time without forage except the limited supply that could be obtained along the route; and [they] are in need of food and rest." The Scouts did not engage in combat. On several occasions they spotted Confederate scouts ahead of them, but drove them off with a few long-range shots.[39]

The Scouts remained with Col. Bertram until March 22, when they were ordered to report to Gen. Canby's headquarters, where they remained for the rest of the campaign. They were with Canby when his

37. Robert V. Johnson and Clarence C. Buel, eds., *Battles and Leaders of the Civil War*, 4 vols. (1887-88; facsimile reprint, New York: Thomas Yoseloff, 1956), vol. 4, p. 411; Max L. Heyman Jr., *Prudent Soldier: A Biography of Major General E. R. S. Canby* (Glendale, CA: Arthur H. Clark, 1959), pp. 227-29.

38. Trimonthly Report of Lt. Knowles, Mar. 1-10, 1865.

39. Trimonthly report of Lt. Knowles, March 1-10, March 10-20, 1865.

Lt. Knowles and the Scouts accompanied General Canby's forces to Mobile Bay in late March 1865, where they were assigned to pursue retreating Confederates and search for contraband cotton. (*Harper's Weekly*, April 29, 1865)

forces besieged Spanish Fort on March 26. After the fort fell, Knowles's men remained in camp for a few days, "obtaining a portion of the rest for [our] horses, made necessary by continued service and the bad roads over which they have been obliged to pass."[40] They stayed in camp during the first days of April, carrying Canby's dispatches, until Confederate General Dabney H. Maury and his remaining 4,500 men retreated from Mobile on the night of April 11. The city fell into Union hands the following day. After the city was taken, the Scouts remained with Gen. Canby, going out on several short expeditions.[41]

After the fall of Mobile, a succession of events brought the war in the west to a close. Gen. Robert E. Lee had surrendered his army on April 9, and Gen. Joseph E. Johnston followed suit on April 26. The remaining Confederate forces east of the Mississippi were surrendered by Gen. Richard Taylor on May 4, after he realized that further resistance would be futile and wasteful. Gen. Edmund Kirby Smith and the remnants of

40. Trimonthly report of Lt. Knowles, March 20-30, 1865.
41. Trimonthly report of Lt. Knowles, April 1-20, 1865.

the Confederate forces west of the river finally surrendered on May 26, officially bringing the war to a close.

While the Confederates played their final hand, Knowles and his men remained in Mobile. They engaged in one last scouting expedition on April 24: eleven men headed up the Alabama River, following the route taken by the retreating Confederates a few days earlier. Gen. Canby wanted them to investigate a report that Gen. Maury's forces had left a large number of horses on several islands in the river, and if that was true, to corral them and deliver them to the Union quartermaster. Knowles and his men did not find any horses, but they discovered that several islands contained caches of cotton that had been moved from Mobile before it fell into Union hands. Convinced that the caches belonged to active Confederates, Knowles relayed news of the discovery to Canby, suggesting that troops be sent out to seize the cotton as contraband. Lt. Knowles filed the last of his Trimonthly Reports from Mobile on May 10, 1865, reporting that the entire area seemed quiet, with little evidence of any kind of Confederate guerrilla activity.[42]

Mustered Out

Soon after that May 10 report, Knowles and his Scouts were called back to New Orleans. Waiting for them were their comrades, the fellow Scouts who had been captured at St. Joseph. These men had been released from Camp Ford on May 16, issued rations for six days, and "ordered to prepare to march the next morning." They started out on the morning of May 17, guarded by a cavalry regiment. Lucien Bennett later recalled in his memoir that they were about fifteen miles from Shreveport by May 22: "Early the next morning we heard a commotion in camp. On arising, we discovered that the teamsters who were driving the mules that were hauling our sick were taking the mules and deserting us." The remainder of the entourage continued on toward Shreveport "and found before we reached there that the guard had likewise deserted . . . [leaving] no one except the officer who had command of the guards."

Approaching Shreveport, they encountered "a large army of rebs camped on both sides of the road. They met us at the lines of their camp and furnished us with coffee readymade, sugar, hard tack, ham and many

42. Trimonthly Report of Lt. Knowles, Apr. 20-30, May 1-10, 1865.

things that we had not seen since our capture. We were directed to the neighborhood of the old stockade where we were formerly confined and here they furnished us rations for four days and wood to cook them with." The next morning, the prisoners boarded three steamboats to take them to the mouth of the Red River, where they were exchanged for Confederate prisoners headed up river. That encounter left Bennett with a vivid memory: "Never did the old flag receive heartier cheers than went up from our men," he wrote, "and never did it look so dear to me."

Once exchanged, the prisoners headed down the Mississippi to New Orleans, which they reached on May 27, "and there met the scouts who had just arrived to be disbanded." Together again, the Scouts spent several days enjoying New Orleans and catching up on events since the capture of their six comrades. Following the brief reunion and one last bit of paperwork, Bennett happily reported that the Scouts were "discharged on June 8, 1865 after a service of 4 years and 11 days." Gen. Canby had given the Scouts a choice: they could be discharged, or they could return to their regiment, the 4th Wisconsin, which was on its way to the Mexican border to keep an eye on Confederates, led by Gen. Kirby Smith, who were fleeing south rather than surrendering. To no one's surprise, they chose the discharge, and on June 8, 1865, Earl's Special Scouts were officially mustered out of the United States Army.[43] They had served well, their last year under exceedingly dangerous circumstances, all of which would contribute to a lifetime of retelling.

43. Bennett, "Sketch of Military Service," pp. 18-19.

CHAPTER TEN

The Scouts' Contributions

I N TERMS OF GOODS AND PRISONERS CAPTURED, THE SCOUTS'
achievements are readily measurable. The intelligence gathered by undercover agents, the intimidation of illegal traders and smugglers, and
the creation of a sense of vulnerability among guerrillas and partisans are
more difficult to quantify, but no less significant. In all of these areas they
owed a large portion of their success to three men: Edward Richard Sprigg
Canby, Isaac Newton Earl, and Warren Philby Knowles.

Canby, Earl, and Knowles

Although they shared a commitment to the Union cause, Canby, Earl,
and Knowles were dissimilar in many ways. Canby's image was that of a
stiff — some would say severe — career military man who was a stickler
for protocol. Yet, under that exterior was a leader who showed remarkable operational flexibility. One historian described him as "lacking the
social amenities" of his predecessor, Nathaniel Banks, and quoted U.S.
Treasury agent George Denison of New Orleans, who described him as
a man who worked "quietly and without ostentation . . . very modest
and unassuming." He could be moralistic: he was personally anguished
by wrongdoing, such as the profiteering he observed along the lower
Mississippi River. Perhaps he is best viewed as a professional soldier,
trained at West Point, who had an ability, to use a current phrase, to
think outside the box. On occasion he was even approachable by a mere

lieutenant and willing to sign a personal recommendation for an enlisted soldier.[1]

Isaac Earl, the farmboy volunteer from Wisconsin, was casual about military protocol and unschooled in social and military formalities. As his friend Newton Culver put it, Earl and his brothers "grew up unendowed with the knowledge derived from books but . . . grounded in that of woodcraft." It was knowledge he used regularly when out on scouting ventures, where he was most comfortable. Two photographs taken while he was leader of the Scouts show a young and handsome man, his chin thrust forward in a posture exuding self-confidence. As leader of his corps of Scouts, his usual approach was to charge straight ahead even when odds were not in his favor. More than once he brought his men home safely by leading them straight toward a large foe. Even when the tactic did not succeed, as when he was captured near Clinton, Mississippi, his irrepressible attitude produced escape attempts that ultimately brought him back to his comrades. In other words, he was fearless. Fellow 4th Wisconsin soldier L. C. Bartlett said of him: "He courts danger for the sport of the thing, and he is eminently successful, that is the beauty of the thing. . . ."[2] Earl's behavior and his personality — and even his pose before a camera — suggest a courageous soldier and a loyal companion, one whose impulsiveness might get himself and those around him in trouble, but one whose courage and coolness under pressure could get them out of it as well. He and Gen. Canby, despite their dissimilarities, came together in their understanding of their theater of operations, and in their tactical approach to their mission, with the senior man enabling his subordinate to carry out his unorthodox mission effectively.

Warren Knowles fell somewhere between Canby and Earl in temperament. He was more businesslike and reserved than Earl was, but he shared his predecessor's fervor for prosecuting the war, and Earl's dislike for those whose quest for business opportunities outstripped their zeal for combat. He shared Earl's view that quick action was the watchword of a good Scout. On succeeding Earl, Knowles began by putting the Scouts' paperwork in order, and then he committed himself to leading the Scouts as Earl had done, which meant the following in practice: "[W]henever I landed [I was] to seize and hold all men, mules and horses near the landing to prevent couriers being sent by bypaths to give information." He pursued anyone

1. John D. Winter, *The Civil War in Louisiana* (Baton Rouge: Louisiana State University Press, 1963), p. 388.

2. L. C. Bartlett to the *Evergreen City Times* (Sheboygan, WI), Nov. 12, 1864, p. 2.

who fled. He believed that when he returned there would be time to formally arrest the guilty and for the rest to be "set at liberty."[3]

The Scouts were fiercely dedicated to Earl, and at first Knowles had
difficulty earning the loyalty that they had felt toward his predecessor.
Ultimately, his actions as their leader brought them around to respecting
and following his leadership. Canby also came to respect Knowles's work.
He defended the Scouts when they were accused of theft and misbehavior;
and he kept them in the field, where they thrived, through to the last days
of the war.

E. R. S. Canby continued his military career after the war, often with
responsibility for dealing with small irregular forces of angry, determined
fighters. He commanded several military "departments," beginning with
the Department of Louisiana, and thereafter including the Department of
Washington (Delaware, Maryland, the District of Columbia, and northern
Virginia); the Second Military District (North and South Carolina); the
Fifth Military District (Texas); and the First Military District (Virginia).
Each assignment required him to deal with former slaveholders and
freed slaves, Republican and Democratic politicians, and postwar terror-
ist groups, such as the Ku Klux Klan. Perhaps it came as a relief to him
when the army assigned him to command the Pacific Northwest Department. However, once there, he encountered resentful Modocs, who had
been moved from their northern California homeland to Oregon, where
they reluctantly shared an area with the Klamath, their former enemies.
Canby again found himself engaged in irregular combat when the Modocs
returned to California without permission. Seeking a negotiated settlement, Canby went unarmed to meet with Captain Jack, the Modoc leader,
near Tule Lake, California. Members of both parties were carrying concealed weapons, and when the Modocs were denied permission to remain
in their homeland, Captain Jack and one of his lieutenants attacked and
killed Canby, giving him the unfortunate distinction of being the only U.S.
general killed during the Indian Wars.[4]

After being appointed military head of the lower Mississippi River
valley, Gen. Canby had had his share of problems. He took command of a
retreating and demoralized army after Gen. Banks's disastrous Red River

3. Lt. Knowles to Lt. Col. James Wilson, Jan. 23, 1865 (copy included in Trimonthly
Reports of Lt. Knowles).

4. Max L. Heyman Jr., *Prudent Soldier: A Biography of Major General E. R. S. Canby*
(Glendale, CA: Arthur H. Clark, 1959), pp. 349-84.

campaign, and he worked to restore its esprit. With Earl's Special Scouts as a centerpiece, he attacked the guerrilla activity and the smuggling and illicit cotton trade taking place along both sides of the river, and he managed to keep a difficult situation from becoming chaotic.

On the opposite side of the ledger for Earl's Scouts was the anger toward the Union Army that came from citizens in the Union-occupied region. For their quick and forceful responses to those they perceived as lawbreakers, and their ability to turn up in remote places without warning, Earl and his Scouts were fiercely disliked by most Southern civilians. They often did not differentiate much between legal and illegal traders, guerrillas, and partisans, and they kept all of them on their toes, chasing them, arresting them, and seizing their goods first — and only later sorting out who was acting legally and who was not. For Gen. Canby, who was determined to disrupt illegal trade and keep the Rebels away from the river, the Scouts were an important tool. The Scouts were a major nuisance to those who eagerly anticipated the restoration of commerce between North and South along the Mississippi River. They could, in a matter of a few minutes, "destroy the work of months," or so Thomas Baldwin, of the federal gunboat *Romeo*, complained after Knowles had arrested men who claimed to be licensed traders.[5]

They were known by name along the river. Northern newspapers hailed their actions; the Confederate press reviled them. While many Union military leaders approved of their actions, others, such as Gen. Dana and Gen. Washburn, did not. To Washburn, the Scouts were "the terror of both friend and foe, [they] plunder without discrimination or remorse whoever has the misfortune to fall into their way."[6] Earl and Knowles arrested men they deemed guerrillas and smugglers. They seized animals, boats, wagons, and goods that they regarded to be contraband or items used in illegal trade. In a few short months, they became known from Arkansas's White River to New Orleans.

From a Union perspective, the credit side of their ledger far surpassed the debit, while most Southerners saw the opposite. Few saw them as underachievers. Mediocre performances seldom prompt either praise or disdain. That the Scouts and their leaders earned plenty of both praise

5. Lt. Knowles to Lt. Col. James Wilson, Jan. 23, 1865; Lt. Knowles to Lt. Col. Christensen, Jan. 14, 1865; Acting Master Thomas Baldwin to Cpt. G. C. Dunwell, U.S. steamer *Mustang*, Jan. 12, 1864 (copies included in Trimonthly Reports of Lt. Knowles).

6. Lt. Knowles to Lt. Col. Christensen, Jan. 14, 1865 (copy included in Trimonthly Reports of Lt. Knowles).

and disdain indicates that, to those who encountered, interacted with, or merely observed them, the actions of the men led by Isaac Earl and Warren Knowles were decidedly not mediocre.

"Receipts to the Amount of 600 Thousand Dollars"

Disruption was the Scouts' first and most noticeable effect wherever they ventured. Impulsive, flamboyant, and unsympathetic, they awakened quiet towns, interrogated and arrested suspected guerrillas and smugglers, conducted searches and confiscated or destroyed hidden caches of cotton and other contraband, and gathered intelligence about regular and irregular Confederate troop movements. And they often left embittered Southerners in their wake. Whether their raids and patrols are considered separately or as part of a year-long campaign, the best method for judging their performance is in terms of the material and psychological damage they caused. Of the two, substantive effects are more easily evaluated; but it is impossible to be precise. The quantity of cotton, wool, and tobacco, and the number of prisoners, horses, mules, cattle, and weapons turned over to Gen. Canby's headquarters, can be estimated fairly well (Appendix B). William DeLoss Love claims: "[T]hey captured three hundred and eighty-four prisoners, and seized public property and smuggled goods valued at $1,153,000."[7] Scout Lucien Bennett later claimed the Scouts held "receipts from the quartermaster for property turned over to him consisting of horses, cattle, wagons, etc. to the amount of 600 thousand dollars and an equal amount from an agent of the Treasury Department who was sent to Natchez and to whom we turned over cotton, tobacco, etc. and at the same time we had the receipts from the Provost Marshall for 250 prisoners captured and delivered to him."[8]

Missing documents make it impossible to validate either of these similar estimates. Bennett's claim of two sets of receipts would come to about $1.2 million, which is very close to Love's $1.153 million total. Love's prisoner count is 134 higher than Bennett's, whose estimate is based on his memory — with no supporting documentation. Moreover, Bennett spent the last four months of the war as a prisoner, far from the activities

---

7. William DeLoss Love, *Wisconsin in the War of the Rebellion: A History of Regiments and Batteries the State Has Sent to the Field* (Chicago: Church and Goodman, 1866), p. 908.

8. Bennett, "Sketch of Military Service," p. 13.

and records of his mates. The receipts Bennett speaks of may have been lost when Warren Knowles and all the remaining Scouts were arrested in January 1865. At the time of his arrest, Knowles complained that his trunks were broken into and all papers and money, his own and that of the Scouts, had been confiscated. Later reports do not indicate whether they were ever returned.[9]

Checking the reported value of the goods confiscated and turned over to federal authorities without the Scouts' receipts or Love's unnamed sources would require re-creating totals using the Trimonthly Reports of Earl and Knowles, as well as other sources, such as the papers of Newton Culver and Lucien Bennett; combing through correspondence and reports published in the *Official Records of the Union and Confederate Armies and Navies;* and reviewing contemporaneous newspaper accounts of Earl's Scouts' activities. A reasonably accurate estimate of the total value of goods captured from smugglers, illegal traders, and partisans can be made by accumulating totals gathered from these sources and applying prices and price indexes that prevailed at the time.

The Trimonthly Reports provide the most extensive accounts. Written to provide Gen. Canby with summaries of the Scouts' activities at ten-day intervals, each report contains a roster of the Scouts on the payroll, the equipment on hand, and a summary of events. Usually, the last report for a month also includes totals of the goods and men captured during that month. Because Earl and Knowles turned over the goods they captured to several different authorities, these totals were often incomplete. Earl's reports were cursory and brief; Knowles's were much more meticulous, providing more complete inventories and descriptions of the Scouts' activities.

A careful examination of all the Trimonthly Reports produces the following totals of captured goods: 87 horses, 99 mules, 8 oxen, 19 wagons, 65 boxes of tobacco, 139 bales and 18 bags of cotton, 6 wagonloads (and the wagons themselves) of baled wool, one wagon loaded with mercantile goods, 1,500 yards of cloth, and two river steamers, the *Buffalo* and the *Sylph.* The reports also mentioned the capture of over 100 prisoners but did not list the weapons and equipment captured with them. Nor did they mention the $250,000 in "foreign currency" captured with the riverboat captain and partisan leader Ed Montgomery.[10]

---

9. Lt. Knowles to Lt. Col. Christensen, Jan. 1, 1865; Lt. Knowles to Lt. Col. Wilson, Jan. 23, 1865 (both included in the Trimonthly Report of Lt. Knowles, Jan. 20-31, 1865).

10. Trimonthly Reports of Lt. Earl and Lt. Knowles.

The papers of Scouts Lucien Bennett, Newton Culver, and Byron Kenyon refer to significant quantities of goods not specifically mentioned in the reports. From August to November 1864, Culver recorded in his diary an additional 20 horses, 15 mules, 16 oxen, two wagonloads and several bags of cotton, and over 40 prisoners. Bennett tells of capturing the steamer *Rob Roy*, which was laden with 400 bales of cotton, and another steamer with an unspecified amount of cotton on board.[11] In a letter to his parents dated July 30, 1864, Kenyon, probably referring to the large cache that the Scouts had seized at Fort Adams, reported that they had "captured very near one million dollars worth of cotton already." Kenyon was overestimating. A more reasonable estimate for the 600 cotton bales at Fort Adams would be about $396,000 — still a significant haul. When the information from these three sources is combined with the Trimonthly Reports, the totals are impressive. At the prevailing New York prices in 1864-65, the total value of the goods and currency captured by the Scouts and turned over to the federal authorities easily reaches $1,200,000. Of that estimate, nearly $610,000 was in cotton, wool, and tobacco. The contemporary value for those goods (as of 2010) can be reasonably estimated at about $16,000,000, of which $8,420,000 would be the value of the cotton.[12]

By any measure, that is a lot of cotton, wool, and tobacco. Even given the sievelike restrictions on illegal trade along the Mississippi, it is a remarkable achievement for one small unit. As a part of the total estimated illegal trade along the Mississippi, it was enough to anger traders and smugglers and put them on constant lookout for Lt. Earl and his Special Scouts — but it was not enough to deter them. Illegal activities continued along the river until the war's end. Estimates of illegal cotton traffic alone have been placed as high as $200,000,000, with an estimated $20,000,000 to $30,000,000 in specie and goods passing through Memphis alone. Further downriver, an estimated 500 bales of cotton and 40 barrels of flour passed through the Vicksburg region daily. Evidence gathered by Isaac Earl's agents helped identify contraband dealers at Natchez, Bayou Sara, and Port Hudson and other locations from Baton Rouge to the mouth of the White River.[13]

11. Bennett, "Sketch of Military Service," pp. 13-18; Culver, Diary entries for August 1–October 31, 1864.

12. "Measuring Worth.Com": http://www.measuringworth.com/uscompare/relative value.php. For a categorized account of all goods captured, see Appendix B.

13. J. W. Schuckers, *The Life and Public Services of Salmon Portland Chase* (New York: D. Appleton and Co., 1874), p. 323; Joseph H. Parks, "A Confederate Trade Center under Fed-

Half of the illegal trade along the Mississippi took place in the Scouts' area of operations. Six hundred ten thousand dollars is a small portion of the total illicit enterprise; thirty men constituted an annoyance but not a major threat to the army of speculators. Even with the amphibious mobility provided by steamboats, it would have taken a flotilla of Scouts to adequately patrol the hundreds of miles of river susceptible to illegal trade and guerrilla activity. But Earl's Scouts made their presence felt. Additional carefully selected special units like them, supported by a stronger policy from Washington, would have had a much greater effect. Other Union patrols and gunboat crews arrested guerrillas and smugglers, but Earl's Scouts were the only ones organized and permanently assigned to that type of duty. There was no other group on the river like them. If their aim was to curtail all contraband trade along the Mississippi, the Scouts were doomed to fail from the beginning. If, more realistically, we view them as a small force of men using all the means at their disposal to disrupt the activities of an omnipresent foe, they were a remarkable success.

Not all the Scouts' captured articles can be measured for their material value alone. The fourteen regimental flags captured in October 1864 are the best case in point. Their value lay in the pride and satisfaction derived from returning them to the units who had lost them to the Confederates. Their recapture received a great deal of favorable publicity for the Scouts — from New Orleans all the way to Washington, D.C. — when it was included in Gen. Canby's report to Gen. Halleck. Similarly, the value of captured Confederate mail shipments, intelligence gained by infiltrating Confederate lines, and the capture of officers like Cpt. Edward Montgomery and Maj. W. F. Springer was in the demoralizing effect such captures had on the Trans-Mississippi Confederacy. The reports of Lts. Earl and Knowles concerning Confederate troop movements, which they gained from captured Confederate mail and Earl's secret civilian agents, also aided Gen. Canby as he deployed troops.

The Scouts ranged far afield in their quest for information. Their most remarkable journey was their twenty-three-day excursion up the Mississippi as far as central Arkansas, posing much of the time as Rebel partisans and soldiers. The expedition produced an evaluation of cotton trade in the area as well as an assessment of Confederate troop strength. Because of the

---

eral Occupation: Memphis, 1862-1865," *Journal of Southern History* 7 (1941): 310; John K. Bettersworth, *Confederate Mississippi: The People and Policies of a Cotton State in Wartime* (Baton Rouge: Louisiana State University Press, 1943), pp. 180-81.

latitude provided their leader, the Scouts were often able to go places and gather information inaccessible through regular army channels.

Speaking only in terms of dollars and cents, prisoners captured, or information gathered ignores another important contribution of the Scouts. Though it is impossible to measure the psychological impact, it must be considered. Only a few accounts of Southern reactions exist. Occupation troops are seldom, if ever, popular with the inhabitants of the area they occupy. The Scouts' successes in diverting and disrupting illegal trade aroused intense feelings. The South's cause was in grave jeopardy by mid-1864, but supporters in the valley of the Mississippi River still clung tenaciously to the Confederacy. These states had contributed large numbers of men and material goods to the Confederate cause, and most Southern residents hated the Union soldiers, whose blue uniforms served as reminders of an increasingly desperate situation. Extremely proud men, as dedicated to the Union and its preservation as Southerners were to their independence, the Scouts evoked negative reactions wherever they went. They treated the people they confronted as guilty until proven innocent. To them, "due process of law" was as an abstract concept. They gathered evidence in any way they deemed necessary and occasionally meted out immediate punishment, arresting prisoners and seizing or destroying large quantities of goods after only cursory investigations.

Earl and Knowles secured knowledge of illegal trade and Confederate operations from a variety of sources. In addition to posing in civilian clothes as Rebels, they used undercover agents. For a time, Lt. Earl employed female spies, including his future wife, Jane O'Neal. Some of these operatives were listed in the Trimonthly Reports, but others remained unnamed. Desire for revenge, tempered by fear, followed the Scouts wherever they went. When they were in uniform, they seemed to take perverse delight in cavalry charges through small villages. Who can deny that a charging squad of soldiers, some firing their pistols, would arouse strong feelings in the citizenry? Out of uniform, they succeeded in blending into the local population on several occasions. The Scouts also often used captured materials in their continuing battle with smugglers and unlicensed traders. Seized horses and tack that did not carry the "US" brand enabled them to hide their Union affiliation.[14]

14. Lt. Earl to Headquarters, July 30, 31, August 10, 1864, List of Letters Received, Department of the Gulf, Military Division of West Mississippi, Record Group 393, National Archives Building, vol. 62, pp. 135-36.

The animosity they engendered cost the Scouts their leader and later led to their brief imprisonment in New Orleans. The death of Isaac Earl seems to have been an ambush, either in response to the Scouts' sudden appearance in Fayette, or based on intelligence that they were in the area. Confederates, too, had their information sources concerning Union plans and troop movements. When Earl was gunned down, it appears that he had been recognized and was the only target; no one else was injured, and only two shots were fired. Correspondence sent shortly after Earl's death speaks of Southerners' avowals to square accounts with the Scouts and their leader for their raids. Later, when Warren Knowles and the Scouts were arrested, the letters and affidavits of accusation revealed bitter feelings on the part of both Southern civilians and several Union officers, an indication of the Scouts' success in disrupting illegal trade. An ineffective unit would not have earned the wrath of so many.[15]

Gen. Canby was pleased with his Scouts' successes, and he included accounts of their achievements in his reports to Washington. After the very productive month of November 1864, Canby recommended Isaac Earl for brevet promotion to major. It was approved, but it did not arrive until after Earl's death. The Scouts were Gen. Banks's idea but Gen. Canby's creation; on occasion they reported directly to his headquarters in New Orleans when they had particularly significant captives or material. They represented a gamble by Canby; when the gamble proved successful, he, too, deserved credit.

Gen. Canby came to rely on the Scouts. When he began an offensive against Mobile at the end of the war, he sent Lt. Knowles and his men to serve as scouts and couriers and later as a special detachment from his headquarters. After the city had been secured, and Canby had returned to New Orleans, the Scouts performed duties around Mobile similar to those that earlier earned them recognition along the Mississippi River.

Counterbalancing all these credits were some significant entries on the debit side of the Scouts' ledger. Earl's biggest failure was his inability to get along with fellow Union officers. His clash with Col. Embury Osband is the most glaring example. Osband commanded a 1,900-man expedition, and Earl's refusal to follow his orders bordered on insubordination. At the same time, if Earl's men had not charged ahead of the main force, they

---

15. Brig. Gen. Brayman to Lt. Col. Christensen, Dec. 9, 1864; Lt. Comdr. R. L. May to Gen. Dana, Oct. 31, 1864; O.R., I, 41, 4, pp. 340, 810. The letters and affidavits are found in the Trimonthly Reports of Lt. Knowles, Jan. 10-31, 1865.

would not have captured several Confederate soldiers. The problem was touchy, and Gen. Dana's decision to send the Scouts in another direction was clearly the wisest course. Warren Knowles also had his problems. He clashed with the commander of a Union gunboat over a cotton-trading expedition, and it took intervention from Gen. Canby's headquarters to settle the matter. Knowles was more diplomatic than Earl would have been, but when charges were brought, he defiantly maintained that he and the Scouts were acting in accordance with Gen. Canby's orders.

It can also be argued that the Scouts did not show proper respect for the rights of loyal Southerners. There were Southerners in the Scouts' employ — and Earl and two other Scouts married Southern women — but in all cases involving what they regarded as suspicious behavior, their procedure was to arrest the persons involved and confiscate their goods before examining any evidence the individual might muster in self-defense. On several occasions the accused produced trading permits — to no avail.[16] Both Earl and Knowles were determined to carry out their orders to the fullest, regardless of their effect on military-civilian relations in occupied areas along the river.

There also is reason to question the tactical judgment of Lts. Earl and Knowles. Neither man had any special preparation for his unusual assignment, and they both made mistakes. They both led commands into engagements against numerically superior foes; Earl was captured several times and Knowles had six men taken prisoner. Earl's first experience of being captured came at Port Hudson before the Scouts were organized. Later he and virtually his entire scouting patrol were taken prisoner near Baton Rouge. He learned from these experiences, and in later expeditions he turned his men away from confrontation with larger Confederate forces. Warren Knowles's education was more traumatic: the first patrol he led after assuming command ended with six men captured and another wounded. Failures such as these did not occur often, but they did happen, and they must be acknowledged.[17]

Wherever they were, the Scouts plunged headlong into new adventures each day. They did so without hesitation, permitting themselves few second thoughts. Why? They all must have had courage and self-

16. Bennett, "Sketch of Military Service," pp. 14-15.

17. For a recent discussion of the pros and cons of anti-insurrection forces, see Max Boot, *Invisible Armies: An Epic History of Guerrilla Warfare from Ancient Times to the Present* (New York: Liveright Publishing, 2013), pp. 313-17.

confidence that outweighed natural fears. These are attributes of any good soldier. But the Scouts were motivated by other considerations as well, and those motivations differed from man to man. For some, such as Miller Graham, who saved almost every cent of his pay, it was a matter of earnings, and that motivation was probably true of other Scouts. Enlisted men who joined the Scouts received $60.00 a month, and the three squad leaders received $75.00. At that time the army pay scale started at a monthly rate of $16.00 for a volunteer private. The possibility of nearly a fourfold raise was not something for a soldier in the ranks to regard lightly.[18] Others, such as William Smylie, Johnny Hays, William Laughman, W. D. Mead, and M. Bowers, were Southerners who either had Union sympathies or felt that they could best improve their status — and earn $50.00–$75.00 per month — by casting their lot with the Union. For still others, men of the 4th Wisconsin Cavalry, such as Newton Culver and Lucien Bennett, for example, the Scouts provided an opportunity for adventure and the chance to make a more personal commitment to the war effort while serving under officers they knew and held in the highest regard.

Over four million men took part in the Civil War. For most of them, the only action they saw was as part of a large Army. A few, such as Earl's Scouts, whether by design or force of circumstances, engaged in special duty. Brought together by different motives, the Scouts carried out their duties efficiently. When the war was over, they returned to their homes in the classic citizen-soldier way, with memories few others could claim. Their greatest satisfaction lay in the knowledge that they had performed well.

18. A discussion of life in the ranks, including pay rates and the cost of special rations, can be found in Philip Van Doren Stern, ed., *Soldier Life in the Union and Confederate Armies* (Greenwich, CT: Fawcett Publications, 1961), pp. 154-64; see also Bell Irvin Wiley's two volumes, *The Life of Johnny Reb: The Common Soldier of the* Confederacy (Baton Rouge: Louisiana State University Press, 1943); and *The Life of Billy Yank: The Common Soldier of the* Union (Baton Rouge: Louisiana State University Press, 1971).

"Good Service"

O N DECEMBER 18, 1883, A GROUP OF CIVIL WAR VETERANS, TWO decades removed from their time together in the Union Army, gathered in Colby, Wisconsin, to organize a Grand Army of the Republic (GAR) post. Once they had dispensed with the usual reminiscing and inquiries about the health and recent activities of fellow veterans, and possibly after offering a toast or two to those no longer with them, they set about electing officers and selecting a name for their new post. In this they were not different from countless other Union Army veterans. Wisconsin alone had sent more than 80,000 soldiers to the Union Army, and once the war was over, a majority joined veterans organizations as a way to sustain the camaraderie they shared as soldiers, and to provide needed physical, emotional, and financial support after the war.[1] For Union Army veterans, the GAR became a dominant social and political force. In Wisconsin alone, 320 communities had at least one GAR post at one time or another.[2]

Once formed, each GAR post selected a namesake they believed em-

---

1. Richard N. Current, *The History of Wisconsin*, vol. 2, *The Civil War Era, 1848-1873* (Madison: State Historical Society of Wisconsin, 1976), p. 334. Wisconsin's total number of draftees and recruits totaled approximately 91,000, with the difference accounted for by reenlistments. Colby was a small transportation and retail depot founded immediately after the war on the route of the Wisconsin Central Railroad in the center of the state. A few years later, the little village established its place in history as the home of Colby cheese, a milder, softer cousin of the better-known cheddar.

2. The GAR founded 404 separate posts in Wisconsin; Milwaukee led the way with twelve. Thomas J. McCrory, *Grand Army of the Republic, Department of Wisconsin* (Black Earth, WI: Trails Books, 2005), p. 67.

Many members of Earl's Scouts maintained contact after the war. Charles Baker attended an 1898 veterans'
reunion, where he wore a ribbon identifying himself
as a member of "Canby's Scouts."
(Photo courtesy of Michael Martin)

bodied soldierly performance at its best. At the suggestion of Nathaniel
White and Joshua Porter, who had served with Lt. Isaac Newton Earl in
Company D of the 4th Wisconsin Infantry, the Colby veterans named their
post to honor the exceptional young soldier who hailed from nearby Dell
Prairie and had been killed near Fayette, Mississippi, in November 1864.
White thought so highly of Isaac Earl that he named his only son, Earl,
after his late comrade.

By the time that GAR post was founded and named, Earl's exploits
had received considerable public attention. During the war, newspapers
around the country picked up reports of his adventures and repeated them

for their readers. In Wisconsin, the *Milwaukee Sentinel* printed soldier's letters that provided accounts of Earl's Special Scouts, as did smaller local newspapers, such as the *Evergreen Times* in Sheboygan. Nationally, the *New York Times* gave his activities an occasional eastern audience, while Southern newspapers like the *New Orleans Times-Picayune*, the *Vicksburg Herald*, and the *Natchez Courier* took less flattering note of the Scouts' exploits.

Postwar Lives and Families

Earl's Scouts reestablished their civilian lives quickly when they returned from the war. They certainly could not forget the fighting and death at Port Hudson, and the loss of their leader at Fayette; but most returned home and picked up the strands of their previous existence at the close of hostilities. Like other veterans on both sides, the Scouts gathered often to recall their wartime experiences, joining GAR posts and attending reunions with old comrades. On at least one occasion, the former Scouts wore distinctive ribbons that identified them as members of Canby's (Earl's) Scouts.

Census data and veteran's pension files in the National Archives provide information that one can use to reconstruct the general nature of the Scouts' lives after the war.[3] Pension files indicate that foremost in the minds of the returning soldiers were the women they had left behind. By 1870, fifteen of the nineteen for whom files are available had married; eleven of those marriages took place in 1866, only one year after they had mustered out of the Union Army. Although most of the men married hometown girls, John Adams and Henry Stafford, like Isaac Earl, married Louisiana women.

Like many couples of their day, the Scouts and their wives tended to have large families. The eight children of Nelson and Ellen Porter, and the six children of Luther and Mary Struthers made up the two largest

---

3. I consulted the following pension files: John A. Adams, No. WO452883; Charles Baker, No. C2557974; Lucien Bennett, No. WC634317; John Billings, No. SO785654; Newton Culver, No. SC383647; Philip Dougherty, No. SO1421616; I. N. Earl, No. WC72262; Charles Fenlason, No. WC786216; Miller Graham, No. SC373888; George S. Hays, No. XC2668762; William Hine, No. WC831085; William Jewell, No. SC202241; Warren P. Knowles, No. WC264730; Nelson Porter, No. WC768576; Jacob Ripley, No. WC741022; Andrew Ryan, No. WC261741; Henry C. Stafford, No. WC631020; Luther Struthers, No. WC952005; Nathaniel J. White, No. WC897091.

families. Almost all the Scouts initially settled with their new families in the Midwest. However, by the end of the century, seven of the nineteen had ventured west, part of the great migration that continued through the twentieth century. Newton Culver, Luther Struthers, and William Hine ended up farthest from Wisconsin: Struthers lived for a time in Medford, Oregon, Hine in Bellevue, Washington, and Culver spent the last years of his life in Pasadena, California. Other Scouts made their homes in Iowa, Montana, and Kansas. Only three of the Scouts went east: Culver lived for a time in Saginaw, Michigan, before returning to Wisconsin and eventually moving to California; Lucien Bennett lived in Phoenix, New York, between 1866 and 1869; and Nelson Porter, who was born in Vermont, returned to the northeast when his first wife died. He remarried and lived for more than forty years in Victory, New York.

The Scouts were not remarkable in the occupations they chose after their service: farming was the primary source of income for six of the veterans, while three men earned their livelihood as schoolteachers; other occupations listed were clerk, insurance agent, trapper, sailor, storekeeper, and newspaperman. The pension files also offer clues about the health of the men and, in some cases, their families. At the time of their request for pension, veterans could list any ailments that might qualify them for additional assistance. Most men — or their widows — did not apply until the last two decades of the nineteenth century, and we can assume that before that they were in generally good health. The exceptions to this pattern were Nathaniel White, Lucien Bennett, Miller Graham, Jacob Ripley, and Newton Culver. White's head wound bothered him throughout his postwar life, and eventually he would have surgery to remove a minié ball that was imbedded in — but did not penetrate — his skull. Bennett claimed to suffer from "asthma and disease of the lungs," which he contracted while he was a prisoner of war in 1865; he provided a series of affidavits declaring that his problem was so severe that he could not sleep unless he was sitting. Likewise, Graham said that he suffered from war injuries that he incurred while a prisoner at Port Hudson. He said that his incarceration had resulted in "catarrh and resulting slight deafness of both ears and resulting loss of memory." Ripley, who died in 1912, was injured as a Scout in a fall from his horse in 1864. This chest injury plagued him the remainder of his life, and it was listed on the attending physician's certificate as the cause of his death forty-eight years later. Similarly, Newton Culver was injured in a fall from his horse while riding advance for the Scouts, and he cited the injury many years later in his pension application.

If the Scouts had expected a monetary reward for their special services, they did not receive it in the form of larger pensions. Although most
of them received pensions in their declining years, the amounts were the
same as those received by other veterans of similar rank. Most of those
payments began under $10.00 per month, and even at the time of their
death the sums were generally $40.00 per month or less. Surviving widows
and dependent children continued to receive payments after a Civil War
veteran's death. As the wife of Isaac Earl, Jane O'Neal Earl unsuccessfully
sought a pension increase in 1927, near the end of her life. In some cases
pension payments continued into the 1930s and beyond. Nelson Porter
had a mentally disabled daughter for whom a claim was filed in 1940 by
her sister. John Billings and Phillip Daugherty were, without a doubt, the
most frustrated pension claimants. Billings's request was denied because
he was listed as a deserter in 1863 and at the end of the war was, according
to Union Army records, "a deserter at large" — and thus not eligible for
a pension. This despite the fact that other records clearly indicate that he
was a properly enrolled, active member of Earl's Scouts. Phillip Daugherty's claim was rejected because, although he was known to have served
with the Scouts, he had never been formally inducted as an enlisted member of the Union Army.

Jane O'Neal Earl

Jane O'Neal's story is unlike any other associated with the Scouts, and not
merely because she provided intelligence about guerrilla activities in the
Baton Rouge area *and* formed a romantic link with Isaac Earl that led to
their marriage in late October 1864.

By the time Jane married Isaac, the war had already brought dramatic
changes to her life. Union soldiers had taken over Baton Rouge in mid-
1862, and had repelled subsequent Confederate efforts to retake the city,
leaving residents to carry on their lives under rules established by the
unwelcome Union Army. It was also in 1862 that her brother Henry died
in Virginia of an illness that he contracted within months of donning a
Confederate uniform; that same year her father was killed in the lawless
region east of Baton Rouge.

As 1863 began, Jane and her mother were doing their best to hold together their family and farm. No matter how they may have felt about the
circumstances that precipitated it, the war and the Union Army it brought

to Baton Rouge were a reality. In the latter months of 1863, O'Neal met Earl and agreed to provide information about guerrillas and Confederate troops in the Baton Rouge area. Perhaps the deaths of her brother and father — and her family's need for income — triggered Jane's decision. In any case, as the fall of 1863 wore on, the mutual attraction between Jane and Isaac made her decision to cooperate with Union troops easier. She continued to work with Earl in 1864, traveling beyond Union lines to learn more about the activities and intentions of Confederates who were active close to the river. Only when her role as a Union informant was revealed, shortly before she and Earl married, did she cease her espionage activities. After Isaac was killed, Jane remained in Natchez, separated from her family but close to the men her husband had led. Soon after the war ended, on January 16, 1866, she married twenty-four-year-old Lieutenant George O. Ellsworth, an officer with the 6th U.S. Colored Heavy Artillery, and moved with him to the upper Midwest, where she lived, far from her Baton Rouge roots, for the next fifty-five years of her life. She returned to Baton Rouge in 1921 with her grandson and spent her last years with her sister.

The way Jane O'Neal spent those fifty-five years away from her family suggests how deeply the circumstances of war had affected her life. George Ellsworth had been born in Albany, New York, and had with his family merged into the stream of migrants who made their way from New York and New England to the upper Midwest in the decades before the Civil War. In 1861, Ellsworth answered President Lincoln's first call for volunteers and enlisted, as one of the state's original three-month volunteers, from Walworth County, Wisconsin. He was a member of the 1st Wisconsin Infantry. Discharged two months later for "disability," he next enlisted and served for two years with the 96th Illinois Infantry before receiving a commission as 1st lieutenant with the 6th U.S. Colored Heavy Artillery in January 1864. He remained with the black artillery unit until it mustered out on May 18, 1866.

Jane and George Ellsworth moved several times after the war, living in Topeka, Kansas; Mason City, Iowa; and Rock Island, Illinois. According to census records and her obituary, Jane became the foster mother of one daughter (possibly two daughters) sometime during the 1880s. Census records identify a daughter named Pearl, born in 1881; the other daughter is mentioned only in Jane's obituary, and no name is given. Nowhere are the parents of Pearl and her sister identified. They may have been the children of Jane and George, though Jane would have been forty-four years old in 1881. More likely she and George provided a home for the orphaned children of relatives or friends.

George Ellsworth's reluctance to return to Walworth County, Wisconsin, after the war was explained two decades later, when Jane learned that he had previously married — and never divorced — a woman named Lucy Daniels there. Jane's widow's pension declaration indicates that she discovered in 1884 that George "had a previous wife still living and no divorce," and it declared that George and Jane were divorced effective January 1, 1885, in Mason City, Iowa. She would later declare that the marriage was annulled on May 7, 1886, in Rock Island, Illinois. In any event, the girl(s) stayed with Jane, while George left for Minneapolis, where he married eighteen-year-old Clara Bair in 1887. He died in Minneapolis in 1926.

By 1895, Jane and Pearl had also moved to Minneapolis, and had taken Earl as their last name. For the remainder of her life, Jane bore the surname of the man to whom she was married for only six weeks, sometimes listing herself as "Jane" and other times as "Jennie" Earl. On January 25, 1900, Jane's daughter Pearl married Christian Jorgenson in Minneapolis, and Jane moved in with her daughter and new son-in-law. Christian and Pearl had three children, two daughters, Ruby Anna and Maybelle Bernice, both of whom died in infancy, and a son, Orville, who survived to adulthood and remained close to his grandmother. Christian Jorgenson died before 1910, leaving Jane, Pearl, and three-year-old Orville living together in Minneapolis. By 1920, Pearl had also died, and Jane and her grandson moved to Baton Rouge to live with Jane's younger sister, Alice LeBlanc.

In Jane O'Neal's Veteran's Widow Pension File is a scribbled, partially illegible letter that she wrote in 1927, seeking a pension increase: "[M]y eyes are bad and I am almost helpless, perhaps you can't read this [letter] if you can do anything for me. . . . I am ninety years old. . . . I am almost paralysed. . . . My husband [captured] over half a million dollars." Her request was denied. Like so many Civil War widows, she could only wonder what kind of life she might have had if her husband had not been killed in that war.

O'Neal family historian Gary O'Neal, whose father's generation knew her as "Aunt Jane," remembers hearing his father and aunts referring to Jane as "an old woman perpetually dressed in black sitting on [her sister] Alice LeBlanc's front porch." She was on that front porch on July 31, 1928, when she fell as she rose from her chair, breaking her hip and arm. Anna Jane O'Neal Earl died a day later at Baton Rouge General Hospital at the age of ninety-one. As testimony to the importance she attached to her brief marriage to Isaac Earl, he is listed as "husband" on her death certificate, and the name on her tombstone is Jane Earl.[4]

A Final Word

When we study the Scouts' service records, pension files, obituary notices, census data, and other bits of information, a picture emerges of ordinary men who, save for one short period, led unspectacular lives. Like all federal soldiers who entered the army in the war's early years, they were volunteers — not draftees or hired replacements. The Southern civilians and black laborers hired by Isaac Earl and Warren Knowles did not qualify for pensions and thus are very difficult to track after the war.

Does the accumulated information about the Scouts offer any hints about their motivation and performance as soldiers? There are some interesting clues. Perhaps the very lack of flair that characterized the prewar and postwar lives of these men holds the key to their behavior. They were

4. I searched the following sources for information on Anna Jane (Jennie) O'Neal: *Sixth Regiment, United States Colored Heavy Artillery:* http://www.nps.gov/civilwar/ search-regiments-detail.htm?regiment_id=UUS0006RAH0C (accessed Apr. 2013); *Compiled Military Service Records of Volunteer Union Soldiers;* National Archives and Records Administration, Washington, D.C.; Microfilm Serial: M1818; Roll 115; Ancestry.com. *United States Federal Census* [database online], years 1850, 1860, 1870, 1880, 1900, 1910, 1920, for Anna Jane (Jennie) O'Neal, Pearl O'Neal, George O. Ellsworth, Christian Jorgenson, Orville Jorgenson (accessed 2012-2013); Ancestry.com. New Orleans, Louisiana Death Records Index, 1804-1949 [database online]. For Archibald H. Campbell: Ancestry .com; *U.S. National Homes for Disabled Volunteer Soldiers, 1886-1938* [database online]; for George O. Ellsworth (accessed Apr. 2013): Ancestry.com. *Minnesota, Death Index, 1908-2002* [database online]; for George Orville Ellsworth (accessed Apr. 2013); Ancestry.com. *Minnesota, Marriages Index, 1849-1950* [database online]; for Pearl Earl and Christian Jorgenson: FamilySearch.org. *Minnesota, Births and Christenings. 1840-1980,* for Ruby Anna May and Maybelle Bernice Jorgenson (accessed March-May, 2013); FamilySearch.org. *Mississippi Marriages, 1800-1911, index,* for Jane O'Neal and Isaac Earl; Ancestry.com. *Minnesota, Territorial and State Censuses, 1849-1905* [database online], for Jennie Earl, Pearl Earl/Jorgenson, Christian Jorgenson (accessed April 2013); Ancestry.com. *Mississippi Marriages, 1776-1935* [database online], for Jennie O'Neal and George Ellsworth, accessed April 2013; Ancestry.com. *U.S. City Directories, 1821-1989* [database online], Minneapolis, Minnesota, 1897, 1899; St. Paul, Minnesota, 1911; Baton Rouge, Louisiana, 1924; for Jennie Earl (accessed April 2013); FamilySearch.org. Louisiana Death Index, 1850-1875, 1894-1956, index, for Jennie Earl (accessed March 2013); Louisiana State Board of Health, Certificate of Death for Jennie Earl, No. 10194; National Archives and Records Service, Washington, D.C., Pension Claim of Jeannie Earl, No. WC72262.

solid, responsible young men who volunteered to redress what they saw as a grievous wrong to their nation. They were initially angered by those who sought to break up the United States, and later even more angered by those who used such a cause for their own profit. When afforded an opportunity, they were more than willing to administer punishment to those they perceived to have violated the United States Constitution, as well as the written — and unwritten — canons of war. Their sense of loyalty to their country, coupled with their sense of personal responsibility to preserve the Union, was quite likely at the base of their decision to join the Scouts. They joined the war effort because they saw it as their duty, and after the war they carried out their obligations as husbands, fathers, and community members with the same sense of commitment. This is the key to understanding Earl's Scouts: they were men who could be relied on by their comrades and trusted to do their best, and they expected the same from others. They were citizen-soldiers in the fullest sense of the term.

Articles Captured by the Scouts

Item	Amount	Item Value	Total Value
Cotton	879 bales[1] 38 bags (398,040 lbs.)	$1.50 per lb.[2]	$597,060
Wool	6,000 lbs.	$1.00 per lb.[3]	$6,000
Tobacco	90 boxes[4]	$50.00 per box[5]	$4,500
Horses	107	$165.00 each[6]	$17,655
Mules	114	$180.00 each[7]	$20,520
Oxen	24	$225.00 each[8]	$5,400
Wagons	21	$300.00 each[9]	$6,300
River Steamers	4	$50,000 (1)[10] $35,000 (3)	$165,000
Small Boats	4	$1,000[11]	$4,000
Confederate Currency	$1,250,000		$62,500
Foreign Currency	$250,000[12]		$250,000
Misc.[13]			$16,250
Total			**$1,155,185**

1. This total includes the 600 bales that were seized at Fort Adams; it also includes 40 bales that Lt. Earl burned in Arkansas, and an estimated 100 bales in the caches Knowles found near Mobile. It also includes two wagonloads of cotton that Newton Culver recorded in his diary as being captured near Natchez (Culver, Diary, pp. 3-4.) Cotton bales were calculated at 440 pounds each, and cotton

bags at 310 pounds per bag. Charles Burkett and Clarence Poe, *Cotton: Its Cultivation, Marketing, Manufacture, and the Problems of the Cotton World* (New York: Doubleday, Page and Company, 1908), p. 222; and *Encyclopaedia; or a Dictionary of Arts, Sciences, and Miscellaneous Literature . . .* (Philadelphia: Printed by Thomas Dobson, at the Stone House, 1798), vol. 5, pp. 487-88.

2. The cotton price used here is an average of the prices for the last six months of 1864 at New Orleans. James E. Boyle, *Cotton and the New Orleans Cotton Exchange* (Garden City, NY: The Country Life Press, 1934), p. 180.

3. This is the wholesale price listed at New York as of January 3, 1865. *The American Annual Cyclopaedia and Register of Important Events of the Year 1864* (New York: D. Appleton and Company, 1869), p. 188.

4. Boxes, one of three methods of packaging tobacco for transport, weighed between 100 and 120 pounds. Joseph Clark Robert, *The Tobacco Kingdom* (first published, Cleveland: The Arthur H. Clark Company, 1928; facsimile reprint, Gloucester, MA: Peter Smith, 1965), p. 224.

5. In 1860, tobacco boxes sold for approximately $25.00 per box. By 1864, the consumer price index for farm commodities had risen by 85 percent. Applied to tobacco prices, the $25.00 per box in 1860 becomes $46.25. This figure is used in the above table. Information for the 1860 price was taken from Robert, *Tobacco Kingdom,* pp. 209-26. The consumer price index information comes from a U.S. Bureau of the Census publication, *Historical Statistics of the United States, Colonial Times to 1957* (Washington, DC: Government Printing Office, 1960), series E, pp. 148-56.

6. In the last year of the war, the United States War Department was paying $144 to $185 for cavalry horses, and from $161 to $185 for artillery horses. An estimated value of $164 is used for all horses captured by the Scouts. Paul W. Gates, *Agriculture and the Civil War* (New York: Alfred A. Knopf, 1965), p. 185.

7. In 1865 the War Department was paying between $170 and $190 for mules. I use $180 as the figure here. Gates, *Agriculture and the Civil War,* p. 185.

8. The estimated price of oxen used here ($225) is based on cattle prices found in Gates, *Agriculture and the Civil War,* pp. 180-81.

9. There is little on which to base a value for the captured wagons. None of the reports carries a description of the wagons captured, other than to describe them as large freight wagons. When the price for other farm implements is considered (mowers rose as high as $180), the estimate of $300 that I use here does not seem unrealistic. Gates, *Agriculture and the Civil War,* p. 245.

10. Information regarding the value of steamers on the Mississippi's waters is taken from Frank Donovan, *River Boats of America* (New York: Thomas V. Crowel Company, 1966), pp. 90-92; and Louis C. Hunter, *Steamboats on the Western Waters: An Economic and Technological History* (Cambridge, MA: Harvard University Press, 1949), pp. 110-12, 307-8. The *Rob Roy* is valued at $50,000 and the three smaller vessels at $35,000 each.

11. The small boats captured by the Scouts are not described in enough detail to make an accurate appraisal. The figure of $1,000 used here is based on the knowledge that they were used to ferry goods across the Mississippi and thus must have been of substantial size.

12. By the middle of 1864, Confederate currency had depreciated to the point where $1 in gold brought nearly $20 in currency. I use a ratio of 20:1 here. E. B. Long, with Barbara Long, *The Civil War Day by Day: An Almanac, 1861-1865* (Garden City, NY: Doubleday, 1971), pp. 727-28.

13. This category includes the large number of miscellaneous items the Scouts acquired during their forays: 1,500 yards of cloth, a wagonload of hats, goods taken from the Douglas plantation, weapons taken from captives, harnesses and saddles from captured horses, a large amount of rope, $60 worth of liquor, and $175 seized from one prisoner who offered it as a bribe for his release.

APPENDIX B

Roster of the Scouts

Adams, John John Adams was a private from Company B of the 4th Wisconsin Cavalry. He resided in Ripon, Wisconsin, prior to his enlistment in the Union Army on November 17, 1863. He joined Earl's Scouts on October 27, 1864, and was with them until he was discharged at the expiration of his enlistment on April 20, 1865. He mustered out of the Union Army on May 28, 1866, but apparently remained in the South, where in 1867 he married Annie Hart in New Orleans, Louisiana. Adams died in 1883.

*Baker, Charles A corporal from the 4th Wisconsin's Company I, Charles Baker was born in Saratoga, New York, in 1843, and lived in Ridgeville, Wisconsin, before he joined the Union Army on April 24, 1861. He was one of the original twenty-one men selected by Lt. Earl on June 13, 1864, and he served with the Scouts until he was captured at St. Joseph, Louisiana, on December 23, 1864. He was sent to the Confederate prison camp at Tyler, Texas, where he remained until the end of the war. Mustered out of the army on June 8, 1865, Baker moved to Iowa City, Iowa, after the war and married Caroline Blackwell in 1869. The couple had four children. Caroline died in 1906, and Baker married Minnie Hindman in 1908. He died in Iowa City in 1910.

*Bennett, Lucien B. Born in Schroeple, New York, in 1837, Bennett was a resident of Burns, Wisconsin, about thirty miles northeast of La Crosse, and was working in a lumber camp near Neilsville, Wisconsin, when he enrolled in the Union Army on May 28, 1861. A member of Company I of the 4th Wisconsin Cavalry, he

---

*Indicates a member of the first group of Scouts to volunteer.

served with them until he joined Earl's Scouts on June 13, 1864. He was captured at St. Joseph, Louisiana, and spent the final months of the war at Camp Ford in Tyler, Texas. Mustered out of the Union Army on June 8, 1865, Bennett suffered from asthma and lung problems throughout his adult life, which he attributed to his time as a prisoner of war. After the war he returned to his boyhood home of Phoenix, New York, where he married Sarah Jessup in 1866. She died two years later. Following her death, Bennett returned to Wisconsin, and then moved on to Minnesota in 1871, working as the foreman of a railroad work crew, and later as a clerk. In 1884 he married his brother's widow, Mary Mott, and the couple had four children. Perhaps hoping that clean, cool air would ease his asthma, he moved with his family to Pillager in northern Minnesota, where he engaged in the lumbering and newspaper businesses. Bennett wrote a memoir of his Civil War experiences before he died on February 1, 1907.

*Billings, John Known for his distinctive red hair, Billings was a private from Company K of the 4th Wisconsin Cavalry. A native of Brothertown, Wisconsin, at the time of President Lincoln's call for volunteers, he enlisted in the Union Army on May 20, 1861. When Lt. Earl issued his first call for scouts, John Billings answered and served with Earl's Scouts until his enlistment term expired on November 22, 1864. After a visit to Wisconsin, he returned to the 4th Wisconsin and reenlisted for another term on March 13, 1865. After the Civil War ended, he was stationed with the 4th Wisconsin at Brownsville, Texas, guarding the Mexican border. Billings moved to Fond du Lac, Wisconsin, at the end of his tour of duty in Texas, and married Josephine Martin in 1866. The couple had no children. Billings was unable to get a veteran's pension because of a desertion charge on his record; that charge was probably a result of his having left the 4th Wisconsin to join Earl's Scouts without receiving a proper discharge. In 1894, he resided at the National Soldiers Home in Milwaukee.

*Bills, Spencer A private from Company H of the 4th Wisconsin, Bills gave Oconto, Wisconsin, as his home when he enlisted on May 16, 1861. He was wounded in the battle of Port Hudson on June 14, 1863. Among the first group of volunteers to join the Scouts, he was returned to his regiment on November 22, 1864, for "misconduct." He was mustered out of the Army on July 8, 1865.

*Culver, Newton H. Culver was the Special Scouts' first historian. He sent detailed letters to his hometown newspaper during the war, and he maintained a daily diary during his entire tour of duty. In 1916 he wrote a history memorializing Lt. Earl and the Special Scouts.

Culver lived in Sheboygan Falls, Wisconsin, when he enlisted as a private in Company C of the 4th Wisconsin Cavalry on June 3, 1861. Born in 1841 in Van Wert, Ohio, he had moved with his family to Sheboygan Falls before the war. Culver joined Earl's Scouts on June 13, 1864, and served with them until his tour of duty expired on October 27, 1864. After returning to Sheboygan Falls, he married Mary A. Wilder and settled down to life as a farmer — perhaps with his father — until 1869, when he and Mary moved to Iowa Falls, Iowa; later they lived in Plymouth, Wisconsin (1871 to 1873), and then in Saginaw, Michigan, where Mary died in 1884. Culver and their three children — Mary, Halbert Earl (who was named for Culver's regimental colonel and the commander of the Scouts), and Harrison — continued to live in Saginaw. In 1889 he married Catherine Taylor, and in 1896, together with Culver's youngest son, Harrison, the couple moved to Pasadena, California, where Newton worked as a ditch tender for the Rich Hill Water and Mining Company. They later moved to Montana, where Culver worked as a teacher. Culver was bucked from his horse while he was an advance scout with Earl's Scouts, and he suffered a fractured coccyx that left him with permanent discomfort and caused him to walk "stooped and bent over" later in life. He received an invalid's pension for that injury. Following Catherine's death, Culver returned to Pasadena, California, where he died in a soldiers' home in 1920.

*Earl, Isaac Newton The man who led the Special Scouts enlisted in the Union Army on June 24, 1861, citing Dell Prairie, Wisconsin, as his home. He was promoted to corporal on April 18, 1863, and he was made 2nd lieutenant on July 28 of the same year. He was twice captured and imprisoned by the Confederates. The first time was during the siege of Port Hudson; he escaped and returned to his regiment. His second capture came on January 11, 1864; but once again he escaped and returned to his regiment on April 30. While he was captive, he was commissioned first lieutenant by Gov. Lewis of Wisconsin. Earl was mustered out of the service in May 1864 so that he could accept Gen. E. R. S. Canby's commission to lead the Special Scouts. He fulfilled that role until he was shot in an ambush in late November 1864 in Fayette, Mississippi. Earl later died in enemy hands. On December 2, 1864, he received a brevet promotion to major for his "meritorious and valuable services" as a scout. Although he died before learning of the promotion, it did figure in the pension amount his wife, Jane O'Neal Earl, received after the war.

*Fenlason (Fenalson), Charles W. A private from Company G of the 4th Wisconsin Cavalry, Fenlason gave Farmington, Wisconsin, as his home when he joined the Union Army on November 2, 1861. He joined the Scouts on June 18, 1864, and served with them until they disbanded. His right leg was wounded at St. Joseph,

Louisiana, on December 23, 1864. Discharged on June 8, 1865, he married Emma Ayers, who, like him, was originally from Maine but had moved to Osceola, Wisconsin, in 1866. A lumberman when he enlisted, Fenlason taught school in nearby Taylors Falls, Minnesota, after the war. Later, he was superintendent of schools in Pipestone, Minnesota. In 1887 he and Emma moved to Rocky Ford, Colorado, where he died in 1914.

*Graham, Miller (Millen) "Old Graham," as Charles Baker referred to him, was a private from Company I of the 4th Wisconsin Cavalry. He was forty-five when he enlisted in the Union Army on April 25, 1861, giving Sheldon, Wisconsin, as his home. Like Lt. Earl, Graham was captured and escaped during the siege of Port Hudson. He joined the Scouts on June 13, 1864, and served with them until February 28, 1865. He returned to the 4th Wisconsin at that time and was mustered out of the service on July 9, 1865. He lived in Kansas for a few years after the war and then moved to La Crosse, Wisconsin, where he ran a grocery store. "Old Graham" died in September 1904 at the age of eighty-eight.

*Harris, Edward A. Edward Harris was a private from Company G of the 4th Wisconsin Cavalry. He enlisted in the Union Army from Platteville, Wisconsin, on May 6, 1861. Taken prisoner on September 29, 1863, he later returned to his regiment. He joined the Scouts on June 13, 1864, and served with them until they were disbanded.

*Hatch, Lewis C. Like Lt. Earl, Lewis Hatch was from Dell Prairie, Wisconsin. He enlisted in the Union Army on April 22, 1861, and rose to the rank of sergeant in Company D. He joined the Scouts on June 13, 1864, and served with them until his term expired on December 13, 1864. Although it is not known whether they were related, Isaac Earl and Lewis Hatch spent time together as youngsters: both lived with Earl's uncle Elisha Crosby while they were teenagers.

*Hays, George S. (Hayes) A private from Company G of the 4th Wisconsin Cavalry, Hayes listed Osceola, Wisconsin, as his home when he joined the Army on May 20, 1861. He joined the Scouts on June 13, 1864, and served with them until his term expired on December 13, 1864. He married Lucy Brawley in 1870; they were the parents of one daughter, Eunice, born in 1885. After farming near Osceola for several years, the couple sold their rural property and moved to St. Paul, Minnesota, to operate a boarding house. Hays died in 1894 and was buried in his native Osceola. Following her husband's death, Lucy continued to operate the boarding house.

*Hine, William S. Hine, who was born Cairo, New York, in 1836, served as principal musician and bugler with the regimental band of the 4th Wisconsin Cavalry until 1863, when he returned to Company I, the group with whom he had entered the service. He suffered a serious injury at Port Hudson in May 1863, breaking the ends of his tibia and fibula in a fall. In part because of the injury, he later received a $20-a-month pension. He joined Earl's Scouts on June 13, 1864, and served with them during their entire existence. After the war, in September 1865, Hine married Lucy Campbell, who, like him, was a native New Yorker. The couple had one adopted daughter, Adelaide, born in 1886, and they lived in Osseo, Wisconsin, where Hine operated a farm until 1880, when they moved into town. They remained in Osseo until 1908, when they moved to Bellevue, Washington, where Hine listed his occupation as a trapper. Hine died in 1917, and his wife in 1927.

*James, Albert W. James was originally a member of the 4th Wisconsin Infantry band before transferring to Company D as a corporal in the 4th Wisconsin Cavalry. He enlisted in the Union Army from Columbus, Wisconsin, on May 1, 1861, and became a Special Scout on June 13, 1864. He remained with the Scouts until they disbanded.

*Jewell, Samuel A private from Company G of the 4th Wisconsin Cavalry, Samuel Jewell enlisted in the Union Army from St. Croix Falls, Wisconsin, on June 3, 1861. He became a Special Scout on June 13, 1864, and remained with the Scouts until they disbanded.

Jewell, William William Jewell joined his brother, Samuel, with the Scouts on October 1, 1864, and also served until the end of the war. Like Samuel, he was a member of Company G of the 4th Wisconsin Cavalry, and had enlisted from St. Croix Falls, Wisconsin, in June 1861. After the war, Jewell, his wife Anna, and their four children lived on a farm near Bloom City, Wisconsin, in Richland County. After Anna died, Jewell married Isabell Griffin in 1883. He died in 1912.

*Kent, William D. A private from Company G of the 4th Wisconsin Cavalry, Kent was a resident of Osceola, Wisconsin, when he enlisted in the Union Army on April 12, 1861. Prior to the war he had engaged in steamboating on the St. Croix and Mississippi Rivers, experience that made him especially valuable to the Scouts. He lost partial sight in one eye on July 15, 1862, when he was hit by an exploding shell fragment while he was a sharpshooter aboard the gunboat *Tyler* during the Yahoo River expedition. One of the original volunteers to join the Scouts, Kent served with them during their entire existence, until he mustered out of the Union

Army on June 8, 1865. After the war he returned to Osceola, where he operated a successful mercantile business for a time. In 1893 he moved to the mining town of Wardener, Idaho. "Captain Kent," as he was known, died in Wardener in 1904.

*Kenyon, Byron S. Like William Kent, Kenyon was from Osceola, Wisconsin. He enlisted on May 20, 1861, and was a private with Company G of the 4th Wisconsin when he joined Lt. Earl's Scouts on June 13, 1864. Kenyon also served with the Scouts during their entire existence and was mustered out on June 8, 1865. Kenyon's family saved many of his letters, which describe his service in the 4th Wisconsin and Earl's Scouts. Copies are available at the Port Hudson State Historic Site, Jackson, Louisiana.

Knowles, Warren P. Knowles's record during the Civil War is much like that of Isaac Earl. He volunteered at the beginning of the war, entering the Union Army as a corporal in Company G of the 4th Wisconsin Infantry on July 2, 1861. Thereafter, he was promoted to sergeant in September 1862 and to 2nd lieutenant on August 24, 1863. He was discharged after fulfilling his three-year obligation; but he reenlisted with a 1st lieutenant's commission from Gov. Lewis of Wisconsin on May 24, 1864. Knowles took command of Earl's Scouts on December 8, 1864, after Isaac Earl was killed, and he was their commander until the end of the war. Knowles remained in the army longer than most of his men. He would later claim a disability caused by the fatigue due to "scarcity of officers," lack of rest, and "necessary food." After the war, he returned to the 4th Wisconsin and served with them on the Mexican border until his discharge on May 28, 1866. Upon returning to Wisconsin, Knowles married Emma Nichols in 1868, and became a teacher, lawyer, and successful businessman. He died on May 29, 1889, after an extended illness. Warren P. Knowles, his grandson and namesake, was a Wisconsin state senator from 1941 to 1954, lieutenant governor from 1954 to 1965, and governor of Wisconsin from 1965 to 1971. Another grandson, Robert Knowles, served as a Wisconsin state senator from 1955 to 1975.

*Porter, Nelson A private from Hudson, Wisconsin, Porter was a member of Company G of the 4th Wisconsin Cavalry. He joined the Scouts on June 13, 1864, and served as clerk for the group during its entire existence. On occasion, he would remain in their Natchez headquarters while the Scouts were out on the river. When he mustered out on June 8, 1865, Porter returned to Wisconsin and married Harriet Wetherby. Both Porter and his wife were originally from the state of New York, and when Harriet died on September 24, 1870, he returned to his prewar home and married her sister, Ellen, in 1873. The couple had eight children. Their disabled daughter, who was "never able to attend school and has to have constant care," was the last member of a Scouts' families to receive a Civil War pension. In his pension application, Porter reported that he contracted typhoid fever while working on "Grant's ditch" in 1863; and though he worked as a carpenter and farmer after the war, he claimed that the malady affected him the remainder of his life. Porter died in Victory, New York, on July 14, 1913.

*Ripley, Jacob Ripley was a corporal in Company F of the 4th Wisconsin Cavalry. He joined the Union Army from Walworth, Wisconsin, on April 24, 1861, and served until June 8, 1865. He joined the Scouts on June 13, 1864, and served with them until they were disbanded. After the war, he returned to Walworth and married Mary Elizabeth Derr in July 1865. The couple remained in Walworth until 1869, when they moved to Chicago and lived there for seven years, before settling with their four children in Monmouth, Iowa, where they lived for thirty-three years. When their children were grown, Ripley and his wife moved to the Seattle, Washington, area in 1910. Ripley had suffered a chest injury when he was thrown from a horse while serving with the Scouts, and he was plagued by ill health after the war. In 1891, when he successfully applied for a veteran's invalid pension, he listed his assets as a log house valued at $200, a cow worth $20, and $20 worth of household goods. His injury was cited as contributing to his death in Seattle in 1912.

Rowin (Rowen), Archibald Rowin was a private from Company I of the 4th Wisconsin. He joined the Union Army from Baraboo, Wisconsin, on April 23, 1861. He became a member of the Scouts on October 1, 1864, and served with them during the remainder of the war. Following the war, he married Lucy Hammond in 1867 at Union Center, Wisconsin. Like several other Scouts, Rowin and his wife headed west and were living in Collins, Oregon, when he applied for a disability pension, claiming an injury suffered while clearing a trail for artillery in 1862, when an ax head from a fellow worker's tool flew off and hit him, breaking bones and cutting his foot. Rowin died in 1903, following a paralytic stroke; Lucy died eleven years later. The couple had no children.

*Ryan, Andrew W. Ryan was a native of Marine-on-St.-Croix, Minnesota, who crossed the St. Croix River to enlist with the 4th Wisconsin Cavalry on May 23, 1861. As a member of that small community on the west bank of the St. Croix River in the heart of lumbering country, he was familiar with river work before he joined the Scouts. Serving with Company G when he decided to join the Scouts on June 13, 1864, Ryan remained with the Scouts during their entire existence. When he mustered out of the Army on June 8, 1865, he returned to Marine-on-St.-Croix, where he married Celia Conner, widow of William Conner, in 1870. The couple had two daughters, Celia, born in 1873, and Elizabeth, born two years later. Ryan moved with his daughters to nearby St. Paul, Minnesota, after his wife died on April 12, 1884. Three years later, Andrew Ryan died suddenly on December 30, 1887, while driving his sleigh.

Shaw, James M. Shaw enlisted in the Union Army on June 8, 1862, and was assigned to Company I of the 4th Wisconsin Cavalry. He joined the Scouts on July 1, 1864, but because of a bureaucratic mix-up, he was officially listed as an Army deserter on July 31, 1864.

Simpson, Lewis A. A private from Company I of the 2nd Wisconsin Cavalry, Simpson gave St. Louis, Missouri, as his hometown when he enlisted on April 18, 1862. He joined the scouts on August 22, 1864, but was returned to his regiment on November 22, 1864, for "misconduct." Remaining with the regiment, he was mustered out of the Union Army on April 18, 1865.

*Stafford, Henry C. Born in Chicago in 1844, Stafford was working in a Black River Falls sawmill when he enlisted on May 28, 1861. One of the original twenty-one men to volunteer for duty as a Scout, Stafford, a private from Company I of the 4th Wisconsin Cavalry, was named squad chief by Lt. Earl on November 1, 1864. He held that position until the Scouts were disbanded. Wounded in his right foot in the spring of 1865, he received a $10 invalid's pension after the war. Stafford married Mary Sanchez of Baton Rouge in June 1865, and he worked as a carpenter, mechanic, and laborer as the couple moved from Eau Claire, Wisconsin, to St. Paul, Minnesota, in 1886, and then to Iron River, Wisconsin, in 1906, where he died that same year. Mary continued to live in their small cottage until her death in 1919. The couple had no children.

Struthers, Luther A private from Company C of the 4th Wisconsin, Struthers joined his Sheboygan Falls friend Newton Culver as one of Earl's first Scouts on July 26, 1864. Having enlisted in the Army on June 3, 1861, he served with the Scouts until his term expired on November 22, 1864. Described as the largest man among the Scouts, the six-foot, one-inch Struthers's size certainly assisted him in his postwar farming occupation. Born in Canada in 1839, Struthers had moved to Wisconsin with his family before the war. After the war, Struthers married Mary Beseck on February 25, 1865, soon after he had been discharged and returned home. The couple had six children and moved several times, always making their way west. They lived in Alexandria, Minnesota, then in Iowa, and then Larimer

County, Colorado, before settling in Medford, Oregon. Injured in a shooting accident in 1916, Struthers lost the use of his right hand for the last ten years of his life. He died in 1926 at the age of eighty-seven, one of the Scouts' longest-living members.

*Van Norman (Van Orman, Vanorman), Charles R. Charles Van Norman was born in April 1838 in Willsboro, in Essex County, New York. He gave his residence as Grand Meant, Wisconsin, when he enlisted as a private in Company F on April 26, 1861. He suffered a head wound from an exploding shell while serving on the gunboat *Tyler* on the Yazoo River, on July 15, 1862. One of the original volunteers, Van Norman joined the Scouts on June 13, 1864, and served until they were disbanded. He was mustered out of the Army on July 8, 1865, and moved to Pilot Mound, Minnesota, in 1866, where he married Janette "Nettie" Hammer. Following their marriage, the couple made their way progressively west, living for a time in Fremont Township, Cavalier County, in northeast North Dakota, on the Canadian border. The couple had three children, who "all died when small," and while in North Dakota they adopted a daughter, Virginia, who was twelve years old in 1900. By 1910, Charles, Nettie, and Virginia were living near Portland, Oregon, where Charles and Janette died within five months of each other in 1918.

*Wait, Nicholas Born in Canada in 1837, Nicholas Wait initially joined the 4th Wisconsin Infantry on May 7, 1861, as a private in K Company from Chilton, Wisconsin. He left the 4th in November 1862 to join a regular army artillery unit, where he remained until joining Lt. Earl and the Scouts at Natchez, Mississippi, on June 13, 1864. He served with the Scouts for the duration of their existence.

Wallace, Frank L. Wallace was a private from Company I of the 2nd Wisconsin Cavalry and, like the other member of the 2nd to serve with the Scouts, he got himself into trouble. He joined the Scouts on August 22, 1864, and on November 22 of that year he was sentenced to forfeit one month's pay for "misconduct." However, he was allowed to remain with the group, and he served until they were disbanded.

White, Nathaniel J. Born in McKean County, Pennsylvania, Nathaniel White came to Friendship, Wisconsin, in Adams County, in 1854. A private from Company D of the 4th Wisconsin, White's place of enlistment was Geneva, Wisconsin, on May 4, 1861. He was later promoted to sergeant. He joined the Scouts on August 22, 1864, and on December 23 was wounded by a minié ball that lodged in his skull, and he was captured in the Scouts' ill-fated raid on St. Joseph, Louisiana. The wound caused him to lose strength on his left side. Although it was removed by a surgeon in the 1870s, he continued to suffer weakness and seizures for the rest of his life. After his capture, White was sent to Camp Ford in Tyler, Texas, where he remained until the end of the war. After his release at the end of the war, White returned to Wisconsin and his family home in Friendship, before moving to nearby Colby, where he married Josephine Loomis in 1875, and then operated a retail business. When it came time to name the GAR chapter in Colby, White championed naming it the Lieutenant Isaac N. Earl Post after the Scouts' founder and leader. White remained in Colby until his death on October 4, 1920.

Woodward, Albert Woodward was also among the men who were captured at St. Joseph, Louisiana, and sent to Camp Ford. He had enlisted from Weyauwega, Wisconsin, on June 15, 1861; he served in E Company of the 4th Wisconsin prior to joining the Scouts on August 29, 1864.

Southern Civilians

Bowers, M. Bowers was a Southern civilian who joined the Scouts on August 8, 1864, for secret assignments. He was paid $60.00 per month, plus travel expenses, until he was dropped from the roster of the Scouts on December 10, 1864, because his services were no longer needed.

Carlin, John W. Carlin, a twenty-five-year-old Irish immigrant from St. Louis, became a Scout on October 22, 1864, and served only two months before he was captured at St. Joseph, Louisiana, on December 23, 1864. Unlike the other Scouts who were captured at St. Joseph and remained in Confederate hands until the end of the war, Carlin's name reappears on the rolls of the Scouts on February 1, 1865. No reason is given for his reappearance. He then served with the Scouts until they were disbanded.

Cook, Sidney M. Like J. W. Carlin, Cook is a mystery. His name does not appear on the roster of either the 2nd Wisconsin Cavalry or the 4th Wisconsin Cavalry, the only Wisconsin units in the lower Mississippi Valley. It must be assumed, therefore, that he was one of the Southern civilians whom Lt. Earl recruited. (This assumption will also be made of other men whose circumstances are similar.) Cook joined the Scouts on August 27, 1864, and served with them until they were disbanded.

*Daugherty, Phillip Daugherty joined the Scouts on June 1, 1864, and served with them until December 1, 1864. His mother served as cook for some of the Scouts when they were in Natchez. After the war, Dougherty applied for a pension, listing Baker, Louisiana, as his home. His claim was rejected because he had not been a regularly inducted member of the Union Army.

Franklin, Thomas Franklin joined the Scouts on August 27, 1864, and served with them until they were disbanded.

Hays, Johnny Hays was a sixteen-year-old Southern boy who joined the Scouts on October 27, 1864. He served as an orderly to Lt. Earl, and was captured when the latter was shot in Fayette, Mississippi. Charged by the Rebels with being a spy, he managed to escape and return to the Scouts, bringing with him information regarding the circumstances surrounding Lt. Earl's death. He left the Scouts on March 16, 1865, and remained in Mississippi after the war.

Laughman, W. J. Laughman joined the Scouts on July 12, 1864, and served with them until they were disbanded the following spring.

Mead, W. D. Mead served with the Scouts from July 12, 1864, until December 1, 1864. At that time Lt. Knowles dropped him from the muster roll for failing to report regularly.

Mulloy, James Mulloy joined the Scouts on October 24, 1864. He was at the center of the controversy that resulted in the Scouts' confinement for a time in January 1865. He was accused of stealing large amounts of money from a man whom the Scouts detained. When the other Scouts were acquitted and returned to their former status, Mulloy was still incarcerated; but he rejoined their ranks on May 11, 1865, just as they were being disbanded.

Netterfield, Harmon (Herman) Born in Ohio in 1837, Netterfield joined Bayles's Company A, 1st Battalion of Rifles, Missouri Infantry in 1861, and was still serving in that battalion when he joined the Scouts. He served as a regular member of the Scouts throughout their existence. After the war, he moved to Wisconsin, where, according to the 1870 and 1880 censuses, he lived in St. Croix County with his wife, Sarah, and two children. Since the largest single group of Scouts (ten) came from St. Croix County, it is not a great stretch to conclude that Netterfield decided to come north after the war with fellow members of the Scouts.

Porter, Samuel R. Porter joined the Scouts on July 1, 1864, and remained with them for the duration of their existence.

Roberts, John E. Roberts served with the Scouts for only a very brief time. He gave his hometown as Natchez, Mississippi, when he joined their ranks on December 11, 1864. No one named John E. Roberts is listed in the 1860 Natchez census. The closest man by that name is John Roberts of Port Gibson, about forty miles north and east of Natchez. That John Roberts was the thirty-five-year-old father of ten children who may have found the $60 per month that the Scouts were paid a tempting opportunity in the devastated Mississippi economy of 1864. In any case, John Roberts had the shortest active tenure of any Scout. Just twelve days after joining them, he was captured at St. Joseph, Louisiana, and he spent the remainder of the war as a prisoner of war.

Smylie, W. R. Smylie was a deserter from the 20th Mississippi Cavalry, where he had been a first lieutenant. He became a Scout on October 5, 1864, and he served as a guide until March 10, 1865.

Southwick, Joel Southwick joined the Scouts on July 26, 1864, and served with them until the end of the war.

Black Laborers

Hardman, James Hardman was employed by the Scouts at a rate of $10.00 per month. He joined them on August 1, 1864, and served until February 10, 1865.

Harper, Mack Harper joined the Scouts on February 10, 1865, when James Hardman left. He was employed at the same rate as was Hardman, and remained with the Scouts until they were disbanded.

Haygood, Josiah Haygood joined the Scouts on August 15, 1864, and stayed with them until they were disbanded.

Johnson, Thomas Johnson joined the Scouts on August 15, 1864, and served with them until they were disbanded.

Jones, Alick Jones was employed by the Scouts at a monthly rate of $10.00. He joined the unit on December 22, 1864.

Keeney, Matthew Keeney joined the Scouts on August 1, 1864, and served with them until they were disbanded.

Parker, C. H. Parker joined the Scouts on August 8, 1864, and served with them until they were disbanded.

Stewart, Thornton Stewart was a wagoner who was hired by Lt. Earl on September 1, 1864, and worked for the Scouts at a rate of $15.00 per month until they were disbanded.

Webster, Daniel Webster was hired by Lt. Earl on August 1, 1864, and served until the Scouts were discharged.

Williams, Jerry Jerry Williams was hired by Lt. Earl to serve as saddler, that is, to maintain and repair the Scouts' saddles and other leather equipment. He was paid $40.00 per month from September 23, 1864, until the unit was disbanded.

Selected Bibliography

A Note on the Sources

The first book-length accounts of the Scouts' achievements came soon after the war ended. In two books describing Wisconsin units in the Civil War, authors E. B. Quiner and William DeLoss Love call attention to the number of prisoners and goods captured by Earl's Scouts and chronicle their raids up and down the lower Mississippi. Several decades later, former Scout Newton Culver published an article that adds important detail. Most recently, regimental historian Michael Martin includes a chapter on the Scouts in his history of the 4th Wisconsin.[1]

In the second half of the twentieth century several historians, mindful of the U.S. Army's highly visible missions around the world, began to look more closely at the Civil War in the west from the perspective of small tactical units in occupied territory. They recognize the role of Southern guerrilla and partisan resistance and look more carefully at the response of Union generals. Richard Brownlee led the way with

1. E. B. Quiner, *The Military History of Wisconsin: A Record of the Civil and Military Patriotism of the State in the War for the Union* (Chicago: Clarke and Company, 1866), pp. 922-23; William DeLoss Love, *Wisconsin in the War of the Rebellion: A History of Regiments and Batteries the State Has Sent to the Field* (Chicago: Church and Goodman, 1866), pp. 907-9; Newton Culver, "Brevet Major Isaac N. Earl: A Noted Scout of the Department of the Gulf," *Proceedings of the Historical Society of Wisconsin* (1917): 308-38; Michael J. Martin, *A History of the 4th Wisconsin Infantry and Cavalry in the Civil War* (El Dorado Hills, CA: Savas Beatie, 2006), pp. 353-91; Michael J. Martin, "Canby's Special Scouts," *Military Images* (March/April 2006): 24-27.

Gray Ghosts of the Confederacy: Guerrilla Warfare in the West, 1861-1865 (1958), a groundbreaking look at Civil War irregular warfare in Kansas and Missouri. Later, Michael Feldman's *Inside War: The Guerrilla Conflict in Missouri during the American Civil War* (1989) changed the point of view, looking at irregular war in Missouri from the perspective of its federal occupiers and their counterinsurgency operations. Union policy and guerrilla action are tied together in Mark Grimsley's *The Hard Hand of War: Union Military Policy toward Southern Civilians, 1861-1865* (1995), which explores how policy evolved from "restraint" to "pragmatism" to "directed severity" intended to demoralize civilians and force the restoration of the Union.

Daniel Sutherland edited a book of essays entitled *Guerrillas, Unionists, and Violence on the Confederate Home Front* (1999), which features a state-by-state look at the Southern home front, including important content on guerrilla activity and Unionist sentiment. Two years later, Darl Stephenson published *Headquarters in the Brush: Blazer's Independent Union Scouts*, a useful counterpoint to earlier books that extol the achievements of Captain Richard Blazer's adversary Colonel John S. Mosby. Blazer's Scouts represented a unit similar to — but larger than — Earl's Scouts.

Recent years have seen increased attention to Union responses to insurgents in occupied areas. Stephen Ash's *When the Yankees Came: Conflict and Chaos in the Occupied South, 1861-1865*, investigates both occupiers and occupied, concluding that, as Union occupation became more aggressive, Southern guerrilla resistance became more determined. Andrew Birtle's *U.S. Army Counterinsurgency and Contingency Operations and Doctrine, 1861-1941* (2003), advances the contrary position: that Union policy-makers stiffened their policies in response to guerrilla fighters and those who supported strong home-front resistance to occupation forces. Robert Mackey brings guerrilla war closer to the center of Civil War interpretation with his conclusion, in *The Uncivil War: Irregular Warfare in the Upper South, 1861-1865* (2004), that instead of a "shadow war," guerrilla conflict was a central part of Southern strategy. Four years later, Mark E. Neely Jr.'s *The Civil War and the Limits of Destruction* (2007) argues the contrary: that guerrilla activity had only a limited effect on Union policy decisions. However historians view its role, they agree that guerrilla activity increased — and Union policy became tougher — in the war's last years.

In 2009, two new books continued the increased interest in guerrillas, Union occupation policy, and counterinsurgency strategies and operations. Clay Mountcastle's *Punitive War: Confederate Guerrillas and Union Reprisals* places responsibility for the Union's increasingly "punitive" reaction to guerrilla warfare more on soldiers in the field than on their superiors. According to Mountcastle, Union soldiers in the west grew more and more angry with the violence of the guerrillas, and they took upon themselves harsh retaliations against civilians and their property before top leaders enacted policies. Daniel Sutherland's *A Savage Conflict: The Decisive Role of Guerrillas in the American Civil War* is the most complete analysis of guerrilla war to date. Sutherland says that examining guerrillas and irregular warfare is critical to understanding the course of the war and its resolution. He demonstrates that Confederate leaders viewed guerrilla warfare as a part of their cultural tradition and incorporated it into their war strategy, but out-of-control guerrillas undermined their government's legitimacy among its own people and in European capitals.

A. Primary Sources

I. MANUSCRIPT COLLECTIONS AND PUBLISHED REMINISCENCES

Bacon, Edward. *Among the Cotton Thieves*. Detroit: The Free Press Steam Press and Job Printing House, 1867.

Baker, La Fayette C. *History of the United States Secret Service*. Philadelphia: Published by the author, 1867.

Basler, Roy P., ed. *Collected Works of Abraham Lincoln*. 8 vols. New Brunswick, NJ: Rutgers University Press, 1953.

Bennett, Lucien B. "Sketch of the Military Service of L. B. Bennett, Private, Co. I, 4th Wisconsin Infantry." Area Research Center, Wisconsin State University, River Falls.

Benton, Fred. Collection. Center for Southeast Louisiana Studies, Southeastern Louisiana University.

Culver, Newton. Diaries (1861-1864) and letters. Manuscripts at State Historical Society of Wisconsin.

Flint, Jerry. Papers. Area Research Center, University of Wisconsin, River Falls.

Kenyon, Byron. Letters, Port Hudson State Historic Site, Jackson, LA.

Johnson, Robert V., and Clarence C. Buel, eds. *Battles and Leaders of the Civil War*. 4 vols. 1887-1888. Facsimile reprint, New York: Thomas Yoseloff, 1956.

Marshall, Albert O. *Army Life: From a Soldier's Journal, Incidents, Sketches, and*

Record of a Union Soldier's Army Life in Camp and Field: 1861-1864. Joliet, IL: Printed for the author, 1884.

Sherman, William T. *Memoirs of General William T. Sherman.* 2 vols. New York: Appleton, 1875.

Wooldridge, Captain Fielding L., comp. *Names of Steamboats.* Pott Library Special Collections, St. Louis Mercantile Library, University of Missouri, St. Louis.

II. Newspapers and Periodicals

Adams County Times, Sept. 20, 1929. "Early Days in Adams County as Told by Mrs. S. W. Ferris." Adams County, Wisconsin, WiGenWeb site: http://www.wiroots .org/wiadams/index.html (accessed Jan. 15, 2012).

The American Annual Cyclopaedia and Register of Important Events. New York: D. Appleton and Company, 1861-1865.

Baton Rouge Advocate, July 23, 1984.

Evergreen City Times. Sheboygan, Wisconsin. 1860-1865.

Harper's Weekly. New York. 1861-1865.

Moore, Frank, ed. *The Rebellion Record: A Diary of American Events.* Vol. 1. New York: G. P. Putnam, 1861.

Natchez (Mississippi) *Courier,* 1860-1865.

New York Times, 1861-1865

Philadelphia Inquirer, June 9, 1863, reprinted in website of the Donald G. Butcher Library at Morrisville State College: http://localhistory.morrisville.edu/sites/ unitinfo/cowles-david.html (accessed Sept. 6, 2012).

Quiner, E. B., *Correspondence of Wisconsin Volunteers, 1861-1865* (10 scrapbook vols. of Wisconsin Civil War–era newspaper clippings of soldier correspondence). Madison, State Historical Society of Wisconsin.

St. Louis Democrat article reprinted in the *Vicksburg Herald,* December 10, 1864.

Vicksburg (Mississippi) *Herald,* 1864.

Virginia City Territorial Enterprise, January 1866.

III. Government Documents

Acts and Joint Resolutions Passed at the Second Session of the Second Confederate Congress. Original in Harvard Law School Library. Facsimile reprint: Holmes Beach, FL: Wm. W. Gaunt and Sons, Inc., 1970.

Certificate of Death for Jennie [Jane] Earl, no. 10194. Louisiana State Board of Health.

Compiled Military Service Records of Volunteer Union Soldiers. National Archives and Records Administration, Washington, DC. Microfilm Serial: M1818.

Confederate Congress. "Proceedings of the First Confederate Congress: First and Second Sessions, Fourth Session." *Southern Historical Society Papers* 45 (May 1925).

Cowles, Captain Calvin D., comp. *Atlas to Accompany the Official Records of the Union and Confederate Armies.* U.S. Government Printing Office, Washington, DC, 1891-1895.

Gibson, Campbell. *Population of the 100 Largest Cities and Other Urban Places in the United States: 1790 to 1990,* Table 9. Working Paper No. 27, Population Division of the U.S. Bureau of the Census, U.S. Government Printing Office, Washington, DC, 1998: www.Census.gov/population/www/documentation/twps0027/twps0027.html/#citypop (accessed May 18, 2012).

Letters Sent, May 1864–June 1865. Records of the U.S. Army Continental Commands, Military Division of West Mississippi, Record Group 393. National Archives and Records Administration, Washington, DC.

List of Letters Received. Department of the Gulf, Military Division of West Mississippi, Record Group 393. National Archives and Records Administration, Washington, DC.

List of Prisoners Received, 1864-65. Records of the U.S. Army Continental Commands, Department of the Gulf. Vol. 410, Record Group 393. National Archives and Records Administration, Washington, DC.

Map of Mississippi River from Baton Rouge to Port Hudson. Records of the United States Army Continental Commands, 1821-1920, Military Division of West Mississippi, Record Group 393. National Archives and Records Administration, Washington, DC.

Maps in Halbert Paine Collection, Record Group 200. National Archives and Records Administration, Washington, DC.

Maps of Baton Rouge to Port Hudson, Mississippi River showing Rodney, St. Joseph, Bruinsburg. Records of the Coast and Geodetic Survey, Record Group 23. National Archives and Records Administration, Washington, DC.

Matthews, James M., ed. *The Statutes at Large of the Provisional Government of Confederate States of America.* First published, Richmond: R. M. Smith, 1864. Facsimile reprint: Indian Rocks Beach, FL: D & S Publishers, Inc., 1970.

Military Service Records of Lt. Isaac N. Earl, Pvt. Joseph Earl, Pvt. William Earl. Records of the Adjutant General's Office, 1780's-1917, Record Group 94, Microfilm Serial: M559, Roll 8. National Archives and Records Administration, Washington, DC.

Muster and Descriptive Roll of Company D of the Fourth Regiment of Wisconsin

Volunteers (Red Book), 1861-1865. Wisconsin Adjutant General's Office, Wisconsin Historical Society Archives, Series 1144.

Official Records of the Union and Confederate Navies in the War of the Rebellion. 31 vols. Washington, DC: Government Printing Office, 1896-1927.

Parish Maps of Louisiana Captured from Confederates, 1865. Records of the Office of the Chief of Engineers, Record Group 77. National Archives and Records Administration.

Provost Marshal General's Office. Letters Sent, July 1864–June 1865. Records of the U.S. Army Continental Commands, Record Group 393. National Archives and Records Administration, Washington, DC.

Records of the Adjutant General's Office (Civil War), Record Group 94. National Archives and Records Administration, Washington, DC.

Records of the Department of Veterans Affairs, Civil War Pension Files. Files of: John A. Adams, No. WO452883; Charles Baker, No. C2557974; Lucien Bennett, No. WC634317; John Billings, No. SO785654; Newton Culver, No. SC383647; Philip Daugherty, No. SO1421616; I. N. Earl, No. WC72262; Charles Fenlason, No. WC786216; Miller Graham, No. SC373888; George S. Hays, No. XC2668762; William Hine, No. WC831085; William Jewell, No. SC202241; Warren P. Knowles, No. WC264730; Nelson Porter, No. WC768576; Jacob Ripley, No. WC741022; Andrew Ryan, No. WC261741; Henry C. Stafford, No. WC631020; Luther Struthers, No. WC952005; Nathaniel J. White, No. WC897091. Record Group 15. National Archives and Records Administration, Washington, DC.

Roster of Wisconsin Volunteers, War of the Rebellion, 1861-1865. 2 vols. Compiled by the authority of the legislature under the direction of Jeremiah H. Rusk, Governor of Wisconsin, and Chandler P. Chapman, Wisconsin Adjutant General. Madison: Democratic Printing Company, 1866.

Smith, Major General William J., and Jason T. Brady. *Report of Special Commission, 1865.* Records of the Adjutant General's Office, 1780s-1917, Record Group 94. National Archives and Records Administration, Washington, DC.

Topographical map of the Country Back of Baton Rouge, drawn by L. A. Wrotnowski, C.E., July 1862. Record Group 23. National Archives and Records Administration, Washington, DC.

Trimonthly Reports Submitted by Lt. Isaac N. Earl and Lt. Warren P. Knowles. Records of the Provost Marshal General's Bureau (Civil War), Record Group 110. National Archives and Records Administration, Washington, DC.

U.S. Bureau of the Census. *Historical Statistics of the United States, Colonial Times to 1957.* Washington, DC: Government Printing Office, 1960.

U.S. Census, 1830: Courtlandville, Courtland County, New York. NARA Microfilm Publication No. 19, Roll 88.

U.S. Census, 1840: Courtland, New York. NARA Microfilm Publication No. 704, Roll 275.

U.S. Census, 1850: Waterloo, Jefferson County, Wisconsin. NARA Microfilm Publication No. 432, Roll 1000.

U.S. Census, 1860: Dell Prairie, Adams County, Wisconsin. NARA Microfilm Publication No. 653, Roll 1399.

U.S. Census, 1860: Population Schedule, East Baton Rouge Parish, Louisiana. NARA Microfilm Publication No. 653, Roll 408.

U.S. Census, 1860: Population Schedule, Fayette, Jefferson County, Mississippi. NARA Microfilm Publication M653, Roll 584.

U.S. Congress, House of Representatives. *Executive Documents, Annual Report of the Secretary of Treasury* (38th Congress, 2nd Session, Vol. 7, No. 3). Washington: Government Printing Office, 1865.

U.S. Veterans' Widows Pension Claim for Jeannie Earl, No. WC72262. National Archives and Records Administration, Washington, DC.

Veterans Pension Files, Records of the Veterans Administration, Record Group 15. National Archives and Records Administration, Washington, DC.

The War of the Rebellion: A Compilation of the Official Records of the Union and Confederate Armies. 70 vols. in 128 parts. Washington, DC: Government Printing Office, 1880-1901.

IV. PICTORIAL ACCOUNTS

Davis, Edwin Adams. *Heritage of Valor: The Picture Story of Louisiana in the Confederacy.* Baton Rouge: Louisiana State Archives and Records Commission, 1964.

Harper's Pictorial History of the Civil War. 2 vols. Chicago: McDonnell Bros., 1868.

Lewis, Henry, and Bertha L. Heilbron, eds. *The Valley of the Mississippi Illustrated.* St. Paul: Minnesota Historical Society, 1967.

Miller, Francis T., and R. S. Lanier. *The Photographic History of the Civil War.* 10 vols. New York: The Review of Reviews Company, 1911.

Moat, Louis S., ed. *Frank Leslie's Famous Leaders and Battle Scenes of the Civil War.* New York: Mrs. Frank Leslie, publisher, 1896.

V. PERSONAL CORRESPONDENCE

Horton, John W. Letter to the author, January 16, 1973.

Way, Frederick, Jr. Letter to the author, November 15, 1972.

B. Secondary Sources

I. BOOKS

Amann, William Frayne. *Personnel of the Civil War.* 2 vols. New York: Thomas Yoseloff Company, 1961.

Anderson, Aaron D. *Builders of a New South: Merchants, Capital and the Remaking of Natchez, 1865-1915.* Jackson: University of Mississippi Press, 2013.

Anderson, Bern. *By Sea and by River: The Naval History of the Civil War.* New York: Alfred A. Knopf, 1962.

Ash, Stephen V. *When the Yankees Came: Conflict and Chaos in the Occupied South, 1861-1865.* Chapel Hill: University of North Carolina Press, 1995.

Ballard, Michael B. *Vicksburg: The Campaign That Opened the Mississippi.* Chapel Hill: University of North Carolina Press, 2004.

Bastian, David F. *Grant's Canal: The Union's Attempt to Bypass Vicksburg.* Shippensburg, PA: Burd Street Press, 1995.

Bearss, Edwin C. *The Campaign for Vicksburg.* 3 vols. Dayton, OH: Morningside House, 1995.

Bergeron, Arthur W., Jr. *Guide to Louisiana Confederate Military Units, 1861-1865.* Baton Rouge: Louisiana State University Press, 1989.

Bettersworth, John K. *Confederate Mississippi: The People and Policies of a Cotton State in Wartime.* Baton Rouge: Louisiana State University Press, 1943.

Birtle, Andrew J. *U.S. Army Counterinsurgency and Contingency Operations and Doctrine, 1861-1941.* Washington, DC: Center of Military History, Government Printing Office, 2003.

Boatner, Mark Mayo. *The Civil War Dictionary.* New York: David McKay Company, 1959.

Boot, Max. *Invisible Armies: An Epic History of Guerrilla Warfare from Ancient Times to the Present.* New York: Liveright Publishing Corporation, 2013.

Booth, Andrew B. *Records of Louisiana Confederate Soldiers & Confederate Commands.* Vols. 1-3. New Orleans, LA, 1920.

Boyle, James E. *Cotton and the New Orleans Cotton Exchange.* Garden City, NY: The Country Life Press, 1934.

Bradley, Isaac S., ed. *A Bibliography of Wisconsin's Participation in the War between the States.* Madison: State Historical Society of Wisconsin, 1911.

Bruce, Robert V. *Lincoln and the Tools of War.* New York: Bobbs-Merrill, 1956.

Bryant, William O. *Cahaba Prison and the Sultana Disaster.* Tuscaloosa: University of Alabama Press, 1990.

Burkett, Charles William, and Clarence Hamilton Poe. *Cotton: Its Cultivation, Mar-*

keting, Manufacture, and the Problems of the Cotton World. New York: Doubleday, Page and Company, 1908.

Campbell, W. D., and I. D. Newell. *History of the Ram Fleet and the Mississippi Marine Brigade*. St. Louis: Buschart Brothers, 1907.

Capers, Gerald M. *Occupied City: New Orleans under the Federals, 1862-1865*. Lexington: University of Kentucky Press, 1965.

Caskey, Willie M. *Secession and Restoration in Louisiana*. Baton Rouge: Louisiana State University Press, 1938.

Catton, Bruce. *The Coming Fury*. Garden City, NY: Doubleday, 1961.

Catton, Bruce. *The Terrible Swift Sword*. Garden City, NY: Doubleday, 1963.

Conclin, George. *New River Guide or a Gazetteer of all the Towns on the Western Waters*. Cincinnati: J. A. and U. P. James, 1851.

Confederate Military History: A Library of Confederate States History. Vol. 10. Atlanta: Confederate Publishing Company, 1899.

Cornish, Dudley Taylor. *The Sable Arm: Negro Troops in the Union Army, 1861-1865*. New York: Longmans, Green and Company, 1956.

Coulter, E. Merton. *The Confederate States of America, 1861-1865*. Baton Rouge: Louisiana State University Press, 1950.

Cunningham, Edward. *The Port Hudson Campaign, 1862-1863*. Baton Rouge: Louisiana State University Press, 1963.

Current, Richard N. *The History of Wisconsin*. Vol. 2: *The Civil War Era, 1848-1873*. Madison: State Historical Society of Wisconsin, 1976.

Dobak, William. *Freedom by the Sword: The U.S. Colored Troops, 1862-1867*. Washington, DC: Center for Military History, United States Army, 2011.

Donovan, Frank. *River Boats of America*. New York: Thomas V. Crowell, 1966.

Easton, Augustus B., ed. *History of the Saint Croix Valley*. 2 vols. Chicago: H. C. Cooper Jr., 1909.

Eaton, Clement. *A History of the Southern Confederacy*. New York: Macmillan, 1954.

Fiske, John. *The Mississippi Valley in the Civil War*. Boston: Houghton Mifflin, 1901.

Gates, Paul W. *Agriculture and the Civil War*. New York: Alfred A. Knopf, 1965.

Gillette, Theodore. *Reminiscences*. Port Hudson State Historical Site, Zachary, Louisiana.

Gluckman, Arcadi. *Identifying Old U.S. Muskets, Rifles, and Carbines*. Harrisburg, PA: Stackpole, 1965.

Gluckman, Arcadi. *United States Martial Pistols and Revolvers*. Harrisburg, PA: Stackpole, 1960.

Goc, Michael, ed. *From Past to Present: The History of Adams County*. Friendship, WI: Adams County Historical Society, New Past Press, 1999.

Gosnell, H. Allen. *Guns on the Western Waters: The Story of River Gunboats in the Civil War.* Baton Rouge: Louisiana State University Press, 1949.

Gresham, Matilda. *Life of Walter Quintin Gresham, 1832-1893.* Vol. 1. Chicago: Rand-McNally, 1919.

Grimsley, Mark. *The Hard Hand of War: Union Military Policy toward Southern Civilians, 1861-1865.* New York: Cambridge University Press, 1995.

Groom, Winston. *Vicksburg, 1863.* New York: Knopf, 2009.

Hammond, M. B. *The Cotton Industry.* New York: Macmillan, 1897.

Hammond's Ambassador World Atlas. 2nd ed. Maplewood, NJ: C. S. Hammond and Company, 1961.

Hawes, Jesse. *Cahaba: A Story of Captive Boys in Blue.* New York: Burr Printing House, 1888.

Hearn, Chester G. *Ellet's Brigade: The Strangest Outfit of All.* Baton Rouge: Louisiana State University Press, 2000.

Hearn, Chester G. *When the Devil Came Down to Dixie: Ben Butler in New Orleans.* Baton Rouge: Louisiana State University Press, 1997.

Heilbron, Bertha L., and Henry L. Lewis, eds. *The Valley of the Mississippi.* St. Paul: Minnesota Historical Society, 1967.

Heitman, Francis B. *Historical Register and Dictionary of the United States Army.* 2 vols. Washington, DC: Government Printing Office, 1903.

Hesseltine, William Best. *Civil War Prisons: A Study in War Psychology.* Columbus: Ohio State University Press, 1930.

Hewitt, Lawrence L. *Port Hudson, Confederate Bastion on the Mississippi.* Baton Rouge: Louisiana State University Press, 1987.

Heyman, Max L., Jr. *Prudent Soldier: A Biography of Major General E. R. S. Canby.* Glendale, CA: Arthur H. Clark, 1959.

History and Catalogue of the 4th Regiment Wisconsin Volunteers. Baton Rouge: Headquarters, 4th Wisconsin Cavalry, 1864.

Hollandsworth, James G., Jr. *Pretense of Glory: The Life of General Nathaniel P. Banks.* Baton Rouge: Louisiana State University Press, 1998.

Holzman, Robert S. *Stormy Ben Butler.* New York: Macmillan, 1954.

Hunter, Louis C. *Steamboats on the Western Waters: An Economic and Technological History.* Cambridge, MA: Harvard University Press, 1949.

Hyde, Samuel C., Jr. *Pistols and Politics: The Dilemma of Democracy in Louisiana's Florida Parishes, 1810-1899.* Baton Rouge: Louisiana State University Press, 1996.

Hyde, Samuel C., Jr., ed. *Halbert Eleazer Paine: A Wisconsin Yankee in Confederate Bayou Country.* Baton Rouge: Louisiana State University Press, 2009.

Illustrated Historical Atlas of Wisconsin. Milwaukee: Snyder, Van Vechten, 1878.

James, Dorris Clayton. *Antebellum Natchez*. Baton Rouge: Louisiana State University Press, 1968.

Johnson, Ludwell H. *Red River Campaign: Politics and Cotton in the Civil War*. Baltimore: Johns Hopkins University Press, 1958.

Kerby, Robert L. *Kirby Smith's Confederacy: The Trans-Mississippi South, 1863-1865*. New York: Columbia University Press, 1972.

Korn, Bertram W. *American Jewry and the Civil War*. Philadelphia: Jewish Publications Society of America, 1951.

Levy, Louis Edward, ed. *The American Jew as Patriot, Soldier, and Citizen*. Philadelphia: The Levytype Company, 1895.

Lewis, Berkeley R. *Small Arms and Ammunition in the United States Service, 1776-1865*. Baltimore: Lord Baltimore Press, 1956.

Livermore, Thomas L. *Numbers and Losses in the Civil War in America, 1861-1865*. Boston: Houghton Mifflin, 1901.

Long, E. B., with Barbara Long. *The Civil War Day by Day: An Almanac, 1861-1865*. Garden City, NY: Doubleday, 1971.

Love, William DeLoss. *Wisconsin in the War of the Rebellion: A History of Regiments and Batteries the State Has Sent to the Field*. Chicago: Church and Goodman, 1866.

Mackey, Robert R. *The Uncivil War: Irregular Warfare in the Upper South, 1861-1865*. Norman: University of Oklahoma Press, 2004.

Main, Edwin M. *The Third U.S. Colored Cavalry: Battles and Incidents of the Third United States Colored Cavalry*. New Orleans: Globe Printing Company, 1908; facsimile reprint, New York: Negro Universities Press, 1970.

Martin, Michael J. *A History of the 4th Wisconsin Infantry and Cavalry in the Civil War*. El Dorado Hills, CA: Savas Beatie, 2006.

McCrory, Thomas J. *Grand Army of the Republic, Department of Wisconsin*. Black Earth, WI: Trails Books, 2005.

McMillan, Malcolm C. *The Alabama Confederate Reader*. Tuscaloosa: University of Alabama Press, 1963.

McPherson, James. *Tried by War: Abraham Lincoln as Commander in Chief*. New York: Penguin Press, 2008.

Milligan, John D. *Gunboats Down the Mississippi*. Annapolis: United States Naval Institute, 1965.

Morris, Christopher. *Becoming Southern: The Evolution of a Way of Life, Warren County and Vicksburg, Mississippi, 1770-1860*. New York: Oxford University Press, 1995.

Mountcastle, Clay. *Punitive War: Confederate Guerrillas and Union Reprisals*. Lawrence: University Press of Kansas, 2009.

Nevins, Allan. *The Organized War to Victory, 1863-1864.* Vol. 2 of *Ordeal of the Union.* New York: Charles Scribner's Sons, 1971.

Nevins, Allan. *The Organized War to Victory, 1864-1865.* Vol. 4 of *Ordeal of the Union.* New York: Charles Scribner's Sons, 1971.

Oates, Stephen B. *Confederate Cavalry West of the River.* Austin: University of Texas Press, 1961.

O'Neal, Gary S. *The O'Neals of East Baton Rouge Parish: The Early Years.* Richmond, VA: Old Favorites Bookshop, 2005.

Parks, Joseph Howard. *General Edmund Kirby Smith, C.S.A.* Baton Rouge: Louisiana State University Press, 1954, 1982.

Pearce. George F. *Pensacola during the Civil War: A Thorn in the Side of the Confederacy.* Gainesville: University Press of Florida, 2000.

Perry, Milton F. *Infernal Machines: The Story of Confederate Submarine and Mine Warfare.* Baton Rouge: Louisiana State University Press, 1965.

Peterson, Harold L. *The American Sword, 1776-1945.* New Hope, PA: Robert Halter, the River House, 1954.

Pierson, Michael D. *Mutiny at Fort Jackson.* Chapel Hill: University of North Carolina Press, 2008.

Porter, David Dixon. *Naval History of the Civil War.* New York: Sherman Publishing Company, 1886.

Pratt, Fletcher. *Civil War on Western Waters.* New York: Henry Holt, 1956.

Quiner, E. B. *The Military History of Wisconsin: A Record of the Civil and Military Patriotism of the State in the War for the Union.* Chicago: Clarke and Company, 1866.

Rains, Gabriel J., and Peter S. Michie. *Confederate Torpedoes: Two Illustrated 19th Century Works, with New Appendices and Photographs.* Edited by Herbert M. Schiller. Jefferson, NC: McFarland, 2011.

Rankin, George. *William Dempster Hoard.* Madison, WI: W. D. Hoard and Sons, 1925.

Reilly, Robert. *United States Military Small Arms, 1816-1865.* Baton Rouge: The Eagle Press, 1970.

Rhodes, James Ford. *History of the United States from the Compromise of 1850 to the Final Restoration of Home Rule at the South in 1877.* Vol. 5. New York: Macmillan, 1893-1906.

Robert, Joseph Clarke. *The Tobacco Kingdom.* First published, Durham: Duke University Press; facsimile reprint, Gloucester, MA: Peter Smith, 1965.

Roland, Charles P. *Louisiana Sugar Plantations during the Civil War.* Baton Rouge: Louisiana State University Press, reprint with new foreword, 1997.

Schuckers, J. W. *The Life and Public Services of Salmon Portland Chase.* New York: D. Appleton and Company, 1874.

Schwab, John C. *The Confederate States of America, 1861-1864: A Financial and In-*

dustrial History of the South during the Civil War. New York: Charles Scribner's Sons, 1901.

Shannon, Fred Albert. *The Organization and Administration of the Union Army, 1861-1865*. 2 vols. First published, Cleveland: Arthur H. Clark, 1928; facsimile reprint, Gloucester, MA: Peter Smith, 1965.

Shea, William L., and Terrence J. Winschel. *Vicksburg Is the Key: The Struggle for the Mississippi River*. Lincoln: University of Nebraska Press, 2005.

Silver, James W., ed. *Mississippi in the Confederacy as Seen in Retrospect*. Baton Rouge: Louisiana State University Press, 1961.

Smith, Jean Edward. *Grant*. New York: Simon and Schuster, 2001.

Speer, Lonnie. *Portals to Hell: Military Prisons of the Civil War*. Mechanicsburg, PA: Stackpole, 1997.

Stephenson, Darl L. *Headquarters in the Brush: Blazer's Independent Union Scouts*. Athens: Ohio University Press, 2001.

Stern, Philip Van Doren, ed. *Soldier Life in the Union and Confederate Armies*. Greenwich, CT: Fawcett Publications, 1961.

Sutherland, Daniel E. *A Savage Conflict: The Decisive Role of Guerrillas in the American Civil War*. Chapel Hill: University of North Carolina Press, 2009.

Taylor, William Banks. *King Cotton and Old Glory: Natchez, Mississippi in the Age of Sectional Controversy and Civil War*. Hattiesburg, MS: Fox Printing Company, 1977.

Tenney, William Jewett. *The Military and Naval History of the Rebellion in the United States*. New York: D. Appleton and Company, 1866.

Thoms, Alston V., ed. *Uncovering Camp Ford*. College Station, TX: Center for Ecological Archaeology, Texas A&M University, 2000.

Walker, Peter F. *Vicksburg: A People at War, 1860-1865*. Chapel Hill: University of North Carolina Press, 1960.

Warner, Ezra J. *Generals in Blue: Lives of the Union Commanders*. Baton Rouge: Louisiana State University Press, 1964.

Warner, Ezra J. *Generals in Gray: Lives of the Confederate Commanders*. Baton Rouge: Louisiana State University Press, 1959.

Way, Frederick, Jr. *Way's Packet Directory, 1848-1994*. Rev. ed. Athens: Ohio University Press, 1983.

Wayne, Michael. *The Reshaping of Plantation Society: The Natchez District, 1860-80*. Baton Rouge: Louisiana State University Press, 1990.

Wells, Robert W. *Wisconsin in the Civil War*. Milwaukee: The Journal Company, 1962.

Williamson, Harold F. *Winchester: The Gun That Won the West*. New York: A. S. Barnes, 1952.

Willis. Henry A. *The Fifty-third Regiment Massachusetts Volunteers: Comprising Also a History of the Siege of Port Hudson*. Fitchburg, MA: Press of Blanchard and Brown, 1889.

Winschel, Terrence J. *Triumph and Defeat: The Vicksburg Campaign*. 2 vols. Campbell, CA: Savas, 1999, 2006.

Winschel, Terrence J. *Vicksburg: Fall of the Confederate Gibraltar*. Abilene, TX: McWhiney Foundation Press, 1999.

Winters, John D. *The Civil War in Louisiana*. Baton Rouge: Louisiana State University Press, 1963.

Wooldridge, Captain Fielding L. *Names of Steamboats*. Pott Library Special Collections, St. Louis Mercantile Library, University of Missouri, St. Louis.

II. ARTICLES

Broussard, Joyce L. "Occupied Natchez, Elite Women, and the Feminization of the War." *The Journal of Mississippi History* 71 (2008): 179-207.

Carter, George W. "The Fourth Wisconsin at Port Hudson." In *War Papers Read Before the Commandery of the State of Wisconsin, Military of the Loyal Legion of the United States*. Vol. 3. Milwaukee: Burdick and Allen, 1903.

Coulter, E. Merton. "Commercial Intercourse with the Confederacy in the Mississippi Valley, 1861-1865," *Mississippi Valley Historical Review* 5 (March 1919): 377-95.

Coulter, E. Merton. "The Effects of Secession upon the Commerce of the Mississippi Valley." *Mississippi Valley Historical Review* 3 (December 1916): 275-300.

Culver, Newton. "Brevet Major Isaac N. Earl: A Noted Scout of the Department of the Gulf." *Proceedings of the Historical Society of Wisconsin* (1917): 308-38.

Erickson, Edgar L., ed. "Hunting for Cotton in Dixie: From the Civil War Diary of Captain Charles E. Wilcox." *Journal of Southern History* 4 (1938): 493-513.

Gieske, Millard L. "Some Civil War Letters of Knute Nelson." *Norwegian American Studies* 23 (1967): 17-50 (Norwegian American Historical Association, Northfield, Minnesota).

Irwin, Richard B. "The Capture of Port Hudson." In *Battles and Leaders of the Civil War*, vol. 3, p. 593. New York: The Century Company, 1887.

Johnson, Ludwell H. "Contraband Trade during the Last Year of the Civil War." *Mississippi Valley Historical Review* 49 (March 1963): 635-52.

Johnson, Ludwell H. "Trading with the Union." *Virginia Magazine of History and Biography* 73 (July 1970): 308-25.

Lerner, Eugene M. "Money, Prices, and Wages in the Confederacy, 1861-1865." *Journal of Political Economy* 42 (February 1955): 20-40.

Martin, Michael J. "Canby's Special Scouts." *Military Images* (March/April 2006): 24-27.

Mitchell, Leon Jr. "Camp Ford Confederate Military Prison." *The Southwest Historical Quarterly* 46 (July 1962): 1-16.

O'Connor, Thomas H. "Lincoln and the Cotton Trade." *Civil War History* 7 (March 1961): 20-35.

Parks, Joseph H. "A Confederate Trade Center under Federal Occupation: Memphis, 1862-1865." *Journal of Southern History* 7 (1941): 289-314.

"The Past and Present." *Fincher's Trades Review* (July 4, 1863).

Roberts, A. Sellow. "The Federal Government and Confederate Cotton." *American Historical Review* 32 (January 1927): 261-75.

Roberts, John C., and Richard H. Webber. "Gunboats in the River War, 1861-1865." *Proceedings of the U.S. Naval Institute* (March 1965): 83-99.

Surdam, David G. "Traders or Traitors: Northern Cotton Trading during the Civil War." *Business and Economic History* 28, no. 2 (Winter 1999): 301-12.

Westwood, Howard C. "The Vicksburg/Port Hudson Gap — the Pincers Never Pinched." *Military Affairs* 4, no. 3: 113-19.

III. WEB SITES

Adams County, Wisconsin, WiGenWeb site, Columbia Rifles Civil War Veterans: http://www.wiroots.org/wiadams/index.html (accessed Jan. 15, 2012).

Alcorn State University Web site: http://www.alcorn.edu/default.aspx (accessed August 24, 2012).

American Memory, Library of Congress, "Journal of the Congress of the Confederate States of America, 1861-1865": http://memory.loc.gov/cgi-bin/query/D ?hlaw:1:./temp/~ammem_Pv2A::#0060830 (accessed May 23, 2013).

Ancestry.com. [databases online].

> *Louisiana Confederate Soldiers Online Database,* Provo, Utah. Original data from Andrew B. Booth, *Records of Louisiana Confederate Soldiers & Confederate Commands.* Vols. 1-3. New Orleans, LA, 1920.

> *Minnesota, Death Index, 1908-2002,* for George Orville Ellsworth (accessed April 2013).

> *Minnesota, Marriages Index, 1849-1950,* for Pearl Earl and Christian Jorgenson.

> *Minnesota, Territorial and State Censuses, 1849-1905,* for Jennie Earl, Pearl Earl/Jorgenson, Christian Jorgenson (accessed April 2013).

> *Mississippi Marriages, 1776-1935,* for Jennie O'Neal and George Ellsworth.

> New Orleans, Louisiana, Death Records Index, 1804-1949, for Archibald H. Campbell.

United States Federal Census, years 1850, 1860, 1870, 1880, 1900, 1910, 1920, for Anna Jane (Jennie) O'Neal, Pearl O'Neal, George O. Ellsworth, Christian Jorgenson, Orville Jorgenson (accessed 2012-2013).

U.S. City Directories, 1821-1989, Minneapolis, Minnesota, 1897, 1899, St. Paul, Minnesota, 1911, Baton Rouge, Louisiana, 1924, for Jennie Earl.

U.S. Civil War Soldiers, 1861-1865, Provo, Utah. Original data from National Park Service, *Civil War Soldiers and Sailors System*, http://www.itd.nps.gov/cwss/, acquired 2007.

U.S. National Homes for Disabled Volunteer Soldiers, 1886-1938, for George O. Ellsworth (accessed April 2013).

Arcadians in Gray: http://www.acadiansingray.com/4th%20Regt.%20Inf.htm (accessed June 28, 2012).

Beauvoir Confederate Soldiers Home: http://www.beauvoir.org/vetshome.html (accessed Sept. 16, 2012).

Donald G. Butcher Library at Morrisville State College: http://localhistory.morrisville.edu/sites/unitinfo/cowles-david.html (accessed Sept. 6, 2012).

CWSAC Battle Summaries, Irish Bend: http://www.nps.gov/history/hps/ABPP/BATTLES/la007 (accessed Jan. 31, 2012).

DeWitt (Arkansas County), *Encyclopedia of Arkansas History and Culture:* http://www.encyclopediaofarkansas.net/encyclopedia/entry-detail.aspx?entryID=819# (accessed Sept. 8, 2012).

Family Search.org.

    Minnesota Births and Christenings. 1840-1980, for Ruby Anna May and Maybelle Bernice Jorgenson (accessed March-May 2013).

    Mississippi Marriages, 1800-1911, index, for Jane O'Neal and Isaac Earl.

Gibson, Campbell. *Population of the 100 Largest Cities and Other Urban Places in the United States: 1790 to 1990*, Table 9; Working Paper No. 27, Population Division of the U.S. Bureau of the Census, U.S. Government Printing Office, Washington, D.C., 1998: www.Census.gov/population/www/documentation/twps0027/twps0027.html/#citypop (accessed May 18, 2012).

Handbook of Texas Online: http://www.tshaonline.org/handbook/online/articles/fwaas (accessed Jan. 26, 2012) (published by the Texas State Historical Association).

Louisiana in the Civil War Message Board: http://history-sites.com/cgi-bin/bbs53x/lacwmb/webbbs_config.pl?noframes;read=12744#Responses (accessed June 28, 2012).

Louisiana's Military Heritage: Battles, Campaigns, and Maneuvers, The Teche Campaign, January-May 1863: http://www.usskidd.com/battles-teche.html (accessed Jan. 31, 2012).

Louisiana's Military Heritage: Battles, Campaigns, and Maneuvers, The Red River Campaign, April-May 1864: http://www.usskidd.com/battles-teche.html (accessed Jan. 31, 2012).

Map of the country between Milliken's Bend, LA, and Jackson, MS. Compiled, surveyed, and drawn under the direction of Lt. Col. J. H. Wilson by Maj. Otto H. Matz and 1st Lt. L. Helmle, 1895, David Rumsey Historical Map Collection, Stanford University: http://www.davidrumsey.com/luna/servlet/detail/ RUMSEY~8~1~26868~1100164 (accessed Aug. 18, 2012).

"Measuring Worth": http://www.measuringworth.com/uscompare/relativevalue .php (accessed Apr. 27, 2013).

Mississippi Confederate Grave Registry: http://mscgr.homestead.com/MSCGRdi .html (accessed Sept. 16, 2012).

Mississippi History Now, Jim Barnett and H. Clark Burkett, "The Forks of the Road Slave Market at Natchez": http://mshistorynow.mdah.state.ms.us/ articles/47/the-forks-of-the-road . . . (accessed May 7, 2013).

Mississippi Steamboat Men in Mark Twain's Writings: http://www.twainquotes .com/Steamboats/Montgomery.html (accessed Sept. 10, 2012).

Mount Clare Museum House: www.Mountclare.org (accessed February 16, 2012).

Old Cahawba, Alabama's First State Capitol, 1820-1826: http://www.cahawba.com (accessed Apr. 7, 2012).

Osband, Col. Embury D.: http://andspeakingofwhich.blogspot.com/2012_03_01 _archive.html (accessed Aug. 21, 2012).

"Paddock, Buckley Burton," *Handbook of Texas Online:* http://www.tshaonline.org/ handbook/online/articles/fpa03 (accessed Apr. 28, 2013) (published by the Texas State Historical Association).

"Parson's Brigade," *Handbook of Texas Online:* http://www.tshaonline.org/ handbook/online/articles/qkp01 (accessed Sept. 12, 2012) (published by the Texas State Historical Association).

Pizzaro, Judith, Roxane Cohen Silver, and Joann Prause, "Physical and Mental Health Care of Traumatic Experiences among Civil War Veterans," in NIH Public Access: www.ncbi.nlm.nih.gov/pmc/articles/PMC1586122/.

Rodenbough, Theophilus F., and William Haskin, eds., *The Army of the United States Historical Sketches of Staff and Line with Portraits of Generals-in-Chief* (New York: Maynard, Merrill, & Co., 1896), U.S. Army Center of Military History Web site, Books and Research Materials: http://www.history.army .mil/books/R&H/R&H-FM.htm (accessed Mar. 21, 2012).

David Rumsey Historical Map Collection, Stanford University: http://www .davidrumsey.com/luna/servlet/detail/RUMSEY~8~1~26868~1100164 (accessed Aug. 18, 2012).

"Skirmish at Gaines Landing": http://www .encyclopediaofarkansas .net/ encyclopedia/entry-detail.aspx?search=1&entryID=6938 (accessed Sept. 9, 2012).

Sixth Regiment, United States Colored Heavy Artillery: http://www.nps.gov/civilwar/ search-regiments-detail.htm?regiment_id=UUS0006RAH0C (accessed Apr. 2013).

U.S. Army Center of Military History Web site, Books and Research Materials: http://www.history.army.mil/books/R&H/R&H-FM.htm (accessed March 21, 2012).

Index